T0283476

THE
POLITICS
OF LIFE

MY ROAD TO THE MIDDLE
IN A HOSTILE
AND ADVERSARIAL WORLD

DOUGLAS E. SCHOEN
with *George Rush*

Regan Arts.

Regan Arts books may be purchased for educational,
business, or sales promotional use.
For information, please contact:
internationalrights@reganarts.com

First Regan Arts edition, June 2024
Library of Congress Control Number: 2023950612
ISBN: 978-1-68245-227-1 (eBook)
ISBN: 978-1-68245-226-4 (HC)

Cover design by Richard Ljoenes
Interior design by Beth Kessler, Neuwirth & Associates, Inc.

Printed in the United States of America
10 9 8 7 6 5 4 3 2 1

TABLE OF CONTENTS

INTRODUCTION

I was about ten years old when my parents decided that my sister, Sarah, and I should see our nation's capital. Touring the District of Columbia, we drove past the Washington Monument and the Supreme Court and visited the Federal Bureau of Investigation, where mugshots of America's Ten Most Wanted kind of scared me. Later, I peered through the iron fence surrounding the White House. I wondered if President Kennedy was home. I recalled that trip three decades later, on a night in February of 1995, when I stepped for the first time into the Executive Mansion. As a Secret Service agent ran a wand over me, I could scarcely believe I was there to meet with President Clinton. With me was Dick Morris, the tenacious campaign maestro who'd helped elect Clinton governor of Arkansas. Morris had been my political mentor when I was in high school. Now he'd turned to me to help the president keep his job. We came in under the cover of darkness because Morris's Republican clients, as well as Clinton's leftward advisers, might have problems with our involvement. The whole business was slightly surreal.

An usher escorted us to a private study off the Oval Office. There I met Bill Clinton. He was aware of my past attempts to defeat him. Showing his uncanny memory, he complimented me on polling I'd done for his opponents in Arkansas years before. I was impressed by his acuity yet taken aback by his affect. On the campaign trail, he'd been eloquent, assertive, magnetic. Now he looked exhausted. Mentally, he seemed to be somewhere else. The commander in chief confided that he felt adrift.

During his 1992 race, he'd effectively portrayed himself as a moderate. The epitome of what analysts were calling "New Democrats," he'd spoken about "ending welfare as we know it"; he'd supported free trade; he'd backed the death penalty; he'd vowed to crack down on crime; and he'd attacked President George H. W. Bush for breaking his "no new taxes" pledge. Once he assumed office, Clinton took the path of least resistance, joining a left-leaning Congress in advancing an economic stimulus bill and an ambitious health care plan that spooked Americans suspicious of big government. In the midterms, Republicans, led by Newt Gingrich, had crushed their Congressional adversaries, ending forty years of Democratic dominance in the House.

The president lamented that he'd lost control of the White House. His more progressive aides were ignoring many of his wishes. They dawdled when he asked them to make staff changes. They refused to push centrist initiatives in Congress, not wanting to "sell out" like-minded House Democrats. Clinton's poll ratings were in the mid-thirties. He was looking like a one-term president. As he gazed into space, I wanted to grab him by the shoulders and tell him to snap out of it.

That night, he asked the billion-dollar question: "What do we do now?"

To be honest, I wasn't sure where to start. But I had a partial answer.

"You've got to move to the right on fiscal issues," I said. "You're perceived as a liberal, big spender. You cannot be reelected with that perception."

Clinton knew this better than anyone. "I'm way out of position," he confessed. "You guys have to get me back to the center."

I sensed he was still skittish about saddling up again with the mercurial Morris—and with me.

INTRODUCTION

"I don't want to read about you in the press," he told us. "I'm sick and tired of consultants getting famous at my expense. Any story that comes out during the campaign undermines my candidacy."

We swore our loyalty, and our silence.

Overcoming his hesitancy, Clinton eventually authorized us to assemble a stealth team to get him reelected. We developed opinion polls that provided unprecedented insight into the psychology of voters and helped us craft resonating messages. Despite fierce resistance from some in the president's inner circle, we helped promote legislation that he could point to with pride. In November 1996, he won by a comfortable margin, becoming the first Democrat since Franklin D. Roosevelt to secure a second consecutive term.

★   ★   ★

Having the president's ear was a high point in my career. More than one client has since asked, "Do for me what you did for Clinton!" Over the years, I've had the privilege of counseling heads of state and business titans around the world. Three of my clients have won the Nobel Peace Prize. I've done my best to help evict dictators, restrain nuclear madmen, and improve the lives of people in need. Along the way, I've developed a set of principles. In my earlier book, *Power: The 50 Truths*, I gave frank counsel on how to attain and retain authority. This book is more personal. It isn't about amassing influence so much as living a happy life. It's a compendium of habits and techniques that have served me well. All my prescriptions have grown out of interactions with people. Some are learned and famous. Others are unheralded, self-taught folks with extraordinary insights.

My adages—call them "Schoenisms"—are all illustrated by anecdotes. Not to sound too grand but, together, they add up to a kind of creed. Its essence is consensus. Self-styled "leaders" often proclaim themselves as "uncompromising"—as though being intractable were a heroic trait. I'd call these people mule-headed, only that would insult mules. Hard-liners like to portray compromisers as weak, slippery ditherers who sit on the fence. To the contrary, charting a center course takes discipline and wisdom. I'm a Jewish guy from New York but, like the Buddha, I've tried to follow "the middle way." I've always been suspicious of extremists. I move incrementally. I weigh everything, sometimes by the ounce.

We live in divisive times. From America to Israel to Ukraine, we are flanked by bellowing bomb-throwers on the left and the right. Yet, like the great Stoic Marcus Aurelius, I believe, "We were born to work together like feet, hands and eyes, like the two rows of teeth." The trick to working together is staying limber enough to wrap your head around conflicting ideas. Let people speak. If you do, chances are you can figure out a workaround where everyone gets a bit of what they want. Cooler heads need to prevail. These Schoenisms may show you how to do it, how to prosper with humility. Take them or leave them, you may find a few laughs. I know this much: these stories are too good for me to keep to myself.

PART ONE

PART ONE

1

LEAVE YOUR ZONE

Every creature on earth has a natural habitat. Most prefer to stay in that habitat. You don't see many camels roaming around the North Pole. Humans also tend to grow where they're planted. But if you want to evolve, if you want to walk upright and get somewhere—be it across the Bering Strait or to a corner office in the C-suite—you'll need to **leave your comfort zone.**

My earliest habitat was quite comfortable. I grew up on Manhattan's Upper East Side, in a rambling apartment off Park Avenue. Every Sunday our family had lunch at the home of my father's parents, Lawrence and Louise Schoen. They lived an idyllic life. Each year they migrated from their summer home in Westchester to their winter home in Palm Beach, spending most of fall and spring aboard ocean liners. The china at their Sunday lunches was so fine that I once bit through a teacup. My father, Andrew Schoen, was a partner at Rosenman, Colin and Freund. One Saturday morning, when I was seven, my father took me to his office. As we were walking in, we passed the firm's co-founder, Samuel Rosenman, a New York State Supreme Court justice and the former White House counsel to Presidents Franklin Roosevelt and Harry Truman.

"Do you see Judge Rosenman working on Saturday?" my father asked me. **"Work all the time. It will serve you well."**

I listened to him, did my homework, and won acceptance to the Horace Mann School. Founded in 1887, Horace Mann has produced lawmakers, judges, diplomats, scientists, writers, artists, entrepreneurs, and other notable people. But it was an abusive place—emotionally, intellectually, socially, and athletically. On my first day of school, when I was eleven, a then-esteemed English teacher, Tek Young Lin, spoke to our class. Lin, who also served as a chaplain and a cross-country coach, said Horace Mann had existed for almost 100 years without us and almost certainly would exist for another 100 years after we left. In other words, each of us should know our place and show obedience. Lin and some other teachers and administrators struck me as strange, and I made a point of keeping my distance from them. It later emerged that several, including Lin and headmaster R. Inslee Clark Jr. were sexual predators. My takeaway: **Don't assume everyone is like you. If something seems creepy, it probably is.**

I loved sports. I was a starting guard on Horace Mann's football team, the Lions, for three years. Honestly, I wasn't much of a player. I was much better at keeping score. I liked statistics—Completed Passes, Field Goals Made, Runs Batted In. My interest in numbers was shared by a scruffy, chestnut-haired kid two classes behind me. He'd do opinion polls of teachers and students. When he was thirteen, he found that teachers supported civil rights more strongly than most Americans. The kid's name was Mark Penn. I'll get back to him later.

I also had a sprouting interest in politics. My parents could be classified as liberals with traditional values. (I don't know if that species exists today.) My father, Andrew Schoen, had a strong sense of right and wrong but believed that your first responsibility was to support your family. If you stuck to established organizations—preferably Jewish—and behaved honorably, things would stay on course. My mom, Carol, was more of an intellectual. After earning her BA from Radcliffe, she did something most mothers-of-two wouldn't have considered in the mid-1960s: she went back to school. She ended up earning a PhD in English Literature from Columbia and teaching college students in New York, England, and Japan. She wrote several books of literary criticism. Besides being a scholar, she was an enthusiastic teacher of English as a Second Language. She had empathy for the drown-trodden, believing that through progressive—but gradual—change, we could achieve a just society in which race and class would be far less important. She drew the line at civil disobedience. When she was a student labor activist, a union leader once told her to cross a police line and get arrested. She asked, "I get what's in it for you. What's in this for *me*?" When she didn't get a satisfactory answer, she went home.

My mother's brother, Jack Bronston, who practiced law with my dad, was an influential state senator in Queens. At family functions, he was always sneaking off to a bedroom to make important phone calls. That struck me as cool. So, in 1969, when I was sixteen, I decided to campaign for Bob Low, a city councilman who went to our synagogue.

While many of my friends were off on European vacations, I boarded the subway to south Brooklyn. It was my first trip outside my comfort zone. Getting on at the D train station, I darted from car to car, observing graffiti artists tagging the motorman's cab; working-class immigrants glaring at young longhairs; African American men sporting the radical chic of Black Panther Huey P. Newton. One train ride gave me a glimpse of the mood shift in the blue-collar boroughs, where people were beginning to doubt that government would or could come to their rescue. Manhattan Democrats didn't seem to hear this grumbling. But as I walked the boardwalk in Coney Island (my compensation included a hot dog and my first knish at Nathan's), I sensed the discontent of voters who'd long been taken for granted by the party. Understanding these voters would become my life's work.

My work that day was to plaster "Bob Low for City Council President" stickers on any surface I could find. I knew that subway authorities prohibited random acts of advertising, including the touting of political candidates. I'd dodged transit police on the trip from Manhattan. But, at the Coney Island station, I stepped straight into the arms of a hefty cop.

"Hey kid," he said, "how much are you getting paid to do this?"

"Twenty-five dollars," I mumbled.

"Not very smart, kid," he said, tapping his head to suggest my own skull might not contain a brain. "The fine for illegally posting bills is fifty dollars."

"So, I could lose money?" I asked, affecting innocence.

He nodded. "Who got you to do this?" he asked.

"Um, a big kid," I said.

He let me off with a warning.

Strolling away from the cop, I thought I'd handled the situation quite smoothly. In hindsight, it taught me the pitfalls of being a smart-ass. **It's good to be clever, but clever only gets you so far**. I'd forgotten, or ignored, my mother's warning to avoid getting arrested. **Self-sacrifice is great—unless it renders you useless.**

2

MAKE THE DEAL

Bob Low ended up losing, but I felt victorious. Handing out campaign leaflets to morning commuters empowered me. I wanted another taste of politics.

The Upper West Side of Manhattan wasn't too far from my home zone. But it felt uncomfortable enough on the cold and rainy fall day when I met Jerry Nadler.

Jerry would go on to serve eight terms as a New York State Assemblyman and, at last count, sixteen terms as a U.S. Congressman, holding the powerful position of Ranking Member of the House Judiciary Committee. On the day we met in 1969 he was twenty-one, fresh out of Columbia. Bespectacled, garrulous, and corpulent, he'd recently won the job of district leader. Looking for foot soldiers, he'd asked me to meet him on a park bench at Eighty-First Street and Columbus Avenue. Why did we have to sit there in a downpour? Jerry claimed to have a message so sensitive that he couldn't chance anyone else hearing it.

It pertained to the Democratic doges of the Upper West Side. Three years earlier, backers of presidential candidate Eugene McCarthy had begun to wrest control of the neighborhood from reformers who only a few years before had banished the last henchmen of the Tammany Hall machine. Now, Nadler whispered, those reformers were about to be toppled.

A bold new regime was forming, spearheaded by a reclusive genius who could analyze political trends like no one before.

"He will be one of the top strategists in America very soon," Nadler declared, "if he isn't already."

Nadler described how this mysterious mastermind and his followers were systematically canvasing and organizing the Upper West Side block by block, "down to individual apartment buildings." He promised that their revolutionary cell would soon hold sway over the neighborhood and, eventually, all of New York City.

Nadler foretold a brave new world of campaigning, in which precise knowledge of voters would become the currency of political power. What made his pitch especially enticing: the veiled prophet behind this vision wanted me to be one of his minions—if I could prove myself worthy.

I told Nadler I would like to hear more.

"We'll be in touch," he said before disappearing into the night.

★   ★   ★

A few days later I received a call. It was The Master.

"Doug?" he said. "You talked to Jerry? Yes? Good. I want you to come over for dinner on Tuesday. You can come? Good. See you at seven."

The caller was impatient, but I did catch his name—Dick Morris.

In the years to come, some would see Dick Morris as the creator and, nearly, the destroyer of Bill Clinton's presidency. Back then he was just another recent Columbia grad who was certain he knew it all. When I arrived at his address, I found a building badly in need of paint and elevator maintenance. I rang his buzzer. The door opened. There stood the Great Oz—a gap-toothed twenty-two-year-old in a rumpled button-down shirt, holding a glass of orange juice. No wonder people called his gang the West Side Kids.

We sat down for some take-out chicken at a folding metal card table that Morris and his wife, Gita, also used for sidewalk pamphleteering. I listened to Morris' plan for marshaling an unstoppable cadre of campaign operatives.

"I know things about political organizing that no one else does," he said. "Sign on, and you'll learn them too."

"But I want to go to Harvard," I told him.

"Give it up," Morris commanded. "Go to Columbia and work for me as a canvasser. I'll give you a block to organize. In two to four years, you'll be a district leader."

As he spoke, Gita listened raptly, making sure his glass was always filled with orange juice.

"You will know every building's issue," he went on. "You will own it. It will be yours."

I felt like I was being lured into a cult. But I could not resist Morris's magnetism. He had a rare intelligence. By the end of the evening, I told him I was in—providing he understood that, if Harvard accepted me, I was going there. Morris grudgingly agreed to my terms.

Soon Nadler and I were spending our evenings crammed into Morris's tiny apartment, using his two phone lines to canvass voters. We'd ask them what mattered to them. We'd push our candidates—my first being Dick Gottfried, a young politician running for the state Assembly.

The West Side Kids were pragmatists. They recognized that, to win, they had to take care of constituent needs better than the incumbents did. For instance, Nadler became an expert on landlord-tenant issues—helping voters keep their rent-stabilized apartments. The Kids also capitalized on national issues. They organized rallies against the Vietnam War and pickets against grocers who sold grapes that weren't picked by the United Farm Workers. The Kids used their research to tailor messages to voters. If a building was a stronghold of radical liberals, we would craft a spiel to the left of Trotsky. If another building had a lot of senior citizens, we'd get up to speed on Medicare and Social Security. No one had ever done such focused and flexible messaging before.

Unlike in the suburbs, you couldn't canvass house-to-house in New York City. You had to figure out how to penetrate apartment buildings. If there was a panel of door buzzers, you'd ring a bunch of them, figuring that someone would assume you were delivering Chinese food. It was trickier if a building had a doorman. In that case, I would breeze into the lobby, announcing that I was visiting, say, Mr. and Mrs. Levy on the sixteenth floor. Once in the elevator, I would head straight to the top floor. It was crucial to start at the top of a building and work your way down—so you wouldn't get tired. Sometimes allies who lived in the building would let me hide out while the dogged doorman sniffed my tracks.

Rather than buzz randomly, we used our research to target the people most likely to vote. In those days, West Side voters weren't satisfied with getting a piece of campaign literature. They wanted a debate! Quite often, we were invited inside to defend our candidates and their positions. Gerard Piel, the publisher of *Scientific American,* once asked me to join his family for dinner. Morris and Nadler frowned on such collegiality. My skills were still suspect. Morris wouldn't even let me canvass Lincoln Towers, a massive apartment complex that was home to many retired teachers. He didn't think I was "mature" enough to handle these formidable debaters.

The West Side Kids compiled a list of 12,000 or so people who'd said they were going to vote. On election day, that list would be checked against the list of those who'd come to the polls so far. If Mrs. Levy hadn't voted yet, a volunteer would call and politely remind her that time was running out. On the final day of the campaign, Nadler even had me calling transients at the West Side YMCA. (The Kids had developed a message for the homeless, promising food at the polls.)

Gottfried won the race handily. But I had a feeling it wasn't because of the guys at the Y. In fact, what clinched the race for Gottfried was a deal Morris cut with fourth-generation Tammany Hall vestige Jim McManus. McManus was the reigning member of a family that had ruled politics in Hell's Kitchen since 1892. In 1970, the McManus Club still controlled about 20 percent to 25 percent of the district. For a West Side leftist to make a deal with McManus was like progressive U.S. Rep. Alexandria Ocasio-Cortez agreeing on anything with her far-right antagonist Rep. Marjorie Taylor Greene.

Only later did I learn that Gottfried and Morris had gone to McManus and asked for his support. For Dick, winning, rather than clinging to ideology, was the point. Some might see this as selling out. But it's worth noting that Dick Gottfried has served in the Assembly for over fifty years, in which time he's championed many progressive causes.

Likewise, Jerry Nadler saw the value in strategic accommodation. Many nights, after he and I would make calls from Morris's apartment, we'd go—Dutch treat—to the Europa Café. The waiter behind the counter would ask Jerry, "The regular?" Out would come a sandwich stuffed with so much roast beef you could barely fit it your mouth. Jerry, who was on his way to tipping the scales at 340 pounds, polished it off without difficulty. In between bites, he would regale me with tales of Democratic party bosses. He was obsessed by Jimmy Hines, who'd controlled patronage in much of Manhattan during the 1920s and 1930s. Linked to mobsters Lucky Luciano and Dutch Schultz, Hines was convicted of racketeering in 1939. Nadler didn't approve of Hines's ethics, but he admired his consummate political skill—the way he managed his enemies and his territory. For Nadler and Morris, seizing power, and maintaining it, was the way to true progress.

★ ★ ★

My father had told me, "You will work every moment that you are not in school. If you do not get a job, I will get you a job. I guarantee you that any job I get you will be less pleasant than one you get yourself." In gratitude for my campaign work, Dick Morris found me a summer job as a surveyor on the Board of Water Supply. There I was, at the age of seventeen, a political appointee earning about $400 a week (over $3,000 today). It was patronage politics at its best! It wasn't quite a "no show" job—more of a "seldom show" job. Even though I'd never surveyed anything beyond some girls I'd hoped to date, I'd tag along with an older guy who'd lug a theodolite into Van Cortlandt Park or over to Randall's Island. I'd wear an orange vest and hold a pole. I'm still not clear what we were supposed to be doing, but whatever it was, we didn't do much of it. We averaged about four hours of work in the morning. If it was raining, we didn't work at all.

Not that Dick Morris gave me any time off. A condition of my getting the surveyor job was that I'd show up at Morris's apartment every night to help Jerry Nadler call voters, to make sure they supported our slate of district leaders. In the afternoons, I'd work for Tony Olivieri, a candidate for the 66th Assembly district on the Upper East Side.

One of my jobs was "constituent services"—solving the problems of citizens Tony Olivieri hoped would vote for him. One of his would-be constituents was a Mrs. Cox, who lived on E. 89th Street in a rundown tenement owned by Eberhart Brothers, one of Manhattan's oldest management companies. Mrs. Cox told me she'd been trying forever to get Eberhart Brothers to paint her apartment. I called Eberhart. After some back and forth, the landlord sent over an older gentleman named Willie to paint her place. I thought for sure we had Mrs. Cox's vote. Oh no! She said

Willie had raced through the painting—giving her a no-primer, one-coat, no-frills job. After inspecting his work, I called Willie and complained.

"This is a crappy, slap-dash job!" I said. "You can barely tell it was painted!"

Willie calmly replied, "Look here, young buck. You spent a lot of time getting me there. But that lady's landlord paid me next to nothing. If I get paid the minimum, you get the minimum work. If Eberhart Brothers wants to pay me more, I'll take my time and give that lady what she wants."

I took Willie's point: **Whenever you hire people, understand their needs as well as your own.**

Tony Olivieri already seemed to have learned that lesson. "Work for my campaign," he promised, "and I'll do everything I can to get you into Harvard."

Tony happened to be a Harvard grad and fundraiser, and he was as good as his word. On my behalf, he called a Harvard interviewer named Rufus Peebles.

"Doug, it's all taken care of," Tony reported back. "Just relax."

Two weeks later I received a letter of admission. (Olivieri also got what he wanted—narrowly becoming the first Democrat-Liberal to win the "Silk Stocking District" in fifty-five years. He became a champion of tenants' rights, health care, and environmental protection—all the while struggling with a brain tumor that claimed his life at age thirty-nine.)

It wasn't that I didn't have the credentials to get into Harvard. But as someone who grew up thinking success was strictly a matter of doing your homework, I was learning that it didn't hurt to have what politicians call "an insurance policy." There are back doors to most institutions, even if it's not immediately clear where they are. If you look, you can find a way in, a path of least resistance. Chances are you'll meet someone who can smooth your way, who can make a deal. **Where possible, make that deal.**

3

DO YOUR FIELDWORK

When I got to Harvard in the fall of 1970, the campus was bristling with dissent. The assassinations of Martin Luther King Jr. and Robert Kennedy were still open wounds. Many students from privileged families were fed up with conventional politics and committed to direct action. Protesting was practically an official major. The previous year, antiwar demonstrators had paralyzed the university by seizing control of University Hall for two weeks. Harvard president Nathan Pusey eventually called in police to evict the students—a move that lit new bonfires of outrage.

I was a buttoned-up kid in a button-down shirt who still believed you could work within the system. But by March of my first year, I got sucked into the political drama.

Conservative members of the Young Americans for Freedom (YAF) had announced a "counter teach-in" to educate the Harvard community on the wisdom of President Nixon's policy in Southeast Asia. The only people more excited than the conservatives by the rally were their left-wing antagonists—the Students for a Democratic Society (SDS). By 1970, the SDS was riven with internal divisions. Leaders of the Harvard chapter saw the YAF event as a way to bind their splintered ranks.

The showdown promised to be as thrilling as the Muhammad Ali–Joe Frazier "Fight of the Century" that same month. The teach-in was due to be held at Sanders Theater, built in memory of Union soldiers who'd died in the Civil War. The night of the rally I headed over there with my dorm-mates Charlie Perkins and Coleman Harrison. The auditorium was packed. Due to speak were White House adviser Dolph Droge and representatives of the governments of Thailand and South Vietnam. Antiwar activists didn't want to hear them.

"U.S. out of Vietnam! Butchers out of Harvard!" they chanted. "One, two, three, four, we got to end this fucking war!"

Overseeing the event was law professor Archibald Cox, who'd been President Kennedy's solicitor general and who would later serve as Watergate special prosecutor. Cox begged the hecklers to let the speakers have their say.

"You cannot deny [freedom of speech] for one man and save it for others," Cox told the mob.

The protestors continued to bark and stomp their feet. They threw paper airplanes, marshmallows, and pennies. After more than an hour of this mayhem, Cox shut the event down.

By now, Harvard's administration had lost its patience with this behavior. The Committee on Rights and Responsibilities was in the process of throwing out fifty-two students deemed to have violated Harvard's code of conduct. Unfortunately for the Sanders Theater protesters, photographers and TV crews had caught all the action. Footage of my friend Coleman Harrison showed him wiggling his fingers in his ears as he called someone onstage a "racist." Coleman was soon summoned to a hearing before Professor Donald G. M. Anderson. The only problem: Coleman had been busted at another protest for allegedly pulling a knife on a cop. I had to call his father, Selig Harrison, a prominent foreign correspondent, who was abroad at the time. It also fell to me to appear on Coleman's behalf before Professor Anderson. I explained that my classmate had been "unavoidably detained" because he was "um, presently incarcerated."

Coleman got off without jail time, but he was suspended from Harvard for a year. Investigators also spotted our pal, Charlie Perkins, among the rabble-rousers. You couldn't miss Charlie; he was wearing a shirt pinker than a flamingo. Charlie received a suspended suspension. To this day, he maintains that I should have been sanctioned—and that I *would* have been if I hadn't worn a nondescript black ski parka. My advice: **Stay seated and wear boring clothes. You can make a difference without making a scene.**

It could have been worse. Around this time, some would-be anarchists lived on the streets of Cambridge. Come winter, Coleman and Charlie invited some of these cold and gamey radicals to crash in their dorm room. These dorm guests espoused a society free from the dictates of money and capitalism. So, Charlie and Coleman shouldn't have been surprised that these light-fingered Bolsheviks "liberated" some of their possessions. Coleman started sleeping with one of this crew—a girl we dubbed Lackey Linda. (Wannabe Marxists were always sneering at "capitalist lackeys.") Only much later did we learn that Linda was an informant in the FBI's infamous Counter Intelligence Program (COINTELPRO), a covert operation designed to "neutralize" political dissidents. Apparently, the FBI figured that even longhairs like Coleman might fall for a honey-trap. Dating tip: **Sleeping alone has its advantages.**

Admittedly, back then, there weren't too many duplicitous vixens aching to seduce me. As a freshman, I had the frustration of living in Thayer Hall below southern charmer Walter Isaacson, who later became editor of *Time*, CEO of CNN, and a bestselling author. Every weekend, I had to listen to high heels climbing the stairs to Walter's room. I wondered how many girls he had up there. Many years later, I confessed my jealousy to him. "There *was* a lot of traffic," Walter recalled, "but not a lot of action. I can tell you now, Doug, very little was happening in my room."

As in all things, Harvard men could be quite competitive about sex. One guy was appalled when a Radcliffe woman informed him that she was dating other people. Vindictively, he leafleted the campus with flyers alleging that his would-be love, who lived in Kirkland House, was a prostitute. Some people mistook this slander for an advertisement. One of my teachers walked into class waving one of these flyers and proclaiming, "They're selling pussy in Kirkland House!" A tenured professor! It was a different time.

Women at Harvard put up with a lot of boorish men. I had a roommate I'll call Steve. Steve was a rich kid with far-left politics. He believed in every person's right to self-determination. Except when it came to a pretty, first-year student he had the hots for. I'll call her Beth. Steve wanted Beth for himself. For several years Beth refused to commit—until Steve became a top editor at the *Crimson*, whereupon he told her she could no longer write for the paper unless she became his girlfriend. She agreed. Apparently, though, she was unaware that Steve's revolutionary principles included a fierce opposition to tennis. He found the sport too bourgeois. Little did Beth realize the danger of playing a few sets with me. She and I were about to head off to the courts one day when Steve returned to our dorm room. Finding her in her white tennis togs, he began to slam her head against a bedpost. I tackled him and pulled him off her. Beth and I made a hasty exit. Amazingly, she was still up for tennis—in fact, more so than ever! We'd just started playing when Steve walked onto the court. Snatching Beth's racket, he whacked all our balls into the Charles River. Beth and Steve went on dating as if nothing had happened. Steve suffered no consequences—even though Beth's brother, a future U.S. senator, knew about the assault—and Steve continued to style himself as a crusading human rights activist.

Be wary of people whose vision of a better world doesn't include reforming themselves.

Getting tear-gassed at demonstrations was never my thing. But, now and then, I did challenge authority. In my first semester, I enrolled in a course in the newly created Afro-American Studies Department. I genuinely wanted to understand our country's history of slavery and the struggle for civil rights. When I showed up for the first class, I discovered that I was the only white student. I didn't mind—in fact, I thought it might be good to feel what it's like to be in a minority. But the visiting lecturer, Hayward Henry Jr., didn't agree. Henry, who later changed his name to Mtangulizi Sanyika, was a twenty-seven-year-old Black nationalist and the first chairman of the Congress of Afrikan People. As soon as he saw me, he said, "Leave!" He didn't think I had the necessary sensitivity to understand the African American experience. He told me I was taking a place that belonged to a Black student. I left, but I complained to the dean of the faculty, John Thomas Dunlop, who later became President Ford's secretary of labor. Dunlop told me Henry's edict was clearly discriminatory—but that I should let it drop. **"Pick your battles, kid,"** he said. It's a piece of advice I still offer to people. Postscript: Henry moved to MIT the following year but returned to Harvard for a 1973 meeting where, one meeting organizer later charged, Henry's inflammatory rhetoric provoked the stabbings of seven other attendees.

I found a much more enlightening teacher in Martin Kilson. The first African American professor to receive tenure at Harvard, Kilson taught government there for four decades. He was part intellectual historian, part ward boss. He sometimes wore a cowboy hat. He had a penetrating mind and a wicked sense of humor. One day I walked into his office to talk to him about a paper. I found him furiously arguing with a Black student about who was responsible for a series of rapes in nearby Medford. Kilson believed the rapists were Black. The student contended whites were responsible. Kilson finally drew himself up and said, "Get your Black ass out to Medford! I want to know what's happening. You're my scout, my courier. Don't just talk. Do some fieldwork!" He then turned politely to me and said, "Schoen, your paper?" It was classic Kilson—irreverent, probing, dedicated to fact over opinion.

I had an odd but delightful relationship with Kilson. From the beginning, he made it clear that he would only have a limited amount of time for me.

"Schoen, there are plenty of professors who will work with you—a smart Jewish boy," Kilson told me. "I have to put my time into the Black students."

He was not being biased or patronizing. Indeed, there were some formidable Black students in our class—among them Robert P. Young Jr., who became a Michigan Supreme Court Justice, and Leonard S. Coleman Jr., later president of baseball's National League and New Jersey's energy commissioner. No one in the class impressed Kilson more than future Harvard professor and 2024 presidential candidate Cornel West, who at seventeen was already sporting a rakish scarf and pipe. West could ride on his intellect. "All of you *other* people are going to have to go out into the field," Kilson told us. "Talk to people, and really work for insights!"

Obeying his marching orders, I headed off to Harlem to research a final paper about how upstart Charlie Rangel had defeated the legendary Rep. Adam Clayton Powell Jr. to win the 18th Congressional District. I did dozens of interviews—talking to community leaders, ward bosses, journalists, and Rangel. Maybe I asked too many questions. One day, I got mugged at knife point and had to beg a bus driver to help me get home. But I was excited by the work. Kilson showed me that I could do serious research. And my shoe leather paid off—he gave me an A+. I later established a fellowship in Kilson's name to fund other students' research.

Don't guess! Do your fieldwork! Ask questions until you get answers.

4

DON'T BACK
LOSERS, UNLESS . . .

By now I'd traveled far afield. I'd learned a lot about politics from Dick Morris and Martin Kilson. But I knew I needed to enlarge my experience. I needed to get even further out of my comfort zone.

From the time of my bar mitzvah, I'd learned that social action was an essential part of a good life. Our rabbi, Bernard Jacob Bamberger, was a vocal advocate for civil rights. My mother was a supporter of the National Association for the Advancement of Colored People and the National Urban League. Together, we'd watched TV coverage of Black students trying to enroll at segregated schools in the South. We'd mourned activist Medgar Evers when he was assassinated in 1963. So, in 1971, when I heard that Evers's brother, Charles, was running for governor of Mississippi, I wanted to help register voters.

Naturally, my parents were a little worried. They remembered that Andrew Goodman and Michael Schwerner, both Jewish kids from New York, had been murdered with James Chaney by the Ku Klux Klan during the Freedom Summer of 1964. Nevertheless, my folks let me go.

Charles Evers was a singular candidate. A college graduate and veteran of World War II and the Korean War, he'd worked as dishwasher, disc jockey, nightclub operator, numbers-runner, bootlegger, and pimp. His brother's assassination remade him and spurred him to carry on Medgar's NAACP work. In 1969, Charles became Mississippi's first elected Black mayor in a century. More combative than Medgar, Mayor Evers hired bodyguards and used strong-arm tactics to enforce boycotts of white merchants in his town of Fayette. Having disclosed his criminal past, he was now primed for higher office.

Arriving in Mississippi at the beginning of the summer, I found a bedroom in a Black neighborhood in Jackson. It was a group house for kids with special needs run by the Reverend Eddie McBride. The fact that Reverend McBride carried a pistol told me something about the political atmosphere.

I did my best to adapt to my surroundings. Every Sunday morning, I'd walk down Pearl Street toward the State Capitol, where I'd pick up local newspapers, like the *Clarion-Ledger* and the Memphis *Commercial Appeal*. Sometimes I'd find the Sunday *New York Times*. I used to get stares. I could understand the locals' confusion: not only was I white, but I may also have been the only person in town who wasn't headed to church. More than a few residents looked at my newspapers and figured I must be the new paperboy.

When I first spoke to Evers's campaign manager, Ed Cole, I mentioned my experience in New York elections.

"Doug," Cole said, "how would you like to be our research director?"

It was a daunting offer. I really wasn't sure what a research director was supposed to do. Luckily, during a trip to the statehouse I stumbled upon Bill Minor, the legendary correspondent for the New Orleans *Times-Picayune*. Minor had been covering Mississippi politics for more than two decades. Unsolicited, he helped me put together policy papers. Each morning I'd darken the door of his tiny, newspaper-strewn office for my tutorial. One day it would be property taxes; the next might be Mississippi's State Sovereignty Commission.

Minor would tell me who to talk to, where to look, sometimes even what to write. A quick piece of advice: **Wherever you go, look for a mentor.**

Pointed by Minor in the right direction, I'd head off to the state archives. Guessing that a nosey Yankee might raise eyebrows, I posed as a graduate student from Tulane University. I tried to blend in wherever I went. One day I visited the Neshoba County Fair. Jimmy Swan, one of Evers's opponents, was campaigning there. The former country music star had run for governor in 1967, promising to save Mississippi from school integration and "the moral degeneracy of total mass integration that Washington has decreed for our children." Swan wore a white suit—just to underscore his supremacy. Supposedly, he was trying to tone down his racist rhetoric in this election. But he was still waving around a book titled, *Take Your Choice: Separation or Mongrelization*. At the fair, he railed against racial intermarriage. I give him one thing: he taught me a new word—*miscegenation*.

Evers's operation couldn't have been more different from that of the disciplined West Side Kids. His white press secretary, Jason Berry, and I were both frustrated with the campaign's disorganization. It didn't help that some of the other northern volunteers didn't seem all that serious about the campaign. They were more like wandering do-gooders—free radicals—who'd come down to check out the scene. Every Monday night, they'd have an "encounter group" where they shared their feelings. There were some heated exchanges between the northern volunteers and the Black Mississippians. One morning, they were having an intense debate. Up till then, Evers had stayed out of the squabbles. But that day, he called us to order. He was a big man whose streetwise bearing told you he took no shit. When he stood to address us, everybody shut up.

"When I worked for Bobby Kennedy, I did what Bob Kennedy told me," he rumbled. "Now, this is *my* campaign. You're working for me. So, you're going to do things my way."

At the time, I don't think I fully appreciated his point: this was *his* time, a Black man in Mississippi was in charge. After his younger brother's murder, Charles later admitted, "Part of the reason I came back to Mississippi was to kill white folks. At times, in those first months back, I just wanted to kill every white man I could." But he'd harnessed his rage and picked up Medgar's crusade, mounting a campaign to help citizens of all colors. He showed that **anger can be a superpower if you use it constructively and rationally.**

Regrettably, Sen. Ted Kennedy and other prominent Democrats wouldn't campaign for him—for fear of antagonizing Southern Democrats or because Evers was running as an Independent, as he had to in a state where the Democratic Party had never supported a Black candidate. (It would be another forty years before a major party nominated a Black candidate for governor in Mississippi.)

Fortunately, there were other brave Black men who came to help Charles. That summer I had the privilege of meeting John Lewis and Julian Bond. One of the last events I attended before going home to New York was a rally in Copiah County. That day, Evers's motorcade set out from Jackson, escorted by a retinue of white police officers. In 1971, in Mississippi, this was practically unimaginable. Two hours later, we arrived at a ramshackle, white wooden church. The room was steamy, and I sensed fear in a congregation that had long been scared away from the polls. I saw that they had a different view of the white cops "protecting" the candidate. Once again, Evers came to the moment from a much higher plane. He spoke like a Baptist preacher—cajoling, haranguing, and imploring his flock to exercise its rights.

"What the hell are you doing if you don't get yourself registered?" he said.

The mood in the room was electric. He'd fired them up. On Election Day, Evers lost badly, garnering only 21 percent of the vote. But he had always been clear-eyed about his chances. He expected to lose. But he hoped that, along the way, he'd start to build a statewide machine that would fight fraud and intimidation in future elections. Evers wasn't running to get elected so much to show his people how to raise their voices and speak their minds. As he said in his previous race, "Hands that picked cotton can now pick the mayor."

Since becoming a political consultant, I've tended to avoid races where I thought there was no chance of winning. But I often remember Charles Evers's lesson:

Winning isn't always the point. A defeat can get you closer to victory. Lose the battle but win the war. Know your goal.

5

KNOW YOUR WHEREABOUTS

I returned to New York in July and went straight to work for City Councilman Carter Burden. Burden's upbringing was as far from Evers's as caviar is from collard greens. An heir to the Vanderbilt fortune, Burden had graduated from Harvard and Columbia Law School. Now, at age twenty-nine, he owned the *Village Voice* and had a stake in *New York* magazine. The *New York Times* described him as "tall, lean, blond, deeply tanned, and patricianly handsome." His wife, Amanda, was a Standard Oil heiress whose stepfather, William S. Paley, had founded CBS. The fun couple's glittering parties made the society columns. Posh as he was, Burden had served as Bobby Kennedy's liaison in New York's inner city. Having campaigned energetically for his council seat, he seemed sincere about improving the lives of his low- and middle-income constituents. He just didn't like to work too hard doing it. Tony Olivieri, the assemblyman who'd helped me get into Harvard, had helped Burden get through Columbia Law School. "You should meet Carter," Tony told me. "But please understand: he's a specialist in getting other people to live his life for him."

Before long, Burden put me to work deciphering New York City's nearly inscrutable finances. The intricacies of the budget were, frankly, stultifying. Fortunately, Burden soon shifted me to another assignment—taking on one of Manhattan's most powerful politicians in one of the toughest slums in America.

The man Carter Burden aimed to take down was Assemblyman Frank Rossetti. Rossetti had been part of the Democratic political machine for nearly three decades. His district in East Harlem had long been a stronghold for Italian Americans. But over the years, they'd been replaced by Blacks and Puerto Ricans. Burden was determined to capitalize on the opportunity this presented. He spent as much as $50,000 of his own money in support of Rossetti's opponent—a young lawyer named Eugene Nardelli. Nardelli's family was from the lower section of East Harlem. He'd boldly moved onto Rossetti's turf to challenge its longtime boss. Nardelli had some potent supporters. Herman Badillo, a local congressman who was mulling a run for mayor, backed him.

What would ordinarily have been an innocuous race for district leadership had turned into a proxy fight for the 1973 mayoral race. If Burden could defeat Tammany Hall's candidate, the Reform Democrat would become the new political boss. And when Burden asked me to serve as Nardelli's campaign manager, I found myself—at age eighteen—in the thick of it.

I'd met Rossetti when I was researching my Harvard paper on Charlie Rangel's win over Adam Clayton Powell Jr. Rossetti embodied everything I hated about politics. He was overdressed, obnoxious, and he talked out of both sides of his month. Nardelli told me that whenever he'd see him, Rossetti would say, "Hey kid, here's a couple hundred bucks, buy yourself a new suit." (Nardelli sniffed that his suits cost way more than $200.) We knew that ousting Rossetti was a long shot. All the same, our little team hit the streets, knocking first on the doors of the remaining Italians— mostly older people. We also leafleted the housing projects that were home to Hispanic and Black voters. Early in the campaign, I made the rookie mistake of bringing a salsa band to a rally at the Lincoln Houses, where most of the residents were African

American. The music was not exactly a hit. Before we knew what was happening, our team was being pelted from the rooftops with rocks and other debris. We beat a hasty retreat.

Rossetti's support didn't just come from his Tammany buddies. He had a few "friends in the neighborhood." Among them was Anthony "Fat Tony" Salerno, a top capo in the Genovese crime family. Salerno oversaw its businesses—which included book-making, loansharking, extortion, and murder-for-hire—from the Palma Boys Social Club at 416 East 115th Street.

Nardelli and I decided it was best to steer clear of the social club crew, since they obviously weren't buying what we were selling. But one day we ignored our own rule and tried canvassing the block where the wiseguys sipped their espressos. Nardelli and I were climbing the stairs of a tenement when we heard a banging sound coming from above. I was already worried about Fat Tony; now this *bang, bang, bang* was getting louder and closer. Nardelli bent down and pulled a pistol from an ankle holster I didn't know he had.

"That's why I carry this," he said, showing me his gun. I guess this was supposed to reassure me. Finally, we looked up and saw a junkie with pinwheel eyes. For some reason, he was thrashing each step with a stick. We let him pass. No wonder my mother stayed awake until I got home.

The Nardelli team continued to campaign hard. We got a high-profile endorsement from former Mayor Robert Wagner as well as from the *New York Times*. Unfortunately, neither endorse-ment mattered as much in East Harlem as the opinion of Antonio "Buckaloo" Ferro. The reputed Genovese underboss spent his days sitting in a beach chair outside a social club at 116th Street and Second Avenue. He wore his pants near his nipples and always had an unlit cigar dangling from his mouth. When Buckaloo put the word out that Rossetti was *his* guy, all bets were off. Suddenly, people who'd put up our posters didn't want to have anything to do with us. A few days before, a candy store owner couldn't have been more supportive. Now he said, "Please don't come in here. It can only cause us problems."

To make matters worse, Carter Burden was MIA. Sure, he was bankrolling Nardelli's campaign, but I could see his heart wasn't in it. The more time I spent with Burden, the more this "socialite" seemed like a profoundly lonely man. He came to work just before noon, locked himself in his office, and spent hours leafing through shopping catalogs. Early in the race, Burden invited Nardelli and our team to breakfast at his apartment in River House, one of the most exclusive buildings in the city. I sat down at an ornate table with Nardelli, his running mate Elba Diaz, and Angelo Guerrero, Elba's working-class husband. Burden's elegant wife Amanda—"Ba," he called her—greeted us, looking like she'd stepped out of *Town & Country*. Then Burden entered—wearing a silk bathrobe. As we discussed the mechanics of the campaign, I could tell this meeting was the last place he wanted to be. He seemed dreadfully bored. Even then, I was old enough to realize that Burden would never be a serious politician. He simply didn't have the passion for it.

Despite the setbacks, I remained hopeful that Nardelli could win. However, on election day, it became clear that Rossetti had outsmarted us. He too had analyzed every voter. He'd stationed his district captains on each block. It didn't hurt that some of his people were also supposed to be overseeing the election. The Board of Elections chairman turned out to be Rossetti's captain for 119th Street between First and Second Avenue. I discovered that Rossetti's people were campaigning *inside* the polling booths on 120th Street. I ran to tell a police officer. He peered at me for a moment then said, "Kid, mind your business."

Nardelli lost the election by a margin of nearly three to one. After his defeat, the long knives were out for him. We heard Rossetti had told someone that Nardelli was "deader than Kelly's nuts," referring to a racehorse that had recently been castrated. Amazingly, Nardelli survived and went on to become a prominent and distinguished judge in New York's State Supreme Court, Appellate Division.

A *New York Times* article kindly described me as his campaign's "young genius." Invoking the name of Tammany Hall's last boss, the reporter dubbed me "the Carmine de Sapio of the New Left." The reporter also observed that, as election results came in, I turned "whiter than a bed sheet that had been washed in Axion, with Clorox added." I'd thought that if you canvassed precisely and carefully constructed your message, voters would see the obvious superiority of your candidate. Instead, the Harvard boy got his ass kicked. I learned that you can't stroll into a neighborhood—even if you grew up a few blocks away, as Nardelli did—and think you have roots there. You can't expect your new neighbors to embrace you as their savior or expect the old guard to play fair. The targeting formulas I'd learned might be the wave of the future. But a ward boss who'd never gone to college taught the "young genius" an enduring lesson: **Brains and money only get you so far. You need to connect with people. Know your whereabouts and assess situations accurately.**

And, for God's sake, don't bring a salsa band to the Lincoln Houses!

6

NO ONE OWNS A GOOD IDEA

Working on campaigns had shown me the important role the media plays in politics. So, I'd started contributing to the *Harvard Crimson*. There was always another demonstration to cover, as well as the never-ending debate over how the Afro-American Studies Department should be run. I reviewed some pizzerias, interviewed some brave classmates who'd organized a Gay Students Association, and delved into the still-unsolved execution-style murder of Joseph Strickland, an investigative journalist and assistant dean. I also wrote a basketball column—"Schoen Tell." One profile focused on recently hired Indiana Hoosiers coach Bobby Knight. It revealed some of Knight's harsh discipline—such as kicking a player who'd been seen sitting on a basketball. "That ball is worth more than you are," Knight told the student. (It would be another twenty-eight years before Indiana finally fired Knight for his abusive behavior.)

I sometimes used my position to right wrongs—particularly if the person wronged was one of my friends. My buddy, Rick Lyon, was an aspiring singer-songwriter. Rick had worked hard to get Bonnie Raitt to play Sanders Theater. He planned to be her opening act. It was going to be his big break. Then Raitt tried to pull out of the concert. I called Raitt's manager and warned him that the *Crimson* would not look kindly on his client if she disappointed her fans.

"You have two choices," I said. "Ms. Raitt can either be destroyed, or she can have over 1,000 people screaming at the top of their lungs." Bonnie Raitt performed. Rick got his shot. The show went so well that Raitt returned a few years later—though, as my classmate (and future U.S. Attorney General) Merrick Garland recalled, her opening act was another up-and-comer by the name of Bruce Springsteen.

Naturally, my favorite beat was politics. Rick's dad was a Washington attorney with pull in the Democratic party. So, Rick and I wangled a Capitol Hill interview in September of 1972 with Sen. Hubert Humphrey, who had run against Nixon in 1968. Humphrey "showed a degree of outrage over the war . . . that he had never shown in his campaign," we reported, adding that Humphrey admitted that Sen. George McGovern's chances of defeating Nixon were "highly questionable." We also interviewed Sen. Thomas Eagleton, whom McGovern had dumped as his running mate the previous month following Eagleton's admission that he'd been hospitalized for depression. Rick and I reported that the chain-smoking Eagleton "appeared tired and worn . . . His deeply set eyes held a dour, almost mournful image." We weren't much kinder to Humphrey, noting his "deeply lined face, [his] sizeable paunch, bloodshot eyes, and the gray hair, which he no longer dyes, of an old man." The two ex-candidates were rewarded for their time with the headline: "The Dustbin of History—View from the Bottom." Recommendation for press secretaries: **Never grant interviews to anyone whose agenda you don't know.**

I also managed to spend ten days following McGovern on the press corps aircraft known as "the zoo plane." I reported how the candidate was making unprecedented use of television to give viewers the impression he was out with the people. In fact, his schedule demonstrated that, on an average day, "he spends less than one hour speaking directly to voters." I chronicled how McGovern's staff made life easy for reporters—providing prepackaged radio soundbites and the help of "media mothers" who "travel on the buses with reporters, flirt with them, serve drinks, and give out the releases" written by male colleagues.

During the primaries, McGovern had run a focused campaign with a clear message: he was against the Vietnam War and for a guaranteed income for every American. But in the general election, I found that McGovern spent "most of his time blasting Nixon without delivering carefully thought-out talks." Already cleaving to the middle, I wrote, "Most people who vote in American presidential elections want a moderate candidate, and McGovern does little . . . to discourage claims that he is a 'radical or extreme' candidate."

McGovern received a gift in October with the break-in at the Democratic National Committee's office at the Watergate Office Building. Even before all the facts were known, McGovern contended the crime was part of a campaign of political spying that led straight to the White House. But, by then, it was too late for him.

For many of my classmates, McGovern's loss was so devastating that it felt like the country had turned against our generation. They blamed his defeat on the racism of Nixon's "silent majority." I sensed a deeper problem, which I began to understand with the help of Daniel Patrick Moynihan.

In the winter of 1972, Moynihan had just returned to Harvard from Washington, where he'd served in the Kennedy, Johnson, and Nixon administrations. The son of working-class Irish Americans, he was raised largely by his mother, who ran a bar in Hell's Kitchen. Moynihan had shined shoes in Times Square while going to high school in East Harlem, just a block and a half from Fat Tony Salerno's clubhouse. After a hitch in the Navy, Moynihan had gotten his PhD from Tufts' Fletcher School of Law and Diplomacy and won a Fulbright to study in England. He'd briefly been a candidate for New York City's mayor. I had ample reason to take him seriously—in part because he took us seriously. (Among the students who lived at his home on Francis Avenue was future Reagan budget director David Stockman, who babysat for the Moynihan children.)

Moynihan taught a refreshingly personal seminar in his living room. The class was less of a Socratic dialogue than a bravura monologue in which the six-foot-five, white-maned Moynihan applied his wide reading and experience to that day's headlines. Epigrams tripped in staccato time from his lips as his eyebrows danced. He even dared to utter what to many in the room was a blasphemy: that Richard Nixon had done some good. Moynihan observed that Tricky Dick had torn a page from the yellowed playbook of British Tory leader Benjamin Disraeli, who in 1867 had flummoxed liberals by granting the vote to people not usually seen as conservatives. Moynihan contended that Nixon, too, was taking liberal issues away from Democrats by expanding on many of their "Great Society" initiatives—like school integration, family assistance, and Black capitalism. At the time, I took Moynihan's claims as the rationalizations of a Democrat who'd sold his soul to a pro-war, Republican administration. And yet I couldn't ignore the growing dissatisfaction of voters—white, ethnic, suburban, Southern—who'd long been the base of the Democratic Party. It was only with experience that I came to appreciate the reliable center route that Moynihan was charting, his instructions for co-opting the other side's issues and building new coalitions.

Never be afraid to borrow—and improve upon—your opponent's good idea. And be prepared to acknowledge where the idea came from.

7

LEARNING THE GRAYSCALE

Besides Moynihan and Kilson, my other great college mentor was Bill Schneider. With his long run as CNN's senior political analyst still in the future, Schneider was a young assistant professor in Harvard's Department of Government. He was fascinated with polling, which was still something of a novelty. Yes, George Gallup and Bud Roper had done political polls since before World War II. But those were usually after-the-fact samples of public opinion. Attempts to divine an election outcome were often doomed by the time the surveys took. (Witness the 1948 polls showing Thomas E. Dewey with an insurmountable lead over Harry Truman.)

Schneider had been frustrated by the divide between academic polling, which was comprehensive but deathly slow, and media polls, which were quick but shoddy. He believed new techniques could replace the wily machine boss with a cadre of data scientists. His class was hands-on. We spent most of the semester writing questionnaires, fielding polls around Boston, and analyzing responses. For me, it was an exciting and eye-opening experience. Polling was like canvassing—with less risk of running into Klan members, drug addicts, and mobsters.

In early 1973, as the New York City mayor's race got underway, Schneider approached *New York* magazine with the idea of a poll that would look inside the head of the Jewish voter. You see, Italian and Irish voters tended to cancel out Hispanic and Black voters. So, the crucial constituency at that time was the Jews, who made up about 30 percent of the electorate in the city's Democratic primaries. Schneider turned to me and fellow Harvard student E. J. Dionne, who had helped me on the Nardelli race and who would go on to be a syndicated columnist for the *Washington Post*. Among our research assistants was Lloyd Blankfein, who'd later become CEO and Chairman of Goldman Sachs. On June 4, primary day, our team conducted 601 interviews with Jewish voters. Our exit polls showed they were sharply divided among four mayoral candidates. But all the evidence pointed toward one conclusion: City Comptroller Abe Beame was likely to be the next mayor of New York City. We'd done an in-depth, academic-style poll—in twenty-four hours rather than six weeks. Veteran political operatives were impressed. Best of all, we turned out to be right.

Among our new admirers was the *New York Times'* Jack Rosenthal. He took Schneider, Dionne, and me to lunch to discuss our work. Over lunch, he offered me and Dionne summer jobs as reporters. Dionne wisely accepted on the spot. I said no, unequivocally. After all, I planned to run the country; others would be reporting on me. It may have been the wrong move. In hindsight: **if you're offered a way into a powerful institution, take it, you dummy!** But by that time, my passion was politics, not journalism. Instead of going to the *Times,* I got my first job as an independent campaign strategist. My client: Father Louis Gigante.

Father Gigante, a Roman Catholic priest, had been one of Eugene Nardelli's most ardent backers. I'd enjoyed his company but hadn't fully appreciated what an intriguing figure he was. His parish, St. Athanasius Church, was in Hunts Point, a neighborhood of tenements at the southern tip of the Bronx. For decades,

Hunts Point had been the first stop for Italian, Irish, and Jewish immigrants who later moved to better homes in Queens or on Long Island. During the 1950s and 1960s, however, that pattern changed. Poor people uprooted by the construction of the Cross Bronx Expressway flooded the area—along with a new generation of poorer, less skilled Puerto Rican immigrants. Desperate people do desperate things. Crime surged. The South Bronx turned into a burned-out, apocalyptic hellscape.

Old-timers too poor to move kept to themselves and tried to keep out of the crossfire. But "Father G"—as he was known in the 'hood—was different. A former hoop star at Georgetown, he mingled easily with the new residents on the basketball courts. He taught himself Spanish so that he could communicate with his new parishioners (one of whom was future Supreme Court justice Sonia Sotomayor). He founded the South East Bronx Community Organization, one of the country's first community development corporations, which ultimately built thousands of affordable housing units.

Father G had made an unsuccessful run for Congress in 1970. Now he was aiming for the City Council and wanted me to be his campaign manager. I believed in his mission. But, till then, I had not been completely aware of his colorful family. Four of his brothers were members of the Genovese crime organization. One of them, Vincent "The Chin" Gigante, would soon become its top boss. Father G didn't say much about his clan's flock of black sheep. He did maintain that "the Mafia" did not exist, at least as the disciplined corporation portrayed by the government. He told me that Vincent, a former boxer, was mentally ill. In fact, a psychiatrist had attested that Vincent suffered from paranoid schizophrenia. FBI agents photographed him muttering to himself as he puttered down the street in his pajamas and bathrobe. The tabloids dubbed him "The Oddfather." Paradoxically, Father G's brothers were aligned with the crew that had opposed

Nardelli and helped reelect Frank Rossetti three years earlier. But now that a Gigante was on the ballot, they were happy to help us—or at least, not interfere.

Father Gigante was looking to represent the Eighth District, which spanned three boroughs. The district's Queens neighborhoods were largely Italian and Irish. Its precincts in East Harlem and the South Bronx had a large African American population, a fast-growing Puerto Rican community, and a dwindling Italian enclave. It also included a sliver of Manhattan's moneyed Upper East Side. This race was the perfect laboratory for all that I'd learned so far—a chance to build a diverse ethnic coalition. It was almost like running a campaign in Mississippi, Puerto Rico, and the Hamptons at the same time.

To meet this challenge, I teamed up again with my pal E. J. Dionne. We decided to try out a relatively new technique—sophisticated, targeted direct mail. Working between classes in the *Harvard Crimson* newsroom, we drafted different messages for each constituency. Queens conservatives received red, white, and blue mailings emblazoned with the American flag—positioning the "patriot priest" as a defender of traditional values. Flyers to East Harlem and the South Bronx praised him as a fighter for the underdog. As for voters on the Upper East Side, they found out that Father Gigante was a champion of . . . recycling.

Remarkably, it worked. Gigante eked out a victory in the Democratic primary and crushed his general election opponent by 8,000 votes. By then, Father G and I had become good pals. I arranged for him to teach a seminar as a fellow of Harvard's John F. Kennedy Institute of Politics. He riled some students by defending the political machine, ward-heeling, and patronage. The *New York Times* ran a front-page story in which he bluntly declared, "I'm in politics to become a political boss . . . I want the power to put good people into government."

He also wanted to help my career. The Gigantes and their associates had been getting legal advice from Barry Slotnick ever since he got The Chin's beloved German shepherd, Bullets, off after he bit a lady. Knowing that I was thinking about law school, Father Gigante suggested that I might replace Slotnick as the family's counsellor. "Barry's a good guy," he said, "but he's not one of *us*. I can trust you. My friends can trust you. We can give you an inexhaustible supply of cases."

I don't know whether Father Gigante was aware of his brothers' schemes. (The Chin admitted in 2003 that he'd faked his "mental incapacity" for thirty-five years.) It's undeniable that the priest made a huge difference in steering kids away from crime and in revitalizing the South Bronx. He certainly taught me as much as any of my Harvard professors.

Most people are self-contradictions—mixtures of light and darkness. Life is about learning the moral gradients—the grayscale—and deciding how much shadow you can live with.

Flattered as I was by Father Gigante's proposal, it sounded a little *too* far out of my comfort zone. I pictured Robert Duvall's character, Tom Hagen, consigliere to the Corleone family in *The Godfather*. Mobsters can be demanding clients. Slotnick successfully defended Joe Colombo before the U.S. Supreme Court but, in 1987, another Colombo boss, Carmine "The Snake" Persico, had a guy beat up Slotnick because, according to an FBI informant, Persico was displeased with his work. In the end, Father G's overture was an offer I had to refuse—politely.

8

FINDING A PARTNER

As my graduation approached in 1974, I knew I wanted to be involved in politics, but I still wasn't sure how to do it. My polling prof, Bill Schneider, suggested I apply to Harvard's Knox Fellowship program. So, I submitted my honors thesis and the work I'd done with him for *New York* magazine and, lo and behold, I got into Oxford University. Hint for undergrads: **Not sure what to do after college? Try more college! Especially if it enhances your life skills. There's no such thing as being over-educated. You often won't know why a class is useful till after it's helped make you a success.**

England would be a little bit out of my comfort zone. Could I hold my own at one of the world's greatest universities? Once I was at Oxford, though, I quickly found a subject that fascinated me. Perhaps because left-leaning British historians thought him best forgotten, there hadn't been a serious biography of Conservative Party politician Enoch Powell. Powell had started life as a classical scholar and poet. Elected as a Member of Parliament, he'd stirred national fury in 1968 with his "Rivers of Blood" speech. Tapping into the resentment of white nativists, Powell augured that immigrants from Britain's former colonies posed a danger to the nation's economy and way of life. Some commentators believed Powell's divisive call to arms fueled the Conservatives'

surprise victory in the 1970 general election. I visited Powell's constituency in war-torn Northern Ireland. His Ulster Unionist voter
base gave me a sense of where populist politics was going, and
the failure of the establishment to understand such movements.

Race-based populism is more relevant than ever. But, at the
time, I was getting a little bored by academia. Fortunately, Bill
Schneider put me in touch with Bob Worcester—now Sir Robert
Worcester—whose public opinion research firm had close ties
to Britain's Labor Party. Once I told Worcester I'd work without
pay, he said the job was mine. Again, I saddled up with E. J.
Dionne, who was at Oxford on a Rhodes Scholarship. We went
to work on a campaign to bring Great Britain into the European
Common Market. Soon, Dionne and I were drafting presentations that Worcester delivered to the Labor Party cabinet. When
the Common Market measure passed, the flinty Worcester was
so delighted he gave us each a whopping £20 bonus.

Still, I missed the hurly-burly of New York politics. Father
Gigante had introduced me to Patrick J. Cunningham, the last of
the Irish clubhouse politicians to lead the Bronx Democratic Party.
When I came back to New York in 1974, I found that Cunningham
was working on behalf of gubernatorial candidate Hugh Carey, a
seven-term congressman. I offered my services. Cunningham must
have known that a campaign, like an army, traveled on its stomach.
One day at his offices, he asked me, "You hungry?"

"Yes," I said.

Reading the mind of a Jewish kid, he asked/ordered, "You'll
eat a roast beef sandwich, coleslaw, and Russian dressing?"

"Sure!" I said.

Cunningham then turned to Stanley Simon, the Bronx Borough
president.

"Stanley," he said, "go out and get the kid a sandwich."

I was slightly shocked that he'd enlisted one of the city's highest elected officials as a delivery boy. But Simon dutifully fetched

me the sandwich. After I'd taken a few bites, he even asked, "Is that okay?"

That sandwich opened my eyes to power in the Bronx. Simon certainly had some clout, but he snapped to when his party boss reckoned that my hunger was more urgent to the cause.

The Carey campaign helped me perfect telephone polling. In the past, pollsters would go door-to-door in selected neighborhoods. By this time, more than 95 percent of Americans had phones. You could gather a representative sample by calling every tenth voter on a registration roll, or by calling randomly generated numbers. The Carey team included Jerry Bruno, an old Kennedy advance man. Bruno put me in charge of a bank of 110 telephones. Needing some help, I remembered Mark Penn, the scruffy kid two years behind me at Horace Mann. Mark was a tenacious character. When Harvard sent him a rejection letter, he went up to Cambridge, marched into the admissions office, and informed its director that he'd made a grave mistake. The director was so impressed with Mark's chutzpah that he let him in. Mark had become the resident pollster at the *Crimson*. As a summer intern for NBC, he'd plotted the network's marketing strategy. Now, as I pondered how to market Hugh Carey, I figured I'd call Mark.

"Hey, Doug," he said. "I expected to hear from you sooner. What took you so long?"

Mark and I were both interested in politics. I was fascinated by policy, strategy, and the human dynamic between candidate and voter. Mark's forte was statistical analysis. I looked for words that could persuade and inspire. Mark was curious about new technology. We hadn't been that close at Harvard, but I felt we could fill each other's gaps.

Find a partner who can do what you can't.

Mark and I enlisted 110 volunteers to handle those 110 phones. The volunteers asked voters whose endorsements mattered most to them. We passed the results up the chain of command. The Carey campaign was thrilled. Carey ended up winning, becoming New York's first Democratic governor in sixteen years. Soon after, Carey named Cunningham chairman of the New York State Democratic Party. Cunningham hired Mark and me to do more polling. Our first survey gauged the appeal of potential Democratic candidates for the 1976 U.S. Senate race. (Among the names we floated was my old professor, Daniel Patrick Moynihan.) Our second poll measured the appeal of potential presidential candidates. Just before we were to begin calling, someone pointed out that we'd forgotten an obscure southern governor. Mark asked me if we should redo the questionnaire. "Nah," I told him. Who'd ever heard of Jimmy Carter?

In between dabbling in New York politics, I was scribbling away on my Oxford thesis on Enoch Powell. Besides earning me a PhD, *Enoch Powell and the Powellites*, was published, favorably reviewed, and became the template for a half dozen later Powell biographies. Still mulling my destiny, I gave my father a call. Little did I know he'd already figured my future out for me.

"Look," he said. "If you go to law school, your tuition will be paid, and you'll have an allowance. If you don't go to law school, you'll be on your own. You're welcome to come to our apartment for family holidays. Other than that, good luck and Godspeed."

So, in 1976, just like my father, I went to Harvard Law School. That same year, Professor Moynihan became Senator Moynihan. To keep myself busy, I asked Moynihan if I could write a biography about him. In his seminar, he'd chided me on my grammar but bestowed an A⁻ on my paper about Charles Evers's run in Mississippi. So, Moynihan said I was welcome to make him my next subject. He did lay down one condition for our first interview—I had to drink Scotch with him. I don't remember much about that interview, aside from my first burning jolt of Scotch. I know Hemingway, Faulkner, and other acclaimed writers were big drinkers, but I believe they succeeded despite their boozing, not because of it. **Don't drink on the job. Your work will survive longer and so will you.**

Meanwhile, Mark Penn, also feeling parental pressure, enrolled at Columbia Law School. In between our legal studies, he and I continued to talk. Our work for Cunningham had begun to attract the attention of other political players. One was David Garth. Garth had begun his career as a sports producer, but by the early 1970s, he'd become the most influential media consultant in the country. He'd put us on his payroll at $400 a week. That was pretty good money in 1976, and Garth hoped to pass the cost onto a client. He had trouble at first but, that summer, he found one.

★   ★   ★

Edward Irving Koch was a junior congressman. In 1973, he tried to run for mayor. Seven weeks into the race, having raised only about $100,000, he was forced to drop out. Now, in 1976, he was back—determined to enlist the services of Garth, the man who'd beaten the Democratic machine in 1965, when he'd made a mayor out of John Lindsay, Koch's predecessor representing New York's 17th Congressional District. Garth would give Koch's campaign instant credibility. Garth, however, had another candidate in mind—Mario Cuomo. Like Governor Carey, who'd made Cuomo his secretary of state, Garth was urging the former Queens lawyer to run for mayor. But Cuomo, later anointed as the Hamlet of American politics, couldn't make up his mind. Garth, in turn, continued to stall Koch. To keep him at bay, Garth told us to field a benchmark poll to gauge Koch's appeal.

Mark and I found that in a hypothetical six-candidate mayoral race, nobody had more than 20 percent support. That was the good news. The bad news: at around 6 percent, Koch was dead last. Koch and his handful of supporters were naturally discouraged. But Mark and I emphasized that there was a path to victory. Voters were angry with Abe Beame. Many believed he'd bankrupted the city and kowtowed to public sector unions and special interests. They wanted a competent decision maker who'd do something to curb crime. Mark and I argued that Koch had a lot of what voters were looking for. He'd opposed the clubhouse system, so he was seen as a reformer. He also talked tough on crime and supported the death penalty. He understood the concerns of middle-class ethnic voters. In short, we believed he could win by styling himself as an outer-borough liberal or, as Koch would later put it, "a liberal with sanity."

When Cuomo finally told Garth he wasn't running, Garth signed on with Koch. Garth had a wide face, a furrowed brow, and a short fuse. He didn't suffer fools. Mark and I didn't have much experience, and we were both technically first-year law students. But for whatever reason, Garth never got around to replacing us. Maybe because we were all Koch could afford. His campaign treasurer, Bernie Rome, often referred to us behind our backs as "those nickel-and-dime researchers"—and sometimes not even behind our backs.

When Koch officially flung his hat into the ring, the media response was less than enthusiastic. Unfazed, Garth started fashioning TV ads that introduced voters to this straight-shooting World War II vet who was socially progressive and fiscally conservative. Garth began to run the ads in late June. At the time, most campaigns saved their ad dollars until the final two or three weeks of a race. One reason for our early blitz was the disturbing rumor that Mario Cuomo had changed his mind. One month later, Hamlet announced that he was indeed a candidate for mayor. Worse still, he'd hired media consultant Jerry Rafshoon. Rafshoon's partner, Pat Caddell, had been at Harvard a few years before me. Working out of his dorm room, Caddell had become nationally renowned for measuring Americans' attitudes about the Vietnam War and racial division. He was the first to understand that you could use polling to *shape* those attitudes. At twenty-six years old, he'd masterminded one of the greatest upset victories in modern American politics—peanut farmer Jimmy Carter's win over President Gerald Ford. No pollster was more famous. But Mark and I had two critical advantages. First, we knew the city much better than Caddell and Rafshoon. Second, we had a secret weapon.

Our first survey for Koch had taken us five nights of polling, just to get enough responses to have a statistically significant sample. Once we had the results, we had to input the data onto punch cards and tabulate the results on a mainframe computer at Columbia University. That took all night—*if* you entered the data correctly. If you made one mistake with a punch card, you had to start again. And we'd get no sympathy from Garth. Rather, he was likely to say, "I don't fucking need you if you can't fucking get me data quickly!"

After several of these mishaps, Mark and I tried to figure out a better way. Mark said, "Let's buy a microcomputer!" This was four years before the launch of IBM personal computers. Microcomputers were seen as expensive toys for hobbyists. A "kit" (assembly required) cost about $1,000—almost $5,000 today.

"Why would we want to spend $1,000 on a computer?" I asked.

"Fine, I'll do it myself," Mark said.

To his eternal credit, he did. Once he got it running, Mark wrote a program that could compile poll results almost immediately. At the end of the process, he had created something that no other political consultant in America had. The microcomputer resided in Mark's two-bedroom apartment room near Columbia. That became our center of operations. After the phone bank operators had completed their work, we'd bring the data back to Mark's pad. We hired several yeshiva students to input the data. Typically, they'd arrive around 10:00 p.m. and finish around

6:00 a.m. Mark's program then cross-tabulated the results. Within an hour, we had something to tell Garth.

Mark's microcomputer didn't just speed up the process. It gave us the ability to evaluate the campaign's strategy every day. Garth could now put an ad on TV during the day, have us poll that night, and get feedback by the next morning. We had invented the overnight tracking poll. Soon Garth insisted that Koch save one hour every morning to film new ads that responded to issues our polls detected.

One potential issue was Koch's sexual orientation. Koch was a lifelong bachelor and a resident of the West Village—home and playground for many gay people. In his first run for City Council, he had campaigned for an end to anti-sodomy laws, full abortion rights, and less restrictive divorce laws. (Opponents nicknamed his platform "SAD.") Whispering had started about his sexuality. Cuomo's campaign denied having anything to do with it. But in some Cuomo strongholds, posters proclaimed, "Vote for Cuomo, not the Homo."

Our polls showed that the public didn't care much which way Koch swung. But Garth worried that it might become an issue later. To stanch the whispers, he sought the help of Koch's friend, Bess Myerson, the first Jewish woman to become Miss America and John Lindsay's Commissioner of Consumer Affairs. Bess soon began showing up to public events with Koch. Garth and Koch even encouraged speculation that romance might be in the air. The Koch campaign was gathering steam.

That summer, it benefited from two tragic events. On July 13, lightning strikes coupled with a Con Edison repair mistake plunged the city into darkness, inciting riots, looting, and arson. Later that month, police found the body of Stacy Moskowitz—the latest victim of a serial killer who called himself "Son of Sam." These terrors shifted the attention of the entire city to public safety. By early August, our polls showed that concern about crime was eroding support for the early frontrunners, Mayor Abe Beame and Congresswoman Bella Abzug. In contrast, Koch, the only candidate who'd run from the get-go on being "tough on crime," was moving up in the polls.

But so was Mario Cuomo. Although he opposed the death penalty, Cuomo had begun to emphasize law and order. Moreover, he'd won an endorsement from the *New York Times.* He had the momentum to win.

But there was a new player in town—a then-obscure Australian press baron named Rupert Murdoch.

Murdoch had recently scooped up the *Village Voice, New York* magazine and, most significantly, the declining afternoon newspaper, the *New York Post.* Founded by Alexander Hamilton in 1801, the *Post* had been known for its excellent arts coverage, the polished columns of Murray Kempton and James Wechsler, and a distinctly liberal point of view. Murdoch changed things fast. Taking on the larger-circulation *Daily News* in the morning, he imported a brigade of Aussies who specialized in the attention-grabbing tabloid style.

Murdoch wasn't just looking for business success. He wanted political power. He wanted to defang the city's unions, which he and others blamed for the city's fiscal crisis. Among other things, Murdoch was looking for a candidate willing to bring into his administration Eddie Costikyan, a Democratic reformer who'd been a loud critic of labor excesses. Murdoch had lunched with both Koch and Cuomo. Garth had arranged for Murdoch to sit down again with Koch at Garth's offices. That day, the air conditioning was broken. Murdoch walked in and looked like his was going to melt. His jacket was over his shoulder; his tie was askew. He and his aides went into a conference room with Koch and his aides. I was not in that room. But, after a half hour, Murdoch and Koch emerged—still sweating but looking very chummy. Shortly thereafter, Koch announced that, if elected,

Eddie Costikyan would be his first deputy mayor. Koch understood you need to **make the deal.**

Murdoch promptly delivered a three-column front page *Post* endorsement of Koch. Our polling showed that Koch's support shot up about 5 or 6 points. More important was the *Post's* coverage during the remainder of the campaign. The *Post* became a reliable champion of Koch, juxtaposing flattering articles and attractive pictures of the balding candidate with vitriolic attacks on his opponents. The *Post's* love affair with Koch provoked more than fifty *Post* staffers to send Murdoch a letter protesting the one-sided coverage. Murdoch responded by inviting those protestors to quit.

Primary election day was September 8. Going into the home stretch, polls conducted by the *New York Times* and CBS continued to show Beame and Abzug tied for first place, with Cuomo and Koch locked in a battle for second. Based on our model of actual turnout, we saw things differently. Within half an hour of the polls closing, we told Koch he would win the primary, with Cuomo coming in a close second. Koch and Garth looked at us incredulously. Although Mark and I were confident in our methodology, we were relieved when Koch received 180,914 votes versus Cuomo's 171,100 votes, with Beame, Abzug, and the other candidates bringing up the rear.

But Koch still hadn't won the Democratic nomination. Since he failed to win more than 40 percent of the primary vote, he and Cuomo were forced into a runoff election. When voters returned to the polls, Koch defeated Cuomo again, this time by a vote of 432,000 to 355,000.

But Cuomo still wouldn't bow out. He stayed in the race as the Liberal Party candidate.

Never assume an opponent's beaten till he's truly beaten. Always be ready to step up your game.

As the final November showdown loomed, Mark and I fielded polls every night. Garth used our results to target messaging. For instance, Black voters heard that Harlem kingmaker Percy Sutton backed Koch; Latino voters heard that Congressman Herman Badillo also supported him. Ironically, Koch himself was almost indifferent to our work. One day, I was in an elevator with him. Trying to make conversation, he asked, "You do polls? *All day?*"

"Yes," I said. "We do polls. All day."

He shook his head, almost sympathetically. He knew we were trying to help him, but he was an old-world politician who mostly listened to his gut.

Hard as we worked, a problem arose in the final weeks of the campaign. Our polls had consistently shown that many voters wanted an outsider. In the primaries, Koch had been that outsider. But now that the political establishment was rallying around him, the dynamic had changed. Voters saw Cuomo as the outsider. Our final poll showed that Cuomo was only 8 points behind Koch. Cuomo's team went on the attack, plastering TV screens with negative ads that attempted to link Koch with former Mayor John Lindsay. It didn't work. Koch edged out Cuomo a third time—712,551 votes to 587,196 votes.

The Friday after the election, the *New York Times* published an opinion piece Mark and I wrote. In it, we discussed how the growing identification of Koch with the establishment during the runoff had almost cost him the election. When our op-ed appeared, Garth went nuts. Not only hadn't we told him we were writing it, but we were kind of blabbing about the inner workings of his operation. And we were sort of taking credit for Koch's victory. Garth threatened to throw Mark's minicomputer out the window. Fortunately, he didn't. Maybe he recognized the little machine was too valuable. Eventually, Garth cooled down.

Before you take a bow, make sure the rest of the cast is onstage—and that they think you deserve applause.

9

LOSERS PAY TOO

From time to time, Mark and I would meet with Koch at Gracie Mansion, home to New York City's mayors. It seemed like only yesterday that I was a high school student playing touch football in the park outside. Koch's victory left Penn and Schoen feeling proud, but also a bit bewildered. We'd been dabbling in politics between our law school classes. Now that we were about to graduate, we wondered what was next. In 1979, there weren't many full-time political consultants. But the fact that we'd vanquished two of the most famous—Rafshoon and Cadell—bolstered our hope that we could make a living doing what we loved. Of course, my father thought we were nuts. He advised me not to waste my Harvard law degree consorting with a bunch of shady politicians—*ganefs*, in Yiddish—who'd probably end up stiffing me.

I still thought it was worth a try. If Mark and I could earn something close to the salary of a law firm associate, we'd be doing okay. Our start-up had no "seed capital," aside from the half-payment clients would give us up front. Our only "angel" was labor mediator Theodore Kheel, who gave us a free office in Automation House, the East 68th Street townhouse where he did his mediating. His only condition was that we rent his phone bank from time to time. Mark and I would sit in that office waiting for our phone to ring. When it did, we'd fall over each other racing to answer it. Could be a client! Did the mail come yet? Any checks?

While Mark cultivated the rumpled, absent-minded air of a young Einstein, I worked the political connections I'd made over the past decade. Fortunately, David Garth was still throwing us work. One of our first post-Koch campaigns was in Louisiana.

I'd gotten a taste of that state four years earlier while visiting my Harvard pal Mike Early in New Orleans. Mike originally studied for the priesthood, but a life of celibacy had lost its appeal by the time he'd met his future wife, Mavis Ann. Shortly after Mike proposed to her, his friends threw him a bachelor party. For entertainment, his buddy Ralph Capitelli, an assistant district attorney, had borrowed several "stag films" from the evidence locker of his boss, Jim Garrison. (In addition to investigating JFK's assassination, Garrison had made headlines cracking down on Big Easy vice.) So, there I was watching my first porn movie on a bedsheet hung from a curtain rod above a window. Suddenly, the doorbell rang. It was the police. We hadn't realized that our skin flick was being projected through the sheer sheet, out the window, and onto a nearby building. Children were seeing engorged body parts three-stories high. Prosecutor Capitelli sprang into action, explaining the circumstances to the cops, who agreed to call off the raid. It was a night rich in irony.

The bachelor party was just one of my eye-opening experiences in the Crescent City. Having won Mavis Ann's heart, Mike hoped to capture a city council seat. With a little help from me, he succeeded. (He held on to the seat for fourteen years.) Mike's previous experience included serving as an aide to Lieutenant Governor James Fitzmorris, known locally as "Jimmy Fitz." When I came to town, Mike asked if I'd like to meet the man. After we exchanged a few pleasantries, the lieutenant governor asked Mike about the economic issue that most concerned him: how much money he was going to pocket for finagling pardons and sentence reductions for convicted criminals. I was struck by his frankness. For all he knew, I was a young lawyer with the Justice Department. Yet Jimmy Fitz chattered about kickbacks like he was ordering a po'-boy sandwich. If he was going to get people out of jail, he wanted what was in it for him!

What brought me back to Louisiana in 1979 was the campaign of Edgar G. "Sonny" Mouton Jr. David Garth's new client was one of the deans of the Louisiana state senate. My task was figuring out how to help Mouton become governor. That spring, I flew down, rented a car, and set out for Lafayette. I knew little about the state's fourth largest city. Had I done a little research, I might have gleaned that Lafayette was the locus of Louisiana's booming oil industry. During the 1970s, no state had more money sloshing around than Louisiana, and much of those petro-dollars fueled politics. Despite this wealth, Lafayette at first appeared to be a ramshackle, bayou town that had seen better days.

I met Mouton at a steakhouse. He was a stubby, bald man with a Cajun accent so thick I thought we'd need a translator. He'd brought along his campaign manager, Eustis Corrigan, whom Mouton jokingly called "Useless Corrigan." Also, there was Mouton's campaign treasurer, a cadaverous oilman named J. Y. Foreman. As I looked over the menu, I tried to keep from staring at the astonishing bouffant toupee perched precipitously atop J. Y.'s emaciated body. I quickly learned that J. Y. was afflicted with cancer. Indeed, Mouton spent much of the meal telling his chief backer, "Don't die on me, J. Y.! Don't die!" The company may have been curious, but the steak was one of the best I'd ever had. As I sliced into my tenderloin, it dawned on me that Lafayette wasn't as poor as I'd thought. I decided to pitch these good ol' boys the full package—a strategy-setting poll for $21,500. They agreed without blinking an eye.

I returned to New Orleans in late May to discuss the poll results. This time I was whisked to an enormous suite at the new Hyatt Regency Hotel. Before my presentation, we met for dinner in the French Quarter. All of Mouton's cronies were there—except for J. Y. Foreman. It turned out J. Y. had in fact died. Despite his passing, the money still seemed to be flowing. At the end of the meal one of Mouton's sidekicks—a man the waiter called "Monsieur Butch"—asked for five long baguettes to go. I must have looked surprised because Monsieur Butch turned to me and drawled, "It's so much easier to buy your bread at restaurants than to have to suffer the indignities of a grocery store." When it came time to pay for the two polls I'd done, he rounded the total up to $22,000. "It's easier to keep count of that way," he told me.

Clearly, the good times were rolling. What I didn't realize at the time, however, was that J. Y.'s death had been a catastrophe for Mouton. Without his moneyman, Mouton had to rely heavily on a figure that even Louisianans viewed with suspicion—Charles Roemer, Governor Edwin Edwards's chief of administration. According to my polls, voters didn't cotton to Mouton's coziness with Roemer. I suggested to Mouton that he needed to redefine himself as a fresh face with new ideas. That meant disassociating himself from Roemer.

"I just can't do that," he told me.

"Why not?" I asked.

"I just can't."

"You have to," I told him.

"You'll have to take this up with Charles's son, Buddy," Mouton told me. So, I called Buddy. I explained the situation. Buddy listened in silence. Finally, he said, "You'll have to talk to my father."

I knew that Charles Roemer fancied himself a skillful pollster and political operative. I also suspected that he wouldn't be too happy to hear that I considered him an albatross. When I called, he and son Buddy listened as I presented my poll results. Neither said a word. Finally, Roemer *père* spoke.

"Listen," he said. "I wouldn't piss across the street for a poll done by people like you who associate with David Garth in New York."

That conversation ended my involvement with the Roemers. A decade later, Charles Roemer was convicted of conspiring with reputed New Orleans mob boss Carlos Marcello to obtain state insurance contracts. (The convictions were later overturned.) Ironically, Buddy Roemer would be elected governor in 1987—managing to portray himself as an "outsider."

I wasn't the only person benefiting from the well-oiled Mouton campaign. When I inquired where I could pick up my payment, I was told to drop by Friday morning at a small French Quarter hotel that served as Mouton's headquarters. I arrived early for breakfast. By 10:30 a.m., more than thirty other people had showed up as well. In the crowd were two of Louisiana's more controversial Black leaders, Don Hubbard and Sherman Copelin. I asked New York writer Jean Nathan what all these guys were doing there. She told me nonchalantly, "Waiting for their walking-around money."

Mouton ultimately finished fifth in the primary. Nevertheless, Louisiana convinced me that there was money to be made in political consulting.

★ ★ ★

Not that it was always easy to collect. In 1979, I thought I'd hit the big time when Sen. Edward Kennedy needed my services. That year, rumors were swirling that the Camelot heir would challenge embattled President Jimmy Carter for the Democratic presidential nomination. Carter's favorability rating had been plummeting. House Speaker Tip O'Neill even declared the nomination was Kennedy's for the asking. Then, in the fall, Kennedy agreed to two interviews with CBS correspondent Roger Mudd. Kennedy apparently expected softball questions. Instead, Mudd dove into the 1969 drowning of campaign worker Mary Jo Kopechne in the Oldsmobile Kennedy had been driving. Mudd further flustered Kennedy by querying him about the state of his marriage. The second interview went even worse. Mudd asked the standard question: "Why do you want to be president?" The candidate's rambling answer was astonishingly incoherent.

It didn't take Ted long to step in it again. When Iranian students stormed the U.S. Embassy in Tehran, Kennedy criticized the Shah of Iran—suggesting to some that the revolt was justified. Rupert Murdoch's *New York Post* splashed Kennedy's picture across its front page with the headline, "The Toast of Tehran."

Trying to deal with the fiasco, Kennedy's brother-in-law and campaign manager, Stephen Smith, called David Garth to ask for advice. Garth told Smith that the campaign should do a poll to assess the damage. Mark and I quickly produced two polls. Smith asked if I could come to Washington to present the results. Excited, I flew down the next day, catching a cab out to the Kennedy homestead in McLean, Virginia. As I walked into the kitchen, I stumbled into a tense scene between Ted and his wife Joan. Their silent hostility was apparent. Kennedy made no motion to rise or shake my hand. Instead, he glumly pointed me to a back room. There I found Smith and the rest of Kennedy's inner circle. I was disappointed that Kennedy himself wasn't participating but went ahead, delivering my takeaways. I said that Kennedy's gaffes were killing his chances. I suggested that he should apologize now, before he went off to campaign in Iowa. Kennedy's advisers listened politely but didn't seem too concerned. At the end of the presentation, Steve Smith thanked me, then asked, "Can I get you a cab back to the airport?"

"No," I replied.

"Oh," he said, puzzled. "Where would you like to go?"

"To your headquarters."

"And why would you want to go there?" he asked.

"Because I want to get paid!"

"Get paid?" he asked.

"Yes," I said. "We need to get paid for the two polls."

A smile spread across his face.

"Oh, so you know our reputation?" said Smith, who also managed the Kennedy family's vast investments. He seemed almost tickled by the clan's notoriety as cheapskates. (JFK reputedly never carried cash, expecting friends and even Secret Service agents to pick up his tab.)

"The bottom line," I said firmly, "is that each poll is $10,000 and we need our money."

Instead of going to National Airport, I took a taxi to Kennedy headquarters—fittingly located in an old auto dealership where used-car salesmen once waited for suckers. I cooled my heels there for several hours until someone produced a check. Call me unreasonable but, at that stage, Mark and I couldn't afford to give thirty to ninety days credit to a Kennedy. As our business got on its feet, we became a little more lenient in our terms. But all too often, after we'd read a candidate's tea leaves, the candidate was in no hurry to pay, particularly if he didn't like the tea leaves, or he ended up losing. Word to the shy: **don't hesitate to demand your due.**

Vigilant as I was about bill payment back then, I was still shortsighted. Around this time, a couple of people helped correct my vision. One was David Garth. He once offered us a candidate who faced an uphill battle and didn't have much of a war chest. I said, "Boy, this guy has real problems." Garth said, "Doug, if he didn't have problems, he wouldn't need you!"

Problems are opportunities. Make it your business to take work other people don't want—and take it seriously, whatever it pays.

Another person who tried to cure my myopia was Democratic strategist Jill Buckley. One day, in her office, Jill was telling me about some up-and-coming candidates she believed could carry the liberal banner. I didn't disagree with Jill's ideals, but I didn't think some of these candidates were electable. I guess she sensed my skepticism. After I'd said goodbye, I was walking toward the stairs when she shouted, "Hey, Doug! I didn't tell you the 11th Commandment of Political Consulting."

"The 11th Commandment?" I asked.

"Yes," she said. **"Losers pay too!"**

Jill meant that, while everybody loves a winner, there was also money to made betting on a dark horse. Even if he came in last. She suggested I do more networking. At her behest, I flew out to North Dakota to meet with some local Democrats— who, even in 1979, were an endangered species in that state. I landed in Bismarck and checked into the Town House Motor Inn. It was November. I was shivering. I decided to take a warm shower. The room was so cold that I turned on the heat lamp in the bathroom. I'm still not sure what went wrong but the lamp exploded—strafing me with scalding shards of glass. Like Janet Leigh in *Psycho*, I watched my blood swirl down the shower drain. It crossed my mind that I might be in the wrong profession.

My lacerations didn't stop me from meeting Byron Dorgan and Kent Conrad. Byron was just twenty-six when he became North Dakota's Tax Commissioner. Kent worked in his office. Byron had lost his bid for Congress four years earlier but now he was ready to try again. I helped him win the first of his six terms as a U.S. Representative. When Byron went to Washington, Kent succeeded him as Tax Commissioner. Around that time, Byron asked if I could do some polling. He said he could only pay me $2,500. I didn't think that was enough. So, I passed. I never heard from Byron or Kent again. Both went on to run for the U.S. Senate, and win. Byron served in the Senate for eighteen years, Kent for twenty-six. I should have done that poll for $2,500. In hindsight:

Make the trip. Take the meeting. Underdogs can become top dogs. Be prepared to compromise for the sake of a longer relationship. Taking less now can mean making more later.

★　★　★

Fortunately, other customers came calling. One was a brilliant politician named Marion Barry. A veteran of the civil rights movement, Barry had been shot near the heart during a 1977 hostage-taking by Islamic militants. He'd survived and gone on to become the District of Columbia's second mayor. In 1982, he was up for reelection and asked Mark and I to do some polling. Barry was smart and charismatic, but I found it odd that, whenever we met, his (third) wife, Effi, joined us. Only later, when Barry's womanizing and cocaine addiction became public, did I appreciate her attentiveness. Our polling helped Barry win a landslide victory. His campaign manager and chief of staff, Ivanhoe Donaldson, was so pleased with our work that he hired us for an exhaustive survey on the issues facing the city. The cost was $45,000. Imagine my shock when, two years later, U.S. Attorney Joe diGenova subpoenaed our records—every letter and phone call—as part of a criminal investigation into corruption in Barry's administration. Mark and I spent a lot of time and money complying. No charges were brought against us. I asked diGenova why Penn & Schoen had been dragged into the case. Apologetically, he explained that, after Ivanhoe Donaldson had paid us $45,000, Donaldson had billed the city the same amount for *his* supposed work on the poll. Prosecutors had at first thought our bill was part of his expense padding.

Barry had given Penn & Schoen a glowing endorsement for our firm's promotional brochure. But more scandals followed—culminating in an FBI sting in which a sometime girlfriend of the mayor lured him into a hotel room to smoke crack. ("Bitch set me up," Hizzoner memorably grumbled.) So, we had to destroy all our Barry-blurbed brochures. Equipment tip: **Invest in a good shredder.**

10

GIVE IT A SHOT

I'd been working with underdogs since my early days in Mississippi and East Harlem. But only in 1982 did I find a longshot with long money.

Frank Lautenberg had helped found the payroll management giant ADP—for which he'd been paid well. He'd used a good chunk of his wealth to best eight other Democratic primary candidates who also had hoped to fill the seat left vacant by U.S. Senator Harrison Williams when the FBI's Abscam sting sent him to jail. Now Lautenberg faced Republican House member Millicent Fenwick, the seventy-two-year-old doyenne of New Jersey politics. Fenwick was known for her jaunty beauty, her ardent support of civil and women's rights, and her fierce opposition to corruption in both parties. CBS anchor Walter Cronkite called her "the conscience of Congress." She was widely seen as the inspiration for *Doonesbury's* noble congresswoman Lacey Davenport. Lautenberg himself reckoned Fenwick might be "the most popular candidate in the country."

To defeat her, Lautenberg turned to us. In our benchmark poll, we found that our client, a little-known businessman, was 25 points behind Fenwick. Teaming up with media consultant Robert Squier, we crafted ads that highlighted Lautenberg's story—the son of blue-collar immigrants; a salesman who'd worked his way up to CEO. The ads improved his numbers. But we could see the positive message alone wouldn't put him over the top. So, we fired off more ads that tied Fenwick to Ronald Reagan (then unpopular in New Jersey) and to the 10 percent unemployment rate. We charged that Fenwick's votes in Congress had cost New Jersey jobs.

We also considered addressing her age. Others in the campaign worried that going negative against a female candidate would boomerang against Lautenberg. Mark and I argued that age was a legitimate issue. Fenwick would be almost eighty at the end of her first term, unlikely to win Senate leadership. Lautenberg, who was fifty-eight, okayed the hit. New ads suggested that Fenwick was out of touch . . . and perhaps a little tetched. We hinted that her pipe smoking (her doctor had told her to quit cigarettes) was an eccentricity that spoke to her "fitness."

Some thought the ads were a step too far, but they worked— just barely. A man who'd never held office—but who had spent twice as much as his opponent—won 51 percent of the vote. We'd played hardball against a woman who may have been the last Republican liberal. In the process, we'd started the political career of another effective progressive. Running for a fifth Senate term at the age of eighty-four, Lautenberg argued that he'd never made an issue of Fenwick's age, only her "ability to do the job." When he died in 2013, he was New Jersey's longest serving senator.

Voters claim they don't like negative campaigns. But it's much easier to persuade voters that somebody's bad than somebody's good. It helps to have a villain. That said, **you can be critical without being vicious. You can win without defiling your opponent's dignity. Even if you're trying to stay positive, you need to differentiate yourself from the competition. Whether it's politics, business, or romance, you need to explain why you're best qualified for the job.**

GIVE IT A SHOT

★   ★   ★

As immersed as I was in politics, I wanted to go deeper. Ever since I saw my uncle, New York State senator Jack Bronston, excusing himself from dinner to make important calls, I'd played with the idea of running for Congress. My serious plotting began when I was twenty-six. Right after graduating from Harvard Law School, I bought an apartment in Forest Hills, Queens. My sole reason for choosing this not exactly swinging neighborhood was that I had identified the congressional seat as vulnerable. It was currently held by Rep. Joseph P. Addabbo. I set my sights on toppling him in the midterms of 1982. But after scoping me out at a voter meet-and-greet at my apartment, Addabbo caught a break when his district was redrawn to exclude heavily Jewish Forest Hills (my base) and include blocks populated by Italian Americans and African Americans (his base). I now found myself living in a district represented by eleven-term "machine Democrat" Ben Rosenthal. He was not an easy target. I decided to hold off. Despite suffering from terminal cancer, Rosenthal proceeded to win a 12th term. Then, one day after Congress was reconvened in 1983, he died. A special election would be held to fill his seat. This was my chance to move into public life.

To run as a Democrat, I needed to have the party's support. That meant kissing the ring of Queens Borough President Donald R. Manes, who was also the Queens Democratic chairman. When we met, Manes surprised me by immediately asking my net worth. Now you might argue that my ability to self-finance a campaign was a legitimate concern. But then he started to bemoan his own net worth—how little the party paid him (though somehow, he could afford a BMW and a house in Jamaica Estates). He pointed out that, as a public servant, he made much less than one of my father's law partners, Sandy Lindenbaum, the dean of zoning attorneys. I got the strong sense that Manes expected me to cross his palm with silver. He was careful not to come right out and say it. But I believe his price was somewhere between his official salary and what Sandy Lindenbaum made.

Manes tried to get me to run instead for the state Assembly. He asked me to talk to his close associate, Michael A. Nussbaum, who suggested we take a walk around Queens Borough Hall. Nussbaum said a "walk-and-talk" was the way they did business in Queens. It reminded me of the way Gambino crime boss John Gotti conducted his business—on the sidewalk, where the FBI couldn't listen in.

I declined Manes's Assembly offer. Knowing I wasn't going to be the Democratic candidate for Congress without paying his toll, I approached Raymond Harding, the powerful head of New York State's Liberal Party. He was willing to put me on the Liberal line. Then he checked with Mario Cuomo, whom he'd helped elect as governor. Cuomo, a resident of the district I hoped to represent, gave me a thumbs down—probably because I'd been Ed Koch's pollster when Cuomo ran for mayor.

At this point I had no choice but to run for Congress as an Independent. I started to wonder if I should keep pursuing this. As usual, my father thought I was crazy. But I reasoned that, with the March 1 election only a few weeks away, it wouldn't take long to learn if this was my future or a folly.

I amassed a war chest of $350,000—close to $1 million today. About $250,000 of that was money I'd saved. Mark Penn helped me out with strategy. So did Hank Sheinkopf, one of New York's canniest media tacticians. I was fast out of the gate with TV ads. I used everything I'd learned—overnight polling, targeted direct mail, and old-fashioned canvassing. I campaigned on subway platforms and at supermarkets.

Manes ended up anointing State Senator Gary L. Ackerman as the Democratic candidate. (A party insider told me they took a brisk walk together on Rockaway Beach.) My former client, Ed

Koch, also backed Ackerman—I guess because Hizzoner wanted to stay in the party's good graces.

I thought I was a better candidate than Gary Ackerman. I was gaining momentum up until he got in the race. But I had a mainstream Democratic platform much like his. I didn't really differentiate myself. And without the backing of a party, a good campaign will only get you so far. I was spending much more of my own money than I ever expected. Every day, I drove past a flapping "Vote for Ackerman" banner that my rival had hung across Queens Boulevard. It was emotionally draining.

But I must have scared the machine. The *New York Times* reported that Manes "poured Democratic workers from throughout Queens into the Congressional District in what he acknowledged was a test of his leadership and traditional organization canvassing against Mr. Schoen's media campaign."

Ackerman won the four-way race, prompting Manes to call it "a victory for the people and the Democratic Party over the media whiz people."

Longer term, the outcome wasn't so good for Manes. Three years later, facing indictment for a raft of kickback schemes, he committed suicide by plunging an eight-inch kitchen knife into his heart. The following year, his friend, Nussbaum, was convicted of soliciting a $250,000 bribe for Manes, though the conviction was overturned on appeal. In 2003, Sheldon S. Leffler, the candidate endorsed by the *New York Times*, was found guilty of scheming to defraud the government in a run for Queens borough president. And, in 2009, Ray Harding pleaded guilty in another corruption case.

Ackerman served for thirty years in the House of Representatives. In 2012, he decided not to seek reelection. He told me that life as a congressman had become so devalued that I should be grateful he won. In fact, he asked if I could help him find a new job.

I can't say I wasn't disappointed when I lost that race. But I don't regret running. It may not have been a practical decision. The tides were against me. But it was what I wanted to do.

If you can't get a dream out of your head, get it out of your system. Give it a shot. You may succeed. You may not. At least you tried.

11

GO GENERAL

Despite my loss, each race gave me confidence—sometimes too much of it. Around this time, I made a presentation to a would-be client and his team. I was impressed with my own performance. Afterward, an older gentleman took me aside.

"Doug, you were great in there," he said. "You hit it out of the park." I beamed. Then he told me to get over myself. His adage (and now mine): **"Even if you are the smartest guy in the room, don't act like it. Don't talk down to people. You can be smart without being a smartass."**

I was getting cocky. Fortunately, I met people who could set me straight. I was once in New Haven making a pitch to a former police chief who was considering a run for office. I told him that Mark and I could do his polling and that I could hook him up with a campaign manager, a press secretary, an ad guy, all sorts of people. This ex-cop and I had been getting along, but suddenly he seemed angry with me.

"Let me tell you something, kid," he said. **"Feed your family first!"**

"What does that mean?" I asked. (I didn't even have a family.)

"You're not hired yet," he said. "You don't have my money. Take care of yourself. Don't do favors for people till you have a check in the bank."

Put another way: **Don't sell others till you've sold yourself.**

The cop's insight was perfected by another unlikely teacher. Arthur Deutsch was born in 1926. He was a poor Jewish kid who never got much of an education. Arthur's drive had built Allied Mechanical Trades, which allowed him to send his son, Peter, to my alma mater, Horace Mann, and then to Swarthmore College and Yale Law School. Peter was barely twenty-five when he approached us about helping him get elected to the Florida House of Representatives. Mark and I agreed to meet Peter and Arthur at Arthur's office in a walk-up on Third Avenue. Arthur was morbidly obese. As he climbed the stairs, he was huffing and puffing and schvitzing like a sauna attendant at the 10th Street Baths. Dozens of keys jangled from his sixty-inch waist. When he finally sat down and caught his breath, he asked me, "Do you know what I do?"

"No," I said.

"I used to be a plumbing contractor," he said. "Then I went into general contracting. The money is in going general. You shouldn't just offer polling. You should do *everything*. **Go general!**"

Here was an untutored man sharing intelligence more useful than much of what I'd heard at Harvard and Oxford. Despite my belief in higher education, I learned that degrees are less important than results.

Wisdom can come from people you don't immediately recognize as wise.

Peter Deutsch ended up being elected to five terms in the Florida statehouse and, after that, to six terms in the U.S. House of Representatives. Taking his father's advice, Penn & Schoen started offering a full menu of campaign services. In the spring of 1984, we reunited with Ed Koch. Facing reelection in 1985, the mayor wasn't looking all that strong. He'd made an ill-considered, gaffe-riddled run for the governorship in 1982 and allowed his relationship with African American New Yorkers to deteriorate. Koch would have to shore up support among his core voters and turn them out in huge numbers. With the old Tammany clubhouse practically boarded up, we had to construct our own machine. Koch tapped his trusted aide, Jim Capalino, as his campaign manager. Jim organized Koch loyalists throughout the precincts. Mark and I did just about everything else. Our offices soon became the campaign's de facto headquarters. We developed a direct mail campaign and set up phone banks. We came up with a novel way to capitalize on Koch's celebrity. Simon & Schuster had just published his book, *Politics*. We convinced him to barnstorm the city, selling autographed copies for $100 each. As usual, he asked everyone he met, "How'm I doin'?" These events proved so popular that they gave rise to a new campaign ritual—the politician's pre-announcement book tour. We also assembled a field organization with thousands of volunteers and raised hundreds of thousands of dollars. That fall, the man once seen as damaged goods crushed his opponents to win a third term.

Our triumph with Koch in '85 showed Mark and I that we could "go general," using all the skills we'd developed over the past decade. By this time, Ronald Reagan was in the first term of his presidency. Mark and I wrote a series of *New York Times* op-eds suggesting how Democrats could survive the Reagan Revolution.

"Most of the Democratic candidates have revised their position to incorporate a more centrist approach to social policy and defense," we wrote in 1984, "but they have not yet convinced the electorate that they are sincere . . . Reaching the middle class and convincing it that the Democrats genuinely care not just about the poor, but about both the blue collar and the white collar workers and their families, is [their] most essential task."

Our strategy resonated for several candidates. Having helped Jay Rockefeller win a U.S. Senate seat in West Virginia, we went to work in Alabama to help Richard Shelby unseat Republican Senator Jeremiah Denton. Shelby, a four-term Congressman, shared our belief that Democrats needed to co-opt Republicans on fiscal matters—take those issues off the table. Denton was a retired admiral and Vietnam POW hero, but we believed he was vulnerable when it came to his lukewarm support for Social Security, his Senate vote to increase his salary, and his lifestyle. (He owned two Mercedes, was seldom seen in Alabama, and made a crude remark about spousal abuse.) Our advertising onslaught quickly shrunk Denton's twenty-five-point lead and, on Election Day, Shelby eked out a narrow victory, helping Democrats regain control of the Senate.

We employed a similar strategy with Evan Bayh, the son of Birch Bayh, U.S. Senator from Indiana and presidential candidate in 1976. In 1985, Evan came to my Manhattan apartment for dinner. Handsome and personable, the twenty-nine-year-old law school grad was eager to carry his father's torch. But Birch himself had lost a bid for a third term five years earlier. Indiana remained an overwhelmingly Republican state. Nevertheless, in 1986, we helped Evan become Indiana's Secretary of State. Two years later, he set his sights on the governor's mansion. To beat the state's lieutenant governor, John Mutz, we picked the weapon Republicans usually use to bludgeon Democrats: taxes.

Indiana voters were mewling about two recent tax increases. Even though the increases went to fund education programs and avert a budget deficit, we portrayed Mutz as a tax-and-spender. Mutz took credit for attracting a $500 million Subaru-Isuzu plant to the state. Bayh accused Mutz of focusing more attention on overseas investment than Indiana's own businesses. Even the *Wall Street Journal* gaped that Bayh "often sounds more Republican than his Republican opponent." For a Democrat in 1988 to have that image in a state allergic to Democrats was miraculous. On

November 8, the thirty-two-year-old Evan Bayh was elected governor by a comfortable six-point margin.

Mark and I had our game down and we believed we could play it anywhere in America. But why stop at America? We were ready for a bigger arena.

PART TWO

PART TWO

12

SCROLLS AND SWISSIES

Though I was raised in a Jewish home, my family never talked much about the State of Israel at the dinner table. I'd once visited relatives who lived there. But I wasn't terribly familiar with the nation's politics. Then David Garth called. He wanted to know if Mark and I would help him rescue the political career of Israeli Prime Minister Menachem Begin.

Begin was more than a politician. Some Israelis considered him a founding father. Others saw him as a remorseless terrorist—the leader of the Jewish guerrilla group, Irgun, which had killed Jewish and Arab civilians in the 1946 King David Hotel bombing. In 1977 Begin had pulled off the biggest upset in Israeli political history by unseating the entrenched Labor Party. He then stunned his critics by working out a peace agreement with Egypt's Anwar Sadat, which won them both the 1978 Nobel Prize.

By 1981, however, Begin's political fortunes had dramatically shifted. Israel's economy had collapsed; inflation was running as high as 133 percent. For two years, poll after poll showed the Labor Party and its leader Shimon Peres with a double-digit lead over Begin and his Likud Party. In March, the *New York Times* predicted Begin was "probably in his final months as prime minister."

We thought he had a chance. Having seen the power of overnight polling in the United States, we believed it could work in

Israel. Since it had never been tried there, we teamed up with a local polling firm, Dahaf. Mark and I set up a meeting with Dahaf's director general, Mina Zemach. Without divulging our client, we explained that we wanted to do daily surveys. She looked at me for a long time before responding.

"CIA or PLO?" she asked.

"What do you mean?" I asked.

"Look," she said, "you're not telling me who your client is and the only people with the money to do this are the CIA and the PLO. I'm going to have to check you out."

Somewhere in the bowels of the Mossad spy agency Mark and I probably now have dossiers. Fortunately, we passed muster. We still had a logistical problem: how to survey a nation that, technologically, was a few years behind the U.S. We came up with a kind of Hebrew Pony Express. Interviewers from Dahaf fanned out across the country. After filling out their surveys, they handed the completed questionnaires to *sherut* taxi drivers, who hot-footed them to us in Tel Aviv. We then loaded the data into Mark's microcomputer—the same one that helped Ed Koch get elected in 1977. Consigned to a dingy room at the Sheraton, Mark and I pored over the numbers. Our only distraction was our TV set's one on-demand English language movie—*The Sting*. We must have watched it thirty times. I'm sure Mark and I could recite Paul Newman and Robert Redford's dialogue today.

We met Begin's campaign manager, Yitzhak Shamir. Five feet tall, he seemed like a nice, grandfatherly man. Always smiling. Only later did I learn that, as a leader of the "Stern Gang," he'd plotted the assassinations of British minister Lord Moyne, UN mediator Count Folke Bernadotte, and Shamir's own compatriot Eliyahu Giladi. Oh, and he'd directed the murder of German rocket scientists working for Egypt. But to us, he was a sweetheart.

Some of Begin's advisers were not inclined to follow our advice. They simply couldn't accept that their own judgment could be trumped by computer read-outs. What mattered was that Begin paid attention to the polls and responded to them. First, his finance minister, Yoram Aridor, helped stem the financial crisis by cutting taxes and allowing subsidies on luxury goods. Almost immediately, prices began to fall. At a time of mushrooming deficits, it was one of the more egregious examples of economic sleight-of-hand I've ever seen. But it worked.

Second, Begin attacked Peres in highly personal terms, calling him a liar and hypocrite and saying that the country couldn't trust the Labor Party on national security.

For some time, Begin had been concerned about a nuclear reactor Saddam Hussein was building in the Iraqi desert. Iraqi officials asserted that it was a power plant. Why would a country with some of the world's largest oil reserves need nuclear energy? Begin understood that the reactor could threaten Israel's existence. So, on June 7, 1981, Israeli jets, flying low over hostile territory, blew it up.

Some of Begin's opponents called the airstrike a political ploy to ensure his reelection. A day or two after the attack, I visited him in his office. He looked exhausted and somber. I told him that his lead in the polls had jumped from 3 points to 9.

"Look," he said, "I didn't do this for political reasons. I know your government is going to condemn me and the world is going to condemn me. But someday you will thank me for doing what I've done. I've kept Saddam Hussein from acquiring nuclear weapons for at least five to seven years. It was the right thing to do; it will preserve peace."

I don't believe Begin ordered the airstrike as a "wag the dog" diversion from his other problems. Yes, it gave him a bump in the polls, but that was short-lived. Clearly, the stakes in this race couldn't have been higher. And its tone couldn't have been nastier. Commentators said it was the dirtiest campaign in Israeli history. There were reports of Likud supporters pelting Peres with eggs and tomatoes. At Likud rallies, the party faithful chanted, "Begin, King of Israel!" The *New York Times* pondered the "Growth of Fascism" in the Holy Land. At the time, I wondered whether Begin was a man of peace or a political opportunist. But, looking back, I do believe the Camp David Accords and his disarmament of a ruthless dictator prove he deserved his Nobel Prize.

Late in the race, we did a poll that asked voters if they'd be more likely to vote for Begin if he appointed Ariel Sharon, longtime commander of the Israeli Army, as defense minister. The response: a resounding "yes." The man responsible for that question? None other than Ariel Sharon. Sharon "got" polling. When the results came in, he harangued us to share the news with the boss. "Tell him," he said. "Tell Begin!" Soon afterward, Begin announced that, if reelected, he would give Ariel Sharon the defense portfolio.

On the eve of the election, every Israeli commentator agreed that the race was simply too close to call. If anything, Labor had a slight advantage. We saw it differently. The morning of the election, Mark and I assured Begin that he would be reelected—by a one seat parliamentary margin. Begin was skeptical. We presented him with our computer printouts—which in those days came out in shiny scrolls. We dubbed them the "Dead Sea Polls." Combing through these tiny scrolls, we tried to convince the prime minister that our prognostication would come to pass.

Begin was encouraged. He urged us to go forth to the unbelievers on his staff and show them the scrolls. We didn't convert many people. After voting ended, Israeli television called the race for Peres and Labor. Joyous crowds of Labor supporters began celebrating their return to power. At Begin headquarters, we were getting dagger looks. "Be patient," we counseled. Israelis, however, are not known for abundant patience. Mark and I began to look for the exits. Luckily, an hour later, Israeli television announced that there'd been a computer error; Menachem Begin had in fact been reelected. His margin of victory was 49 percent to 48 percent—just as we predicted.

★　★　★

Our time in Israel laid the foundation for elections around the world. By 1992, Mark and I had worked in eighteen countries. That November, I heard from Birch Bayh. The former senator sat on the board of ICN Pharmaceuticals. Its founder and CEO, Milan Panić, had quite a bio. Born in Belgrade, Yugoslavia, in 1929, he was fourteen when he'd joined Marshal Tito's partisans in fighting the Nazis. Panić later became a national cycling champion. During the Cold War, he and his wife defected, eventually making their way to Los Angeles, where Milan had used $200 to start his drug company in his garage. Its generic version of the widely prescribed Parkinson's medication, L-Dopa, led ICN to develop the building blocks for thousands of drugs. Panić had become a millionaire many times over. But he didn't forget his homeland. He'd grown increasingly concerned about the man elected as the first president of the newly formed Republic of Serbia.

Slobodan Milošević had promised to replace Yugoslavia's one-party communist system with a democratic multiparty system. He also professed a desire for peaceful coexistence with the other new Balkan republics. Instead, many alleged, Milošević had given his cronies ownership of formerly state-run businesses and used the Serbian-controlled Yugoslav People's Army (JNA) to oppress other ethnic groups. In response, the United Nations had imposed economic sanctions. Milošević knew the sanctions would devastate Serbia's economy and weaken his hold on power. So, he came up with an idea: why not put an American face on his isolated regime? He asked Panić, a successful entrepreneur and U.S. citizen, if he wanted to be Serbia's prime minister.

At sixty-two, Panić was an impulsive man, a gambler, someone fond of the big gesture—or at least that was his act. He had
a touch of the charming rogue. It would be hard to imagine a
more unlikely statesman. Yet, I soon learned, a statesman was
exactly what Panić aspired to be. In many ways, Panić had the
classic first-generation immigrant's outlook on his birthplace: he
viewed it as a rather rinky-dink place, a Mickey Mouse country.
He could see that it was alienating the world and destroying itself
in the process. Panić hoped to sweep in and take charge of the
situation. He received permission from the U.S State and Treasury
Departments to hold a foreign office. That would be the only
assistance he'd receive from the U.S. government.

Panić was not aware then that, as far as Milošević was concerned, lobbying the West to lift sanctions would be Panić's only
job. Milošević had no intention of sharing power with him. That
July, Panić and a team of advisers—mostly non-Serbian pharmaceutical executives—had arrived in Belgrade. His honeymoon
with Milošević didn't last long. The new prime minister promptly
announced that he'd be taking control of the Defense Ministry,
the Interior Ministry, and the Ministry of Foreign Affairs. He
also called for an immediate cease-fire in Bosnia and recognition
of the independence of the disputed Kosovo. In the beginning,
these declarations had little weight. Parliament had to approve
such moves and the ruling Socialist Party was in Milošević's grip.
Still, Milošević quickly recognized Panić as a thorn. Indeed, on
the day of Panić's arrival in Belgrade, more than 100,000 Serbs
marched through the streets to demand that Milošević step down.
To effectively challenge the strongman, Panić would need to gain
the trust of these people.

Birch Bayh had asked me if I'd conduct a quick assessment of
Panić's operations. I'd just weathered a grueling election season.
While Evan Bayh had been reelected governor of Indiana, we were
unable to oust New York Republican Senator Al D'Amato. Our

candidate, New York Attorney General Bob Abrams, had made several costly mistakes during the final stages of the campaign. It had been a frustrating defeat. I wanted a break. Instead of going on vacation, I agreed to go to Serbia. Travel tip: **If you want to take your mind off your problems, visit a war zone!**

My first challenge was getting there. The UN Security Council had imposed a ban on air travel into Serbia, so the U.S. Treasury Department had to grant me special permission. The closest major airport was Budapest. Panić's foreign policy adviser, Jack Scanlon, former U.S. ambassador to Yugoslavia, kindly offered to pick me up there. As we climbed into his BMW, Scanlon introduced me to my first key contact—his chauffeur, Branko, a powerfully built forty-year-old with a big smile. As we began our six-hour journey, Scanlon gave me a briefing on survival in Serbia. He said Branko could help me change money, best done on the black market. Branko could also provide me with information. Moneychangers and others in the underground economy were attuned to shifts in the public mood. It was good to have a Branko.

Whenever you land in a new terrain, find a fixer—someone who can get you out of trouble or, better yet, keep you from getting into it.

We finally arrived in Belgrade. The outskirts of the city were a mishmash of discolored concrete apartment blocks. The center of town was only slightly more attractive. That's where Scanlon and Panić lived in a luxury apartment complex. Scanlon invited me to dinner. As we sat down to eat, he casually suggested that we should watch what we said because his apartment, and indeed the entire building, was undoubtedly bugged.

After a nice meal and a stilted conversation, Branko drove me over to the Hyatt. The lobby was buzzing. Beefy men puffed on Morava cigarettes, guzzled Zaječarsko beer, sipped *rakija* (a sinus-clearing plum brandy) and chewed on chunks of gray boiled meat. Their sullen blond girlfriends looked bored. At

Reception, there was a sign—written in Serbian and English—that politely requested: *"Please Check All Weapons at the Front Desk."*

Apparently, there'd recently been a gangland slaying in room 389. I was in room 391. Back in East Harlem, I'd avoided mobster social clubs. Now I appeared to be living in one.

The next morning, I walked over to Government House, a crumbling Soviet-style office building that housed the prime minister's offices. I introduced myself at the security desk and was taken upstairs to a little office, where I found a stack of polls conducted by local media outlets. Soon after I sat down, one of Panić's aides informed me that it was time for the cabinet meeting. A bit confused, I followed him to a large conference room. There I met Milan Panić. A former cycling champion, he was trim and vigorous. He greeted me warmly and introduced me to his ministers and attaches. He beckoned me to jump into the conversation. It occurred to me that Panić had only a vague idea of what a political consultant was supposed to do. I'd only been in the country for a few hours, and I was already being invited to help govern it. I gingerly suggested that I might be of more use elsewhere. Panić genially acceded. I backed respectfully out of the room, thus ending my career as a Serbian cabinet member.

What I really wanted to do was assess Panić's political standing. The results I had seen indicated Milošević was deeply unpopular, with only a 20 to 25 percent approval rating. Yet almost everyone I spoke to, even Panić's Serbian aides, seemed to believe he was impossible to beat. Were the polls wrong? I decided to conduct one of my own.

For assistance, I turned to Panić's press secretary, David Calef, an American. Calef offered to take me to the public opinion research department at the University of Belgrade. When we got to the campus, we found our way to a brutalist building where no one else walked the dark halls. At first, I thought we'd been given the wrong address. Eventually, we located the head of polling, Liliana Bacovic. She looked as forlorn as her surroundings. I asked if she could conduct a nationwide poll.

"That will be difficult," she said. "It will take time."

"How long are we talking about?" I inquired. (My desire to get away from New York was rapidly yielding to a desire to get out of Belgrade.)

She said it would take about ten days just to field the poll and get the data back. Plus a few more days to collate the data. In total, about two weeks. I gave David a look of despair. He smiled. From his pocket he pulled a large roll of Swiss francs. A few thousand francs exchanged hands and an agreement was reached that we would have tabulated results in a week. Calef's "Swissies" would become an essential lubricant during my time in Serbia. As Panić's efforts to oust Milošević intensified, the rubber-banded roll would give way to a plastic shopping bag. **When traveling in difficult circumstances, bring cash—the harder the better: euros, dollars, Swissies.**

But even an abundance of Western currency could not liberate me from Belgrade quickly. I would have to wait for the poll results. At first, I spent most of my free time by myself. I become a regular at McDonald's. I was surprised when Panić's guys first took me there but, after a brief acquaintance with *kavurma* (pig intestines), I'd come to appreciate Belgrade's version of the Big Mac. I did try to bone up on Serbian culture and politics. A new friend took me to Klub Književnika, a prestigious literary association founded in 1946. My host was an intellectual, but he didn't hesitate to show me the holstered pistols he had under each arm. Wow, I thought, even eggheads packed heat here.

I also met with the president of Yugoslavia, Dobrica Cosic. The respected Serbian writer had once been comrades with Milošević, but he too now believed Slobodan had to go. At seventy, Cosic didn't think he was the man to take him on. I began to sense that Serbia's only plausible savior was Milan Panić. Hearing that he'd be flying to Berlin and Geneva to talk with the UN High Commissioner for Refugees, I asked Calef if I could hitch a ride on the PM's 737. En route, I told Calef that I thought Panić needed to run for president. Calef agreed. On the flight back to Belgrade, Panić was in good spirits. It was Thanksgiving back in the U.S. and he had managed to procure a turkey. Capitalizing on his holiday mirth, I said, "Look, Milan, you're at 70 percent, Milošević is at 25 percent. If you get into this race, I know you are going to win."

He looked skeptical. "You don't understand the situation," he countered. "I'm a Serb; I've been here; and it's not that easy."

Panić's Serbian advisers were telling him that Milošević would never lose—or admit to losing. The pessimists argued that just entering the race would cost Panić his credibility. Failure was inevitable. He might even be killed. (Milošević had already sent troops into his office and detained him for hours at a military checkpoint.)

I didn't buy it. Serbia was an authoritarian regime, but it was not a total dictatorship. There must be elections. The world would be watching.

"I don't have an organization," Panić pointed out. "I don't have a campaign manager."

Serbian law required presidential candidates to collect 10,000 nominating signatures; the registration deadline was only four days away.

Calef jumped in. "If we got you on the ballot, would you do it?" he asked.

Panić responded casually. "Yes, sure."

Then he got up to carve a turkey in the main cabin.

The next morning, I went down to the hotel lobby for breakfast. When the elevator doors opened, I waded into a sea of excited young volunteers. At the center of the action was Calef, with his wad of Swissies. The campaign to defeat Slobodan Milošević had begun.

Calef, a former organizer for the Democratic Party in California, had already turned two conference rooms into our campaign head-quarters. Flip charts adorned the walls. Soon he and others were calling activists and opposition leaders and recruiting students to serve as petition coordinators. Later that morning, Liliana Bacovic delivered our first poll, confirming that Milošević was extremely vulnerable. By Monday morning, Calef's ragtag army of volun-teers had collected nearly 50,000 signatures in support of Panić's candidacy. I was convinced that, on December 20, Europe's last Communist government would fall.

Panić himself seemed a bit mystified by this turn of events. I don't think he'd ever made a conscious decision to get into the race. Nevertheless, he was true to his word. Now that he was on the ballot, he was ready to throw himself into the race.

I developed a strategy that combined the best aspects of Ronald Reagan's 1980 campaign and Bill Clinton's 1992 campaign. Both had run against incumbents with troubled economies. Our message: are you better off now than you were four years ago? Our slogan: "Promena Sad!" ("Change Now!")

But it was dangerous to underestimate Milošević. That fall, his Socialist Party had slipped "poison pill" language into a bill that set residency requirements for the presidency that Panić did not meet. We challenged the requirement in the Serbian Supreme Court, which Milošević did not yet control. On December 5, the court handed down a ruling in Panić's favor.

The next problem was the media. Milošević lorded over the airwaves. Every night, Radio Television Belgrade attacked Panić, questioning his loyalty and portraying him as a tool of the West, sent to infiltrate and destroy Serbia. The only way we could counter this slander was through paid advertising. However, Milošević-controlled stations refused to air our commercials until

Panić was officially certified as a candidate. That meant our first ad wouldn't run until December 10—seven days before campaigning was scheduled to end.

I still thought it was enough time if we could get the right message on the air. Calef turned to his friend Bill Press, former chairman of the California Democratic Party. Press arrived at campaign headquarters after a harrowing overnight bus ride from Bucharest. He looked worse for wear. He'd apparently been one of the few passengers not associated with the poultry business. Chicken feathers clung to his clothes. Nevertheless, he was ready to work and there was no time to lose. Calef located a TV studio on the outskirts of the city. We came to a dark alley. Years of canvassing in East Harlem and Hunts Point told me not to walk down this alley. We did anyway, finding a ramshackle building with a single dilapidated soundstage. It was run by a five-foot-tall Serb named Alek who seemed capable of breathing only through a Camel cigarette. We clearly made Alek nervous. But, God bless him, he later became my Branko, driving me around Belgrade in his twenty-year-old VW bug.

We came up with a TV spot that opened with a picture of Milošević and panned to desperate Serbs queuing up in bread and gas lines. The ad cut to a vibrant and confident Panić, promising voters a healthy economy, peace, and a more democratic society. It was a bravura production given the time and conditions. I saw it as our knockout punch.

It never ran. Radio Television Belgrade banned it as too inflammatory. I was furious. We tried taking out all references to Milošević. Again, it was rejected. Strangely, some of Panić's own advisers seemed relieved. Our Serbian finance chairman explained to me, "You have to understand, if we lose, you will not be here to face the consequences, but we will."

Inklings of foul play were everywhere. One evening during dinner at a posh Belgrade restaurant, a Serbian journalist complimented us on one of our new radio spots. We had come up with the spot just that morning in our headquarters and had not even told Panić about it. Either our offices were bugged, or there were moles among the English-speaking "volunteers" who never seemed to leave.

It was almost impossible to keep secrets. Solution: **If you can't plug a leak, turn on the faucet.** Instead of distributing numbers to a handful of senior campaign staff, I publicized them as widely as possible. My reasons were twofold. First, I wanted to underscore the dissatisfaction of the electorate. Second, I hoped to prevent—or at least reduce—election fraud. We knew Milošević would cheat. We didn't expect to win in the first round. The key was to force him into a runoff. Making our polling public was one way to keep Milošević honest—or less dishonest.

What Panić really needed was international support. Yet all our attempts to secure it were met with polite indifference. I called Cyrus Vance, Jimmy Carter's Secretary of State, who was then serving as a United Nations mediator in the Balkans. I told him Panić could win only if someone sent election observers. Vance was sympathetic but offered no assistance. Nor did we get any help from George H. W. Bush's outgoing administration. Policymakers seemed to view Milošević as a necessary evil, a strongman who could make peace, rather than what he was—the instigator of violence.

"Where is the United States?" Panić would rage, pacing the floor of the suburban villa he had made his home. "Milošević is a killer, and he's going to get away with it. They will regret the day they didn't help me."

Panić campaigned around the country. One of his scheduled stops was Niš, a gritty industrial city that had long supported Milošević. We hadn't been able to send an advance team. It was just the sort of place where Milošević's thugs might embarrass Panić—or worse. But our local supporters assured us Panić's speech would not go unheard. When we pulled into Niš, a crowd of more than 20,000 people greeted us. They cheered wildly and rocked our cars as we left. It took nearly a half-hour to get out of the central square.

Election Day came. Fog blanketed much of the country. In Belgrade, we awoke to find Milošević's graffitists had defaced Panić posters with the letters "U.S.A." As a check against fraud, we arranged morning and afternoon exit polls at 60 voting stations across the country. Those polls showed a huge surge for Panić. The next day, election commission officials announced that, after counting only 19 percent of the votes, Milošević had nearly 57 percent to Panić's 33 percent. We realized Milošević would try to steal the election outright. Panić dismissed those results as invalid "because of fraud, theft, and cheating in the counting of ballots." Election monitors from the Conference on Security and Cooperation in Europe (CSCE) described the election as "riddled with flaws and irregularities." The monitors noted at least five percent of eligible voters, mostly young people, had been barred from voting. Such statements were helpful, but inadequate. The CSCE needed to step in and supervise the vote-counting. Instead, on December 23, most of these observers went home for Christmas. No one was watching the election workers.

On Christmas Eve, the central election commission pronounced Milošević the outright winner. There would be no run-off election. Before leaving Belgrade, I appeared on CNN and *Good Morning America* to talk about the election theft. Back in the United States I continued those efforts. But no one was really interested. Even Panić's advisers shrugged off the steal. Panić's childhood friend Tosha Olic warned me not to be "too strident." On December 29, Communists and ultranationalists teamed up and voted Panić out as prime minister. The threat to Milošević's power was gone.

I'd expected to stay two or three days in Serbia. I ended up spending most of two months. In the weeks after the election fiasco, I wondered whether I should have more forcefully urged Panić to lead his supporters into the streets. Maybe they could have taken control of the capital. But I wasn't experienced at organizing demonstrations. After all, I was the guy who'd stayed seated at that Vietnam teach-in at Harvard. Frankly, I was a bit scared. We didn't have a security team to speak of. We were dealing with war criminals—gangsters in uniform. I had a strong feeling that Milošević's crew didn't check their Glocks at the front desk. Moreover, Panić himself wasn't inclined to storm the barricades—not when the U.S. and the U.N. were content to sit on the sidelines. Much later, Panić confided, "Doug, we were at much greater risk than either of us knew. I was not prepared to put my life on the line when our supposed allies weren't ready to join me." In his defense, I would say, **Martyrdom is overrated. Don't fall on any swords unless there's an ambulance on the way.**

13

INOCULATION

I'd always assumed our clients would be confined to politics. Toppling a dictator was enough of a challenge for me. But Mark believed that what we'd learned could be transplanted to the boardroom.

I'd worked with corporate clients before. In 1979, Ron Maiorana, a former speechwriter for Nelson Rockefeller, asked if we'd help Hess Oil gauge consumer attitudes toward gas station convenience stores. Ron arranged a meeting with Hess president Phil Kramer. I soon discovered I was out of my depth. When Kramer asked how much it would cost for polling and focus groups, I nervously proposed $35,000—a princely sum for two young pollsters. Kramer, somewhat absentmindedly, nodded. Wanting to make sure he was okay with that price, I kept looping back to the number, each time getting the same faint nod. Eventually, I took the nod for a yes and wrapped up the meeting. I was in high spirits but Ron, taking me aside, said, "Schoen, you are a fucking idiot."

"Fucking idiot?" I objected. "I just sold that guy on a $35,000 poll!"

Ron impressed upon me that each of my price-checks gave Kramer the opportunity to change his mind. My lesson:

When you have something sold, shut up and leave!

It wasn't until 1984 that some bad news truly propelled us into the corporate realm. Two years before, Mark had played a critical role in helping Frank Lautenberg win his Senate seat. But some on Lautenberg's staff still regretted the negative campaign, and resented Mark for hatching it. Despite his past success, Mark was abruptly dropped from Lautenberg's team. The experience temporarily soured Mark on politics. He and I both knew corporate clients had much deeper pockets. But it was slightly audacious to think that a small political consulting firm—a *Democratic* consulting firm at that—could compete with the advertising and public relations leviathans of Madison Avenue.

Mark and I recognized the similarities between political campaigns and corporate marketing. The voter was much like the consumer. Building a candidate's name recognition was like building brand awareness. Party identification was akin to brand loyalty. Politicians and companies both competed for the loyalty of swing voters—or, in corporate parlance, occasional buyers. There were differences. In politics, it was winner-take-all. In the marketplace, a company that came in second might still make a decent profit.

Large corporations were also more slow-moving and bureaucratic than a campaign organization. Accustomed to overnight polling and quick decisions, we thought we could do better. Another oil company provided our entrée. In 1985, as Pennzoil and Getty were in merger talks, Texaco swooped in and made Getty a better offer. Pennzoil responded with a lawsuit charging that Getty had violated a binding oral agreement. Texaco had indemnified Getty against any lawsuits arising from their deal. Because of that agreement, a Texas jury said Texaco owed Pennzoil more than $10 *billion*—a staggering ruling that forced the oil giant to file for bankruptcy. During this difficult period, Texaco needed someone to help navigate the political reefs of Chapter 11. Our advice was straightforward: focus on the blue-chip company's long history of high-quality products, satisfied customers, honorable behavior—and how a ridiculously large jury award now spelled doom for Texaco's thousands of employees. The strategy was successful. A torrent of criticism directed at the jury award followed. Our arrangement with Texaco became so important that we made our point man, Mike Berland, a partner in Penn, Schoen & Berland.

Another early corporate client came courtesy of a Republican. Mitch Daniels, a veteran of the Reagan White House, was now president of North American Pharmaceutical Operations for Eli Lilly in Indiana, where he would one day serve as governor. Looking past our political differences, Daniels invited me to lunch at Eli Lilly's cafeteria. He'd been impressed by our work for Evan Bayh. He wondered if we had any thoughts on selling a medication Eli Lilly was about to unveil. It was called Prozac.

Back then, it was rare for someone to admit feelings of depression. Mental illness carried a heavy stigma. While psychotherapy offered some relief, most people didn't have the time and money to take advantage of it. Prozac had the potential to change that. Our first task was to help the company differentiate Prozac from the older generation of antidepressants. For decades, physicians had been prescribing—often mis-prescribing—a wide array of tricyclic drugs. Prozac was the first in a generation of drugs known as selective serotonin reuptake inhibitors (SSRIs). It was critical that Eli Lilly *inoculate* Prozac against any association with these older products. In politics, we called this a "prebuttal"—i.e., a preemptive rebuttal.

We advised Eli Lilly to focus, first, on physicians. We helped develop language to educate doctors about Prozac's ease of dosing, lower toxicity, and milder side effects, based on the years of clinical trials. Our second target audience was potential users. Back in the late 1980s, the idea of marketing a drug directly to the public was novel. Many people now decry the proliferation of prescription drug ads. But it was a fact that depressed people were not getting the help they needed. Many consumers viewed anyone who took antidepressants as "crazy." We advised Eli Lilly to speak directly to the doubters—particularly men, who were less willing than women to talk about their feelings.

We also sought to inoculate the product against future attacks. Given the high occurrence of suicide among people suffering from depression and other mental illnesses, we knew deaths might be "linked" to Prozac. We knew that trial lawyers would come after Lilly. We wanted to ensure that these legal battles occurred in an environment where public opinion was favorable.

Eli Lilly went on to craft one of the most effective marketing campaigns in American corporate history. People suffering from depression sought out Prozac by the millions. As expected, trial lawyers began to accuse Prozac of causing, not only suicide, but also murder, self-mutilation, spending sprees, and nymphomania. But the public was skeptical, as were many juries. By the end of its first decade in the marketplace, sales of Prozac had earned Eli Lilly an estimated $28 billion.

Inoculation had worked. Woe to the company that didn't anticipate possible blowback from its product. Procter & Gamble was initially slow to respond to critics of Olestra, a calorie-free fat substitute. The Center for Science in the Public Interest (CSPI) charged that Olestra's benefits—reducing cholesterol—were outweighed by the alleged risk of abdominal cramping and loose stools. Our response was a campaign that clearly emphasized the product's safety and natural ingredients. P&G immediately recognized the effectiveness of the so-called "political model." Olestra's rollout was salvaged, but it never became the success P&G had hoped for.

★   ★   ★

In some cases, the head of a company was very much like a political candidate. In 1997, Microsoft's marketing head, Mich Matthews, needed help prepping its co-founder, Bill Gates, for a big television interview. At the time, the company was embroiled in a long battle with the Justice Department's Antitrust Division, which alleged it had engaged in anti-competitive practices. Gates had been portrayed as a geek who'd turned into a ruthless robber baron. His advisers believed the public needed to know him better.

Flying out to the company's headquarters in Redmond, Washington, I found a man who wasn't particularly good with people. During one coaching session aboard his plane, we sat opposite each other for twenty minutes before he spoke to me. Finally, he blurted out, "Okay, talk!"

As he flicked his foot up and down, I talked to him about how to relax, smile, and avoid coming off as defensive. We talked about the core values he wanted to get across. At that time, much was being made of his 66,000-square-foot mansion, Xanadu 2.0—recently valued at $131 million. Having done some polling for billionaire Michael Milken during his securities fraud trial, I knew that many people have deep suspicions about the enormously rich. I suggested to Gates that he might demonstrate that he was using his wealth for more than a mansion. Of course, he's become one of the world's great philanthropists. He's also become much more open and affable.

Those coaching sessions evolved into a long relationship with Microsoft. Mark joined me in a strategic study of the brand and its clients. I remember one day, one of their executives called and asked, "Can you guys get reactions to a new product? We're thinking of calling it the Xbox."

Humanizing a company was also the order of the day at America Online (AOL). Back when people were just hearing of the Internet, AOL came up with the enticing offer of unlimited service for the flat fee of $19.95 a month. Thousands of people signed up. Unfortunately, this was in the early days of dial-up connections. During peak hours, many customers got busy signals and cancelled their accounts. Bob Pittman, who'd helped create MTV, had recently joined the company as CEO of AOL Networks. He asked us to help put out the fire. Our research quickly identified Steve Case, co-founder of AOL, as one of the company's biggest assets. People liked his winning, awe-shucks, "boy-next-door" persona. We prescribed a commercial in which Case, wearing a sweater, would make a forthright apology for those annoying busy signals. He promised that AOL was working day and night to fix the problem and investing to upgrade its network. Within three years, AOL's user base grew to 10 million people.

Authenticity works—even if it takes a little work to become authentic.

★   ★   ★

In the summer of 1993, execs at the august advertising firm of Foote, Cone & Belding (FCB) told us it was making a run for AT&T's business. They asked if we'd like to team up—offering us $7,500 to do a poll for their bid. It wasn't a lot of money. But as I'd learned the hard way in North Dakota, *taking less now can mean making more later*. Mark also saw how a multimillion-dollar telecom account could kick us up to the next level.

AT&T's roots run deep—back to company co-founder Alexander Graham Bell's invention of the telephone in 1875. But by the mid-1980s, young companies were competing vigorously for AT&T's core long-distance business. The most aggressive was MCI. In 1991, MCI rolled out a new package—Friends and Family—offering 20 percent discounts to customers who convinced their loved ones to sign up. By the end of the year, AT&T had lost 2 percent of its market share to MCI.

As political strategists, Penn, Schoen & Berland had always been guided by a core set of principles:

1. **Take the offensive and play to win.**

2 **Start yesterday: front-runners tend to be winners.**

3. **Define the issues before others define them for you.**

4. **Keep your finger on the pulse and be ready to respond.**

5. **Let no attack go unanswered.**

So far, AT&T had failed to act on any of these principles. Nearly two years after MCI's attack began, AT&T was still playing defense—and not well. It was past time to hit back. Giving customers a viable alternative to Friends and Family certainly needed to be part of the response, but it wasn't enough. AT&T had to go negative.

Back then, corporate marketers rued direct attacks on competitors. Coke never criticized Pepsi. McDonald's didn't disparage Burger King. The reason: doing so would give the other guy free publicity. Mark and I considered this nonsense. Still, AT&T's brass were cautious. The company had spent a century building its brand. It couldn't risk a backlash.

Two problems bedeviled us.

For decades, companies had relied on focus groups to test and develop advertising campaigns. Politicians relied on them too. The basic format for both was: convene a representative group of people, show them a range of advertisements, have them pick the one they liked best, and figure out what they liked about it. By the early 1990s, however, political consultants had noticed that focus groups were panning negative ads. Yet campaign after campaign demonstrated that negative advertising worked. Was there a more scientific, less offensive way to go negative?

Compounding our AT&T dilemma—ironically—was the telephone. To gather statistically significant information, a phone poll must garner responses from a representative cross sample of the public. Give me 500 people, randomly selected, and I can tell you what the nation thinks about any given issue. But when potential respondents hang up on interviewers, things get more complicated. Yes, you can call someone else, but the chance of sampling error increases as the response rate declines.

We were no strangers to these problems. Now, backed by AT&T's resources, we set out to solve them. To do so, we went to the mall.

It was Mark's idea—based on the striking fact that, back then, 70 percent of Americans shopped at a mall at least once a week. If you chose the right malls, shoppers bore a startlingly close resemblance to American consumers (and voters for that matter). Democrats, Republicans, AT&T customers, MCI customers all went to the mall.

So, our team began buttonholing shoppers as they wandered from Foot Locker to Cinnabon to JCPenney. Mall rats became our lab rats. We showed them MCI ads and AT&T ads. But, more than that, we questioned them about their lifestyle and purchasing habits—finding previously unnoticed niche groups, such as immigrants who made calls to their home countries. Panning in those canyons of consumerism, we discovered a dazzling nugget: many people found MCI's Friends and Family rules too complicated. We advised AT&T to offer tempting discount plans that were easier to understand. They did, and our ad agency partners filmed new ads. When we brought these ads back to the mall, AT&T's message consistently bested MCI's. Our client was still nervous. But with MCI now holding 20 percent of the market and rising fast, AT&T had little choice but to roll the dice.

AT&T soon unveiled its "True" plan—backed by a $200 million advertising campaign based largely on our research. The campaign did go negative—but with a dab of humor. "TrueMath" commercials questioned MCI's math skills—how it calculated savings. By the end of 1994, AT&T had signed up 14 million new long-distance customers. At its next earnings report, it reported record earnings of $4.71 billion.

Our techniques helped save AT&T's most lucrative franchise. But the greatest impact of our work for the phone company came at a different number—(202) 456-1414—the one that rings at 1600 Pennsylvania Avenue.

14

THE REMAKING
OF A PRESIDENT

Penn, Schoen & Berland had been a successful consulting firm for almost twenty years, but we were still waiting for the ultimate invitation—to work on a U.S. presidential campaign. I never would have thought that invite would come from my old mentor, Dick Morris.

I'd lost touch with Dick after college. After all, if I wasn't canvassing, I wasn't useful to him. But in 1990, Mark and I were making a bid to poll for former Texas Governor Mark White, who was mounting a race to return to office. Governor White asked me to send some materials to his strategist, Dick Morris. When I saw the address in Redding, Connecticut, I realized it was a five-minute walk from the summer house my wife Peggy and I had rented. I figured I'd drop off the documents and say hello. Morris and I were soon chatting as avidly as we had in his shabby West 95th Street apartment. Of course, a few things had changed. The card tables and folding chairs had been replaced by French country décor. His wife, Gita, who used to fill his glass with orange juice, had been replaced by his wife, Eileen, who filled it with Sauvignon blanc.

Dick's cheeks were a little ruddier. His allegiances had also become a bit more fluid. Gone were the days when liberal ideology or even political affiliation dominated his thinking.

Now, Dick's main concern was who paid the most. (A house in Provence ain't cheap.) In a field where most political consultants associate exclusively with one party, Morris had gone to work for both Democrats and Republicans, including some of the most conservative members of the GOP, such as Trent Lott and Jesse Helms.

None of Morris's clients had done better than one of his earliest—a young attorney general from Arkansas named Bill Clinton.

Morris had worked for Clinton in his successful first run for governor in 1978. Clinton soon abandoned him but, when he failed to win reelection in 1980, he returned to Morris. Together, the two men restored Clinton's political fortunes and reclaimed the governor's mansion in 1982. Morris didn't work in any substantial way on Clinton's 1990 presidential campaign. Morris claimed he'd refused to join Clinton's famous "war room" because of an argument they'd had in 1990 at the Arkansas governor's mansion. According to Morris, Clinton went so far as to tackle Dick and cock his fist before Hillary Clinton calmed her husband down. Whatever the truth, the two men made up. One magazine compared Clinton to Elvis Presley and Morris to the singer's manager, Colonel Tom Parker. Come 1994, when a disastrous midterm election took both houses of Congress from the Democrats, Clinton again turned to Morris to rescue his floundering presidency.

In January of 1995, I was at Midway Airport in Chicago when Morris paged me. (This was when people carried "beepers.") I called him back from a pay phone.

"Do you want the Clinton campaign?" he asked. "I can get you the whole thing—polling, strategy, media."

It was a mind-boggling offer. Part of me wondered whether Morris was on the level, but I said, "Yes, of course."

"We'll be meeting at the White House at eight o'clock on February 5th," he said.

I quickly checked my calendar and mumbled something about having a prior commitment.

"You'll be there," Morris predicted, correctly.

When somebody important wants to see you, make yourself available, regardless of your schedule.

To be clear, Morris fully intended to run Clinton's campaign. But, like the mighty Oz, he planned to do it from behind a curtain. He knew his Republican clients wouldn't cotton to his working for America's top Democrat. Morris's code name would be "Charlie," a reference to Charlie Black, a prominent GOP consultant—and perhaps a wink at *Charlie's Angels,* in which the master of operations was never seen.

As I told you earlier, I was shocked during my first visit to the White House by Bill Clinton's distracted demeanor, his listlessness. That night I wasn't certain how to help him. But I knew enough not to share that uncertainty.

When someone you want to work with asks you if you can solve a problem, the answer is always Yes.

Having winged my first reply to him, I began to work out the specifics of how he could move back to the center. Throughout the winter and spring of 1995, Morris and I told the president he must commit to a balanced budget. Treasury Secretary Bob Rubin and Vice President Al Gore supported the idea, but Clinton's more liberal advisers—Chief of Staff Leon Panetta, Deputy Chief Harold M. Ickes, and Communications Director George Stephanopoulos—disagreed. They claimed he'd be selling out congressional Democrats. Clinton believed in letting everyone have their say. He once told me, "I don't want to hear what you *think* I want to hear." But I was starting to think he could not control his own staff. I wasn't sure how much influence I had over him. It didn't help my standing to be associated with Dick Morris. Back in the late 1960s, Morris and Ickes had locked antlers in some New York City races. Ickes couldn't let it go. Whenever I suggested he and Dick should put it behind them, Ickes talked like a robot: "I serve at the pleasure of the president. I'll do what he tells me to do." This he said while sticking a pencil in his ear. Perhaps he thought the eraser would drown me out.

Ickes fought us over everything. He disputed our expenses. He refused to give us a long-term contract. Stephanopoulos and Panetta would also do their best to undermine us. In fairness, Morris didn't need to be so brusque with Panetta, who would go on to serve as President Barack Obama's CIA Director and Secretary of Defense. In one meeting with Clinton and Gore, Morris told Panetta, "Leon, Bill's going to do it my way. I'd rather have you cooperate. If you don't, I'll just have to cut you out." Talk about audacity. Of course, Panetta sometimes responded in kind—exiling our ally Bill Curry to an office across the street in the Old Executive Office Building. Panetta told Curry that if he needed his help, he would call. Curry's phone rarely rang.

All this backstabbing and kneecapping told me we needed to recruit our own people—people who agreed with us. Sharing power in Washington is generally seen as a mistake. It means you must share access and credit. But it's better than failing. **When you can't do it yourself, call in reinforcements.**

Even though Morris was ostensibly our commander, it was starting to look like his White House rivals would either push him out or that he would self-immolate. I had to build a team that could, if necessary, outlive Dick Morris. I immediately thought of Mark. His work for our corporate clients could be adapted to Clinton. Morris didn't really know Mark, but he knew he didn't like him. A few years earlier, the two had been in some meeting where Mark had dared to contradict Morris's advice to a client. Morris hadn't forgotten. Morris finally agreed that Mark could dispense his polling insights at the *beginning* of our meetings with Clinton—but then Mark would have to leave. Also, until Morris summoned him, Mark would have to wait in the usher's office.

Not surprisingly, Mark wasn't thrilled. I told Morris that this protocol was demeaning and petty. After much discussion, Morris backed down. Still, he vowed to keep Mark tightly tethered— "like a caged animal."

I next contacted Bob Squier, with whom I worked on the Lautenberg campaign. Squier was one of the top media consultants in Washington. More importantly, he'd worked with Clinton and Gore. He and his partners, Bill Knapp and Tom Ochs, had the type of D.C. connections we sorely needed. I also brought on Hank Sheinkopf, who'd helped me run for Congress, and Marius Penczner, a Nashville producer of music videos. Besides bringing a useful MTV sensibility, Penczner shared the president's love of country music.

Code-naming ourselves "the November 5th Group," we met for the first time on a muggy day in May at Bob Squier's Capitol Hill townhouse. Dick Morris made the introductions. Looking at our host, he noted, "Bob and I have had our ups and downs." That was putting it mildly. Back in 1986, while representing competing candidates in a Florida Senate race, Squier had accused Morris of goosing his client's numbers. He called Morris "the Julia Child of cooked polls." Trying to smooth Morris's feathers, Squier now quipped, "At least I didn't call you Chef Boyardee."

Putting slights and grudges aside, we began to look for ways to lift Clinton out of his hole. We made an oath of secrecy. During Clinton's first two years, low-level, mid-level and high-level aides were constantly talking to reporters. Everybody leaked. The best way to stay on Clinton's good side was to stay quiet. One time, when our group was meeting with him, National Security Advisor Tony Lake came in to update the president on the fate of Scott O'Grady, an Air Force pilot shot down over Bosnia. Lake looked uncomfortable speaking in front of us, but the president reassured him. "These guys don't leak," he said.

Nothing impresses like discretion.

I worked for Clinton for nearly half the year before word of our operation got out. When the *New Yorker*'s Jane Mayer called me to confirm the November 5th Group's existence, I quickly jumped off the phone. I knew that if Ickes thought I was her source, he'd make sure I was fired. I later gleaned that Ickes himself may have been the source. "I confirm you didn't leak," he told us slyly.

★   ★   ★

Even though we hadn't been officially hired, the president seemed to be listening to us. He made an address calling for targeted tax cuts. If we could only get him to back a balanced budget. With the Republicans now controlling both houses of Congress, it was only a matter of time before they sent him their version of a budget, which he'd likely have to veto. If he offered his own balanced budget—featuring less draconian cuts to social and entitlement programs Americans valued—Clinton would have far more credibility on the issue. It took months of persuasion but, in June 1995, he pledged to balance the budget in ten years (three years sooner than the Republican plan).

The president had drawn a clear distinction between himself and his party's liberals. As John Breaux, the moderate Democratic senator from Louisiana said, "The President has been reborn." Dick Morris liked to speak of "triangulation"—positioning the candidate above and between the two parties. It sounded like a pyramid scheme. I didn't see centrism as a calculated tactic. To me, it was the wisest way of governing—of reconciling extremes. The country was trending to the right. Bill Clinton was responding. Few leaders had his combination of spine and heart. If anyone could find harmony in the discordant chorus of voters, it was the man with the saxophone.

★   ★   ★

Republicans never tired of bellowing that Democrats were soft on crime. Clinton had consistently broken ranks with his party on public safety. Highlighting his crime agenda would be a critical first step in rehabilitating his image. We recommended a $2 million ad buy focusing on the president's support of the assault weapons ban and his efforts to put 100,000 cops on the street. No one had ever done this kind of massive advertising more than a year before an election. To test the ads, we went back to the malls where we'd tried out AT&T commercials. We aimed Clinton's ads at swing voters in swing states—Washington, Missouri, Wisconsin, and Pennsylvania. We did *not* run the ads in media hubs like New York, Washington, and Los Angeles. Our goal: fly under the media radar and pitch our message straight to the American people. It was months before the national media caught on to the ads. By then, Clinton's numbers were showing marked improvement.

Meanwhile the Republicans' "Contract with America" budget was making its way through Congress. Clinton had warned the GOP that he'd veto any budget with drastic cuts in Medicare, Medicaid, education, and environmental protection. But the Republicans were sure the hobbled president would sign the bill, rather than shut down the government.

In August 1995, at Clinton's request, we ran several polls based on various scenarios involving the budget and a possible government shutdown. Every scenario led to the same conclusion: stand and fight. One day, I was sitting in the Map Room with Clinton—assuring him we couldn't lose on the budget.

"Poll it again," he said. "I just don't believe it. Test five or six more hypotheses."

Clinton knew he was betting his presidency. Without the support of the rest of his staff, he wanted to be sure he wasn't

111

committing political suicide. But the numbers came back the same. In one poll, by 58 percent to 25 percent, Americans said they would blame the Republicans if the government was shut down.

The trap was set and, amazingly, the Republicans walked right into it. The first government shutdown lasted only a few days, but Clinton's approval ratings rocketed up. Americans now saw him as a strong leader willing to fight for his beliefs. Stubbornly, the Republicans came back for more embarrassment. After weeks of fruitless negotiations, they shut the government down again—this time for more than a month. Again, the White House stood firm. Again, the Republicans paid a heavy political price—none more so than Senator Bob Dole, the presumptive Republican nominee for president. Instead of campaigning in New Hampshire, he was tied down in budget negotiations.

★   ★   ★

Mark and I realized we couldn't expect the Republicans to stumble and bumble forever. The Democratic Party needed to reconnect with middle-class voters. I was eager to find a tool to help us understand voters' concerns. Mark had the inspired idea of looking at the electorate in a more three-dimensional manner—the way we'd done with AT&T. It wasn't enough to understand voters demographically, by traditional parameters as age, race, gender, or party affiliation. Instead, he argued, we needed to examine lifestyle characteristics, attitudes, and values. Mark sought to create a nuanced psychological profile of the electorate. He called it a neuropersonality poll.

Our polling divided the electorate into four distinct parts:

1. the Clinton base (28 percent of voters)
2. the Dole base (18 percent)

3. "Swing I" voters, leaning toward Clinton but still undecided (29 percent)
4. "Swing II" voters, more conservative and less likely to
   support Clinton (25 percent)

We figured that Clinton needed support from 60 percent of
Swing I voters and 30 percent of Swing II voters. Swing I voters were slightly progressive. Swing II voters were fed up with
Washington, supported congressional term limits, and more likely
to scapegoat illegal immigrants, mostly because they competed
with them for jobs. They shared Swing I concerns about economic
fairness, affordable health insurance, and health care for seniors.

Pollsters traditionally saw wealth and age as the defining
variables in U.S. politics. Not so, we discovered. In 1996, the
most important factor was marital status. Families were far
more inclined to support the GOP. So, we needed to focus on
family-oriented concerns like crime prevention, elder care, raising
the minimum wage, and preventing health care companies from
denying coverage.

Now that we understood the issues, we faced the challenge
of crafting the message. We stepped into the field of psychology,
asking questions like:

- Are you the life of the party or a wallflower?
- Do you value common sense or a vision?
- If you were a teacher, would you rather teach fact courses
  or theory courses?
- Are you spontaneous or do you plan?

Voters who saw themselves as intuitive and empathetic
were the most likely to support Clinton. That wasn't surprising
when you consider the president's own personality—the way he
bit his lower lip when he "felt your pain." Unfortunately, the

much-needed Swing II voters made practical, pragmatic decisions based on detailed information. They were interested in results, not grandiose proposals. So, the president would need to make a conscious effort to articulate his arguments differently, depending on his audience.

We thought we could improve our messaging by finding out how voters lived their lives. It turned out that Clinton voters liked HBO, MTV, and *Oprah*; Dole voters preferred *Home Improvement* and *Larry King*; swing voters liked *Seinfeld* and *Friends*. Clinton voters jogged; Dole voters hunted. Swing I voters liked soccer; Swing II voters preferred hockey.

Clinton voters often contradicted themselves: they were the most likely to exceed the speed limit, yet they often were afraid to go out at night. They were health-conscious and liked the great outdoors—that is, when they weren't overeating and shopping. Dole voters were more straightforward: you'd probably find them in church. Swing II voters owned a gun. Swing I had a gay friend. Swing I and Swing II both were about forty years old, had an income of between $30,000 and $60,000, were married, college-educated, moderate, and non-union. Both were afraid. They worried about crime, retirement, technology, illness, and pressure at work.

Both Swing I and II voters liked *60 Minutes*. If we ran Clinton ads during those shows, we'd show the president in less formal settings and lay in some music the Swingers liked—country or rock. Depending on what state the Swing voter was in, we would stick in or leave out mention of the Family Leave Act.

Never had a campaign so carefully dissected the electorate. But we still wondered why so many voters had lost faith in Bill Clinton. The president himself suspected there was more to the problem than the old tax-and-spend label. One day, as we were talking with him about a recent poll, Mark suggested an answer.

"Mr. President," he said. "It's not about economics, it's about values."

For years, Republicans had taken Democrats to task on "family values." But the GOP's conception of values was absurdly narrow—focused on religious issues like abortion, school prayer, or personal morality. The GOP base loved the family values debate. However, it didn't resonate for many Americans, particularly those who weren't that religious.

Mark deduced that Clinton could appeal to this new breed of swing voters by justifying policy decisions in terms of secular values such as "opportunity, responsibility, and community." Clinton could refocus the debate on what we called "public values"—protecting children, caring for elderly parents, safeguarding the environment, looking after the neediest, fighting for equal opportunities.

With the help of our neuropersonality poll, we were able to cast Clinton as a defender of the public values Americans hold dear. The Republicans could keep their moralistic preaching. We leaned into issues like keeping kids away from cigarettes, clamping down on TV violence, improving the nation's schools, expanding opportunities for a college education.

Some may wonder how Bill Clinton could talk about values when many people had called his personal behavior into question. By this time, actress Gennifer Flowers had claimed she and the president had had an extramarital affair. Arkansas state employee Paula Jones had sued him for sexual harassment. But our polling found that public values trumped private peccadillos. Voters seemed willing to overlook Clinton's personal conduct so long as his public character appeared in order. It was a thesis that soon would be severely tested.

The president's reinterpretation of values reached its apex in his State of the Union address in January 1996. Working closely with the White House staff, Mark and I put together a list of more than 100 policy ideas. We then polled each of them. The strongest ones became the stanzas of the president's speech, which he delivered with perfect pitch. Watching him on that chilly night, I felt that we had achieved our strategic goals. We had positioned him to become the first two-term Democratic president since Franklin D. Roosevelt. However, as is so often the case in politics—and particularly with Bill Clinton—surprises were lurking around the bend.

★　★　★

Working for the president took up most of our time. Still, I juggled other clients. One was Clinton's gubernatorial successor, Jim Guy Tucker. Arkansas's governor was on trial for fraud and conspiracy related to investments by the Clintons and associates into the Whitewater Development Corporation. Tucker's legal team had hired me to help with jury selection. From the first, it was clear that this was more than a trial. Special Prosecutor Ken Starr and his investigators were rampant on the scene. One day, at trial, I went outside to the bathroom. When I came back, an FBI official was peering down at the papers I'd left on my seat. Later, I saw Starr seated in the courtroom, holding a Bible as he watched the proceedings. A member of Tucker's security detail pulled me aside. Having previously worked for Clinton, this state trooper told me that FBI agents were grilling other troopers about Clinton's personal life. Starr's probe clearly went far beyond a real estate deal.

When I got back to Washington, I told Clinton what I'd heard. He said friends in Little Rock had shared similar tales of heavy-handed tactics. "We didn't do anything wrong," he insisted. He recognized that he was far from perfect, but he felt that his behavior wasn't too different from that of other presidents. His opponents were just more determined to use his urges to destroy him. It was hard not to feel sorry for him. That said, I've never seen anyone who could compartmentalize problems better than

Clinton. When he set his sights on a goal, he could tune out the snarling wolves.

★   ★   ★

As the campaign entered the final stretch, our strategy sessions settled into a routine—save for the fact that our chief strategist appeared to be losing his mind. Dick Morris had always been a contradiction. He demonstrated extraordinary insight. At the same time, his personality bristled with insecurity and self-absorption. I had long ago learned to shrug off his bombast. Mark and other members of the campaign team were not so understanding. The rise in Clinton's poll numbers bloated Morris's already engorged view of himself. While Mark and I were working, he'd be holding court in his Jefferson hotel suite, doling out tidbits to reporters. In the lead-up to the Democratic convention, Morris pushed Vice President Gore and Governor Evan Bayh to throw out their own speech ideas and deliver something he'd written. Both resisted.

Morris's relationship with Mark remained tortured. Morris obviously envied the applause Mark had won for his campaign insights. Making matters worse, Mark had moved to Washington full-time, working out of a walk-in closet in the White House's West Wing. Morris became obsessed with Mark's whereabouts and activities. "You're like a piece of wood," Morris told him. "I keep pushing you to the bottom of the lake, but you pop right back up." Eventually Morris issued an edict that Mark could not meet with Clinton without Morris's approval. One day, Mark joined a group of staffers in the Oval Office to discuss an important speech. I was in Las Vegas meeting with casino industry clients when I got an urgent call from Morris.

"Get him out of there!" Morris screamed, claiming that Penn had broken the rules. I was at a loss. I wasn't about to call the president's secretary, Betty Currie, and tell her to walk into the

Oval Office and order Mark to leave a meeting with the president of the United States. Morris saved me the trouble. He called the White House and asked that the staff remove Mark. Luckily, the meeting was close to breaking up.

The changes in Morris went beyond this squabbling. Earlier in the campaign, Mark and I would often have dinner at Washington's Old Ebbitt Grill. Morris would usually join us. As time went on, Morris dined with us infrequently. We had no idea what he was doing. Then, during the Democratic Convention in Chicago, the supermarket tabloid *Star* published a story explaining Morris's absences: Dick had been enjoying the services of a D.C. call girl, Sherry Rowlands. *Star* reported that Rowlands had met Morris weekly at the Jefferson Hotel. Photos showed the two kissing on his balcony. Rowlands claimed that Morris liked sucking her toes and that he'd let her eavesdrop on his phone calls with Clinton. She said Morris had called the president "the Monster," because of his temper, and the First Lady "the Twister," because she resembled a tornado.

We were all at the convention when the story broke. This fresh sex scandal threatened to damage the president just as he was due to accept his party's nomination. Everyone knew Morris must resign from the campaign. Everyone but Dick. In a panic, he asked me to come to his hotel room. There, the mysterious genius who twenty-seven years earlier had asked me to join the West Side Kids now paced the floor. He was in no mood to go quietly. He blamed a GOP conspiracy for his downfall. He claimed that he hadn't done anything worse than the president. He railed against "yellow journalism." I sat with him, reminding him how hard we'd all worked to resuscitate Bill Clinton's presidency, and of the harm he could do if he didn't step aside. "Go with dignity," I said. White House Chief of Staff Erskine Bowles joined the intervention. After hours of persuasion, Morris agreed to write his own concession speech.

"While I served, I sought to avoid the limelight because I did not want to become the message," he said in a statement. "Now, I resign so I will not become the issue."

Yet he would not disappear completely. About a week after the convention, Clinton met me, Vice President Gore, and Mark. He told us he trusted us to take charge of his campaign. Following Morris's resignation, Clinton had issued a statement saying, "I am and always will be grateful" to "my friend." I, too, was grateful to Morris for bringing me into the White House, but I told Clinton he must cut ties with Morris. Clinton was silent. I repeated my advice. Silence again. By then, I'd learned that when Clinton doesn't speak, he doesn't agree with you.

I never saw Clinton be anything but respectful of Morris. Yet knowing Dick, I feared that he would turn on "the Monster" when the moment was ripe. First, however, I had my own Morris crisis to deal with.

Not long after his eviction from the campaign, Morris called me with what he said was an offer I couldn't refuse: he wanted me to serve as his secret conduit to Clinton. I politely declined. Then he said he was considering writing a book about his years with Clinton. He asked if I wanted to be the secret coauthor. Again, I demurred. I sensed that, sooner or later, Morris would try to punish me and Mark for our insolence. However, with Election Day approaching, I could no longer worry about Dick Morris. We had a campaign to run. Clinton took our advice and sailed through the campaign, sticking to his centrist positions. He won 49.2 percent of the popular vote, with Bob Dole claiming 40.7 percent and Reform candidate Ross Perot taking 8.4 percent.

I didn't see Bill Clinton in person until the first strategy meeting of his second term. I remembered how, when we started working for a beleaguered president, not a single member of his staff stood up when he entered the room. Now everyone snapped to attention. We'd helped restore his stature poll-by-poll, initiative-by-initiative.

Smart, small plays gain more yardage than Hail Mary passes. One silver bullet may kill a werewolf but, if you want to build a house, you'll need 10,000 nails.

At the end of that meeting, the president pulled me aside.

"Doug," he said, "thanks for all your hard work. I couldn't have done it without you."

Doing a job well may be its own reward but someone else's gratitude gives you the strength to start the next job.

15

WRESTLING
WITH STRONGMEN

In between trips to the White House, I was jetting to other parts of the globe.

I'd been keeping an eye on Turkey since 1994, when Prime Minister Tansu Çiller's True Path Party (DYP) hired us. Our task that year was getting DYP candidate Bedrettin Dalan elected mayor of Istanbul. That local race would have global reverberations for years to come. Dalan had already served as mayor of the fabled city. Having lost to a leftist in 1989, he wanted his job back. He was up against a dozen candidates. Among them was one Recep Tayyip Erdoğan. The mainstream media scoffed at the blue-collar Erdoğan's lack of experience; opponents called him a rube. But I could see he was a rousing speaker. He made appealing promises to fix Istanbul's pollution, traffic, and corruption. Erdoğan represented the Islamist Welfare Party (RP). Although he claimed to be religiously moderate, my clients believed he threatened Turkey's secular Constitution. We ran a commercial that showed a public-school morphing into a Muslim *madrassa*. I was sure the ad would jolt voters wary of the sort of theocracy that ruled in neighboring Iran. But, as in many races, voters were more concerned about their wallets. They blamed Dalan's corruption-tarred party for Turkey's miserable economy. No other issue mattered. Election Day delivered mixed results. Çiller's party narrowly retained power. But Erdoğan defeated Dalan.

My fears came to pass. In 1998, Erdoğan gave a jihadish speech ("the mosques are our barracks, the domes our helmets, the minarets our bayonets and the faithful our soldiers") that got him jailed for four months, ending his mayoralty. Yet he returned even stronger, abandoning overtly fundamentalist rhetoric to get himself elected prime minister and then president. He's now been in power for two decades and counting—ensconced in an illegally built 1,000-room presidential palace. Many who shared my assessment of him reside in jail.

Foresight isn't flawless. The best binoculars won't always stop you from running into a wall.

★   ★   ★

Israel also remained on my mind. In the fall 1995, as Mark and I were consulting for President Clinton, I got a call from Zev Furst, our friend who'd introduced us to Menachem Begin. Furst asked us to do some polling for the reelection campaign of Israeli Prime Minister Yitzhak Rabin. Two years before, Rabin had signed the Oslo Accords with his sworn enemy, PLO chairman Yasir Arafat, on the White House lawn. Rabin hoped Israelis would give him four more years to finish the peace process with the Palestinians. I was excited by the opportunity. On November 3, I was putting the finishing touches on a benchmark poll to evaluate Rabin's popularity. The next day, at a rally in Tel Aviv, a young, right-wing Israeli stepped out of the shadows and pumped two bullets into Rabin. He died a few hours later.

I was devastated. But I still hoped to play a part in continuing his legacy. With Rabin gone, leadership of the Labor Party passed to his foreign minister, Shimon Peres. Though we'd worked with Begin to defeat him in 1981, Peres asked us to stay on board for his race against Likud leader Benjamin "Bibi" Netanyahu. In January 1996 I met with Peres at his spartan office. Buoyed by voter sympathy for Rabin, he was up 17 or 18 points. "I can't lose to somebody like [Bibi]," Peres assured me.

Peres and his team didn't want to exploit Rabin's death. They didn't want to use video that showed Netanyahu using polarizing rhetoric that many Israelis blamed for Rabin's assassination. Instead, Peres wanted to run on his own merits. But for all his accomplishments, the New *York Times* reported, Peres "could never shake the image of an indecisive dreamer and a shifty politician." When four terror attacks left sixty Israelis dead and scores injured, Peres's poll numbers quickly plummeted. A race that few people thought Netanyahu could win was now neck and neck.

We told Peres he must sharpen his hawkish profile. Peres displayed atypical fury when he retaliated against Hezbollah guerrillas by pounding their positions in Lebanon. But the violence only grew worse, and Peres's support dropped further. We told him Lebanon was not the top concern for Israelis. In one meeting, I recommended that he crack down on terrorists and deemphasize the notion of a Palestinian state.

"We should do everything Schoen is saying," he told his campaign staff.

Then he looked at his campaign manager, Haim Ramon, and added, "But I know you're not going to do it."

Ramon shook his head and confirmed, "That's right."

This admission laid bare Peres's irredeemable flaw: for all his gifts, he lacked the drive to win. He seemed to forget that **if you're the boss, act like the boss.**

Instead of taking our advice, Peres developed his own idea on how to turn things around. In the spring of 1996, our polling showed Bill Clinton was more popular in Israel than either Peres or Netanyahu. Peres thought he could bolster his security profile by forging a new defense treaty with the United States. Bypassing the U.S. State Department, one of his advisers asked us to ask Clinton if he'd go for this treaty. We asked. Clinton and National Security Advisor Sandy Berger both thought it was a terrible idea. In their view, it wasn't good for Israel, and it would do little to help Peres politically. Nevertheless, Clinton wanted Peres to win. With his instinctive understanding of Israeli politics, he used me to channel advice to Peres. In fact, Clinton put out a statement that essentially endorsed Peres.

For all of Peres's missteps, the race stayed close. Two days before Election Day, the two candidates engaged in their only face-to-face debate. We begged Peres to make security his focus, but he didn't do it. On election night, Israeli media outlets at first called the race for Peres. Then, just as they had in 1981, these outlets reverse themselves. That night I was in the White House with Clinton and Dick Morris. After the initial call for Peres, Morris urgently tried to arrange a call between the president and the apparent victor. Peres demurred. "I can still lose this," he allowed. In fact, he ended up losing his fifth election by a mere 29,457 votes. The day after the voting, Zev Furst went to Peres's office. He was surrounded by advisers, but Furst demanded to speak to him alone. There was a small bedroom behind the minister's office. Sitting at the end of the bed, Furst told Peres that his advisers had consistently misled him—refusing to carry out his instructions, telling him he was ahead when he was behind. Tears streamed down Peres's face.

★ ★ ★

Despite the disappointment of that election, we remained involved in Israeli politics.

Years earlier, I had met Ehud Barak, then Israel's most highly decorated soldier. We'd intersected in Florida—in, of all places, the offices of SlimFast. Crazy as it sounds, Barak was consulting for the diet program. The founder of SlimFast, Danny Abraham, was a Long Island kid who, after fighting the Nazis in Europe, moved to Israel and fought in the Yom Kippur War. Along the way Abraham met Barak, and later recruited him to help sell SlimFast. Barak quickly took to marketing. Listening to him in a sales meeting, I was impressed by the former Lieutenant General's strategy for helping Americans win their battle of the bulge.

Barak had served as Peres's Foreign Minister. From the day Peres lost his bid to be prime minister, Barak began to plot his own run for the job. In May 1997, he asked us to take the pulse of the Israeli voter. Our results showed that Barak must develop a strong domestic agenda of pocketbook issues. We also found that, while voters admired him, they still saw him more as a soldier than a political leader. After that poll, we didn't hear from Barak and his team for more than a year and a half. Then in the fall of 1998, word leaked that Barak had hired Stan Greenberg, Bob Shrum, and James Carville to run his campaign. We were a bit miffed. But then, shortly afterward, one of Barak's advisers said he also wanted us. Shrum, Greenberg, and Carville would be the public face of the campaign. Zev Furst and I would work behind the scenes. We later learned Barak had hired a French consulting team as well. Yes, at first, we were pissed.

Even if you're angry, remain professional. No temper tantrums. Just do your job. Do what your client has asked to the best of your ability.

Barak explained that, as a military man, he liked having "lots of information from different sources." He never let on what the other consulting teams were telling him. Only when he was ready did he unveil a strategy that brilliantly combined the disparate advice.

There is no such thing as perfect information. Get the best evidence you can find, then act on it decisively.

Despite Barak's self-possession, he seemed almost a secondary character in the election drama. This race was really a referendum on another man—Benjamin "Bibi" Netanyahu. Since becoming prime minister, Bibi had ricocheted from one crisis to another, both personal and political. Relations with the Palestinians reached a new low. Social tensions among Jews—Russians and non-Russians, secular and religious, Sephardic and Ashkenazi—had also grown more acute. The economy was in tatters. According to one of our first polls, by a margin of 66 percent to 27 percent, Israelis thought the country was on the wrong track.

Bill Clinton also viewed Netanyahu with great suspicion. Clinton blamed him for the stalled peace process; he believed Barak would be much easier to work with. Even with everything else on his mind, Clinton found time to pore over our poll numbers and offer Barak advice. Our research consistently showed that direct attacks on Netanyahu's character improved his numbers. During one meeting at the Tel Aviv Hilton, I told Barak he needed to go negative at once. Barak asked Furst to review our data twice before finally instructing his staff to follow our directions.

Netanyahu fired back with claims that Barak would be weak on security. But these swipes didn't land on a candidate who'd personally freed Israeli hostages in daring operations and taken out key terrorist leaders. In the end, Barak won by a 56 percent to 42 percent margin. Israelis had had enough of Bibi, for now.

★ ★ ★

Meanwhile, I hadn't forgotten about Serbia. Having controlled his homeland for seven years, Slobodan Milošević was now president of the Federal Republic of Yugoslavia. Although full details were yet to emerge, his regime had directly supported the displacement of more than two million people and the killing of an estimated

200,000, including more than 8,000 Bosniak Muslims massacred at Srebrenica.

After Milan Panić's ouster in 1993, I tried to persuade him to stay involved with politics. But his stint as prime minister had riled some important stockholders of his pharmaceutical company; retaining control of ICN was now his priority. Yet Panić was working behind the scenes. He paid me to continue polling and to stay in touch with Milošević's opponents.

Around this time, I got to know Richard Holbrooke, the U.S. special envoy who'd negotiated the 1995 Dayton Accords that brought a frail, bandaged peace to the Balkans. Holbrooke sometimes had trouble getting an appointment with the president. He knew I had regular campaign meetings with Clinton; so, one day, he made it his business to sit next to me on a flight from New York to Washington. He hoped I would pass along his intelligence.

Influence depends on access. If you don't have as much juice as you want, get close to someone who does.

I always faithfully passed along Holbrooke's messages. Holbrooke never did get me that seat on the Council of Foreign Relations board, not that I really expected it. But he did once give me some useful advice. "Foreign policy ain't that difficult," he said modestly. "It's mostly practical thinking and common sense—and if you quote me on this, I will have to deny I know you."

Holbrooke and I were on the same page when it came to Milošević. We both feared that the strongman would stop at nothing when it came to punishing ethnic Albanian rebels in Kosovo. My recent polling demonstrated that Serbian nationalist fervor was reaching a boil. As Serbian military and paramilitary soldiers stepped up their "ethnic cleansing" in Kosovo, I decided to take Holbrooke's tip and use my access to the president. Though Serbia wasn't my official brief, I told Clinton that Milošević was a phony tough guy, so scared that he wore a bulletproof vest under his trench coat. To get him to back down, you had to threaten his personal safety. On March 24, 1999, NATO forces finally launched a tentative air campaign against Serbia. The White House hoped Milošević would quickly withdraw from Kosovo. He didn't. Again, I told the president and National Security Advisor Sandy Berger that Milošević would budge only if he thought he might die. "Sandy, I know this man," I told Berger. "I've been working against him since the early 1990s." Before dawn on April 23, 1999, NATO dropped three laser-guided bombs on Milošević's house. Milošević, who switched bunkers every night, wasn't home. But he got the message. His troops pulled out of Kosovo.

Know your adversary and act on his fears.

★　★　★

A few weeks later, I got a call from Milan Panić.

"It's time to finish the job," he said.

"What do you mean?" I asked.

"I went to the National Democratic Institute in Washington and told them to hire you to oust Milošević," he said.

The U.S. Agency for International Development (USAID) had set aside over $40 million to support groups trying to pry Milošević from power. One of them, the National Democratic Institute, funded public opinion polling. With the Institute's financing, we fielded a poll that weighed possible approaches for toppling Milošević. Those approaches were personified by two prominent opposition leaders, who disliked each other almost as much as they hated Milošević.

Zoran Djindjic had studied neo-Marxist theory in Germany before proving himself an adept capitalist by importing machine tools from East Germany. His critics accused him of arrogance and chumminess with mobsters. I saw him as a can-do guy. With funding from Panić, Djindjic had put together a fledgling coalition of democratic parties that had turned out tens of thousands of Serbs to protest the regime. Djindjic thought voting was pointless because Milošević would always find a way to steal an election. He believed a rebellion was necessary.

Vuk Draskovic, a novelist and head of the ultranationalist Serbian Renewal Movement, was a messianic and moody figure. Then again, I might be moody if I'd been imprisoned and tortured. Draskovic insisted on an electoral campaign.

Our numbers backed Draskovic's argument. Two-thirds of Serbian voters wanted Milošević to resign before the end of his term. However, if he refused to step down, Serbs did not want a mass uprising. They wanted an election. That was the good news. The bad news was that most people felt the opposition parties— there were nearly two dozen of them—were "self-interested, uncooperative, likely to fall apart." Voters didn't consider any of the opposition leaders a strong candidate. Draskovic and Djindjic had approval numbers almost as bad as Milošević's.

In October, I flew to Budapest to present the results of the survey to the leading members of the opposition. I arrived at the Marriott to find that most of my results had already leaked out. Djindjic was said to be so upset by my findings that he was boycotting the meeting. Nevertheless, I went ahead. I emphasized that Milošević was vulnerable to a well-organized challenge. The key to victory was unity and a campaign focused on Serbia's calamitous economy.

The audience broke out in a buzz of conversation and argument. Clearly, they were excited by evidence of their dictator's weakness. But they were also skeptical. Some still maintained an election was pointless since Milošević would always find a way to cheat.

I could feel the audience slipping back into the same defeatist stance I'd encountered seven years earlier. I was getting fed up with their squabbling. I may have behaved myself at that Harvard antiwar donnybrook, but now I was angry. Switching from exposition to exhortation, I told the audience that skepticism didn't justify passivity. Milošević could be toppled, I repeated—but only through the electoral process. Win the election first. If he cheats, take to the streets.

An analyst must sometimes become an advocate. When all else fails, stop observing and do something!

The meeting ended without any formal decisions, but I felt my message had been heard.

The next morning, I had breakfast with Jim Dobbins and James O'Brien, Secretary of State Madeleine Albright's special advisers for the Balkans. They found my analysis persuasive. They offered to arrange for me to give a stateside briefing to the Principals' Committee, whose members included the Secretaries of State and Defense. I happily accepted and, a few weeks later, flew to Washington to brief the Committee at the White House.

I'd been to the White House many times by then but, that day, as I was racing through the doorway, flashing lights and a siren went off. Secret Service officers rushed to block my entry.

Fortunately, an even-tempered supervisor came over.

"Sir," the man said calmly, "either you're carrying a nuclear device and we have a serious problem—or you've been to the doctor this morning."

I quickly explained that, in fact, I'd just had a cardiological exam—a dual isotope stress test. Apparently, trace elements still in my body had set off radiation detectors. In Washington, people touched by scandal are often said to be "radioactive." But I really *was*! If ever I needed a warning to take better care of my health, it was the shrieking alarm I'd set off.

I did not address the Principals' Committee that day. The meeting was never rescheduled. Ultimately, someone at the White House decided it would be unseemly for a political consultant, particularly the president's political consultant, to tell the Principals how to beat Milošević. Nevertheless, my memo was widely circulated and discussed. Among those who received a copy was CIA Director George Tenet. Someone from the spy agency asked if I could brief its Yugoslavia analysts. So, radio-active heart tests in the past, I reported to CIA headquarters in Langley, Virginia. The analysts there at first greeted me with warm cordiality . . . that soon turned to hostility. The analysts questioned my assumptions, my methodology, my sample sizes, even my ability to conduct a proper poll. The CIA, they explained, had its own well-funded polling operation to monitor public opinion in Serbia. Its officers insisted I was underestimating Milošević's popular support. Instead of welcoming a new source of information, they resented someone they saw as an uninformed amateur—a political hack—second-guessing them.

After that briefing, the CIA tried to deep-six our polling. Assistant Secretary of State James Dobbins called me. He was concerned about Langley's objections to the electoral strategy.

"How confident are you of your data?" he asked.

"Completely confident," I told him.

He paused then responded, "I agree with you. We're going to stay behind you on this one."

Thanks to Dobbins's unwavering support, USAID and European donors intensified their support for opposition parties.

Then, on July 27, 2000, Milošević caught us all off guard. He called elections for September 24. The opposition was stunned; most observers had expected a vote the following summer. Clearly, Milošević thought he could win.

In early August, I flew back to Budapest for another meeting with the opposition. The ostensible purpose was to present the results of the poll we'd done just before Milošević announced elections. The results were not cheering. Not only were his numbers improving but support for opposition leaders was declining. Too many Serbs still saw the ragtag opposition as incoherent bickerers. They needed to join forces. In my mind, success hinged on Zoran Djindjic. His Alliance for Democratic Change would have to be the core of the opposition. Djindjic was still steamed about my last poll. His standing had further slid when, during NATO's bombardment, he'd fled Belgrade for Montenegro. Though he'd insisted he'd received a credible assassination threat, Milošević's propaganda machine tarred him as a NATO spy.

As the lights dimmed and my PowerPoint slides went up, I scanned the room to see if Djindjic was there. Would he boycott another unity meeting? I was assured he would arrive at some point—probably around 2:00 p.m. 2:00 p.m. became 4:00 p.m. Finally, at a little after 5:00 p.m., Djindjic, with his piercing gaze and silver buzzcut, swept into the hotel, accompanied by five burly bodyguards. Everyone stopped and watched him enter. Even other opposition leaders viewed him as a figure more significant than themselves. An aide informed me that Djindjic wanted to speak with me privately. The two of us stepped into a little function room piled high with chairs. With a cool look that divulged nothing, Djindjic gestured for me to sit down.

When I'd last seen him in Washington in 1997, he spoke little English. Now, he asked, flawlessly, "I can't win, can I?"

"No," I said.

Politicians rarely like to hear they can't win, but Djindjic received the news calmly.

I pressed on. I told him we must find someone who could carry the opposition banner but who didn't have high negatives. This candidate needed to have strong nationalist credentials, but he couldn't be complicit in Milošević's crimes.

"What about Koštunica?" Djindjic asked.

It was an intriguing question. Vojislav Koštunica was the leader of the smaller Democratic Party of Serbia. A prickly law professor, he was an ardent nationalist—critical of both Milošević and NATO. Most people knew little about him, but that meant his unfavorability ratings were low.

"If you get him, you get the nationalist votes, plus you get a clean new face." I told Djindjic. "How are your relations with him?"

"Not good," Djindjic admitted. "But I can serve my purposes by making him the candidate—and of course it will serve his purposes as well." He went on, "I will control the campaign, but I will need your messages and advice to do this."

I was startled by the extent to which our thinking was now in sync. We agreed that this time, we would make sure the election stayed won.

One powerful tool could be the exit poll. However, after his near loss against Panić, Milošević had pushed through legislation banning exit polls. But there was no legal obstacle to doing what is called a "quick count"—deploying people to observe voting and tabulation and then report the results back to campaign headquarters in real time. It would take an enormous effort, but it was the only way to guard against fraud. Over the next two months, USAID and the Democratic Opposition of Serbia (DOS) would train nearly 30,000 poll watchers.

We developed a slogan: "Gotov Je!"—meaning, "He's Finished!" Everybody knew who "he" was. U.S. taxpayers paid for 2.5 million stickers with the slogan, as well as for 5,000 cans of spray paint that student activists used to emblazon anti-Milošević graffiti on walls across Serbia. We advised Koštunica to get out of Belgrade and into the provinces. After a few weeks of pressing the flesh in smaller towns, he was leading Milošević by roughly 40 percent to 25 percent.

Sunday, September 24 was Election Day. To preempt any effort by Milošević to claim nonexistent levels of support, the opposition started the day by announcing the results of our latest poll showing Koštunica winning by 56 percent. Opposition volunteers posted at every polling station kept a running tally of the voting. Results were emailed back to the USAID-funded tabulation center in Belgrade and fed into the computer bank. Just after midnight, after the polls were closed and the results had been double-checked, Koštunica called a press conference to announce that he had won a clear majority.

The government seemed caught off guard. Milošević hadn't foreseen that the opposition would conduct its own parallel vote count. At first, the regime was silent. Only after several days did the Milošević-controlled election commission assert that neither candidate had won more than 50 percent and that a runoff election would be necessary.

The opposition now faced a difficult choice: should it agree to a runoff, giving Milošević two more weeks to maneuver for an advantage? Or should it risk a bare-knuckles confrontation with the government? Taking a poll, we found that more than two-thirds of respondents believed Koštunica had won. Our poll gave the green light to act now instead of risking a runoff.

The Democratic Opposition of Serbia announced plans for a general strike. Miners, workers from idled factories, provincial mayors, and others had already pledged their allegiance. On October 5, hours before daybreak, convoys of anti-Milošević protestors from across Serbia set off for Belgrade. The regime ordered cops and soldiers to block their passage. But confronted by angry—sometimes armed—throngs, security let them pass. It later emerged that Djindjic had also reached out to figures in the police and the army, as well as to underworld figures, to reassure them that a new government would view them sympathetically—if they stayed out of the final showdown with Milošević.

By the early afternoon, thousands of people had converged in front of the Federal Parliament. These weren't just student protestors. There were fed-up politicians, like Mayor Velimir Ilič of Čačak who brought roughly a thousand men, many of them former soldiers. Belgrade's mayor, Milan St. Protić, led a group that overran a police station and handed out weapons to supporters.

Around 3:00 p.m., a protestor drove a bulldozer up to the doors of Parliament. Its guards stood down. Milošević had banked on the loyalty of security force commanders. But they too fell in with the "Bulldozer Revolution." On October 6, the Butcher of the Balkans met with Vojislav Koštunica and publicly accepted defeat. Koštunica took office as president of Yugoslavia the following day.

The opposition had taken a huge gamble based on a single poll. Public opinion research had helped achieve what untold diplomatic missions, international peace conferences, and thousands of bombs had not—it had ended the Balkan Wars. *Washington Post* correspondent Michael Dobbs called it "the first poll-driven focus-group revolution."

Data can give courage to your convictions. Persuasive research is a call to arms.

Our effort cost a fraction of the price of a military intervention. If only the U.S. had spent the money seven years earlier, when Panić ran, thousands of people might still be alive.

Support democracy! It's cheaper than its alternatives and it lasts longer.

Two weeks after Milošević's ouster, Secretary of State Madeleine Albright wrote to thank me for my unexpected contribution to peace. "This may be the first-time polling has played such an important role in setting and securing foreign policy objectives," she noted.

But regime change is an ongoing process. It didn't take long for the relationship of coalition partners Koštunica and Djindjic to fray. In May of 2001, Prime Minister Djindjic defied President Koštunica by sending Milošević to stand trial at The Hague. In 2003, Djindjic won the power struggle when Serbia and Montenegro approved an arrangement that eliminated Koštunica's position as president of Yugoslavia. But by then, Djindjic had made too many enemies. On March 12, 2003, as he walked out of a building in Belgrade, a sniper's bullet pierced his heart. Investigators ruled his assassination was likely a collaboration between organized crime and former members of Milošević secret police. Clearly, Serbia remained a rough neighborhood.

Nevertheless, my work in Serbia helped me develop seven principles for toppling dictators:

- **Unity is critical.** A unified opposition needs to be in place before an election begins.

- **Harness discontent.** Opposition leaders must translate popular dissatisfaction into active support.

- **Use public opinion polls to identify key issues and then craft simple messages.** Use focus groups to make sure the messages appeal to critical constituencies. Then repeat them again and again!

- **Expect to be smeared as the lackey of a nefarious outsider.** Deflect this attack by focusing on the issues voters care about most (and that made the regime vulnerable in the first place).

- **Use tracking polls.** It's the only way to monitor whether your message is getting through. Positive poll numbers help keep the opposition unified.

- **International pressure is critical.** Play to the media, particularly the international media.

- **Prepare for theft.** Winning the election doesn't necessarily mean taking power. You need a plan of resistance that mobilizes the opposition and neutralizes at least some of the people with guns.

Every campaign is unique. But you can adapt these principals to battlefields big and small, foreign and domestic. Maybe you have an autocrat in your town or your office.

Take on a despot when he first threatens you. Bullies only get bigger.

16

OBEDIENCE TRAINING

Mark and I continued to work for Bill Clinton on policy initiatives during his second term. Our first focus was Social Security reform. The president recognized that, as the vast number of aging Baby Boomers retired, it would be harder to make good on the government's obligations to them. We believed that investing the Social Security Trust Fund in equities, rather than just bonds, could be a better way to build wealth. It would be a hard sell—liberal Democrats were adamantly opposed to this idea. But putting the Social Security Trust Fund on a safer foundation would be a historic achievement.

It was not to be. The vagaries of the stock market certainly played a role. But the bigger problem was the president's relationship with White House intern Monica Lewinsky. Clinton first faced the question of whether he'd had "sexual relations" with Lewinsky during a deposition by lawyers for Paula Jones, an Arkansas woman who'd claimed he'd exposed himself to her. Determined that Clinton would not escape, Jones's lawyers encircled him in a long, tightly knotted definition: "A person engages in sexual relations when the person knowingly engages in or causes contact with the genitalia, anus, groin, breast, inner thigh, or buttocks of any person with an intent to arouse or gratify the sexual desire of any person." Clinton replied flatly: "I have never had sexual relations with Monica Lewinsky." In his mind, Clinton had slipped the definition's bonds as smoothly as Houdini. As he saw it, he was the passive recipient of oral sex. It was a tortured legalism that has haunted him ever since. But, as he later confided to me, he had to play for time to save his presidency.

Staving off impeachment forced the president to protect his left flank and keep Congressional Democrats loyal to him. I remember Clinton calling me in the summer of 1998 shortly after I'd returned from an overseas trip. It had just been announced that he would appear before Special Prosecutor Ken Starr's grand jury. As an attorney, I knew Clinton's appearance could put him in further legal jeopardy. I asked why he'd agreed to testify.

"I need to protect my base in the House," he said with a sigh.

Even his supporters wanted him to explain his actions. Stonewalling the prosecution, as Richard Nixon had done, would likely condemn him to Nixon's fate. At first, the president seemed to believe he could ride out Lewinskygate, as he had earlier sex scandals. But the daily drip of revelations was taking a toll on, among other things, his marriage. One day I was in a meeting with the president when First Lady Hillary Clinton poked her head into the room. She said she was taking their Labrador retriever, Buddy, out for a walk.

"I'll take him out," her husband said.

"No, no," Hillary said. "I'll take him. You're busy with your political advisors."

"I have plenty of time," he insisted.

"No, you don't," she countered.

The room had enough tension to charge a nuclear submarine. In my reading of the subtext, Bill wanted to assure Hillary that their family life mattered to him. Perhaps he thought that walking Buddy might get him out of the doghouse. But Hillary didn't seem ready for that.

Luckily, Clinton had the good fortune to have a foe in Newt Gingrich. The House Speaker happened to be having his own extramarital affair, with a House staffer twenty-three years his junior. Though the GOP controlled both chambers of Congress, Clinton survived the impeachment proceedings. Our private polling showed that the Republicans had badly misread the mood of voters, who were less troubled by Clinton's peccadillos than by partisan warfare. With the economy humming, Mark suggested a 1998 midterm election slogan: "Progress Over Politics." The electorate seemed to agree with the message. The Republicans lost five seats, the worst midterm performance in sixty-four years by a party not holding the presidency.

★   ★   ★

I'd gotten to know Vice President Al Gore as well as I could during Clinton's first term. During the 1996 presidential race, one of my key responsibilities was winning his home state of Tennessee. Unfortunately, neither Clinton nor Gore was terribly popular there. We did our best to find Christian conservative ministers who'd endorse Clinton. By emphasizing law and order, we joked that we out-"Republican-ed" the Republicans. And still, Clinton-Gore barely won Tennessee. In the second term, I continued to do most of Gore's polling. For nearly three years, I would huddle with him and his core advisers at least once a month. I'd publicly defended him on national television during a mini scandal over allegations of improper fundraising by the vice president's office.

Yet Gore could be oddly detached. In one of our early meetings, he and I were alone in his office. During a lull in the conversation, he started surfing the Web. Attempting to break the silence, I asked him a question about Serbia. He looked at me as if to say, "Why would you want to talk about *that*?" Gore's core political principles seemed oddly unsettled. He professed a desire for new approaches but rarely took the suggestions Mark and I made. In early 1999, we did an elaborate message poll to help him develop themes for his upcoming presidential run. His wife, Tipper, came to one of our presentations. I was sitting next to her as Mark gave a solid pitch for holding on to the high ground Clinton had claimed. Tipper looked at me and said, "Can you put this into plain English, please?"

There could be nothing plainer than the logic of taking credit for the Clinton-Gore accomplishments—low unemployment, low crime, low inflation, record economic growth, welfare reform, middle-class tax cuts, a record budget surplus. But after the Lewinsky affair came to light, Gore began distancing himself from the Clintons and their advisers. Mark and I became suspect. Relations between the vice president and the First Lady were already fraught. So, the Gore camp wasn't pleased when Mark began to work on Hillary's nascent New York senatorial campaign. Mark also dared to tell Gore directly that he should embrace and expand on Bill Clinton's achievements. Bob Shrum, who had been working on the Gore campaign, later confirmed Mark's honesty caused Gore to fire him.

★ ★ ★

My rapport with Gore wasn't much better. So, as the 2000 election cycle approached, I moved on to other contests. None kept me busier than the New Jersey senate race.

New Jersey was a curious state politically. Although it had been trending Democratic by the late 1990s, it had a Republican governor and a Republican legislature. Many Democrats blamed this vexing logjam on one man—former Democratic governor Jim Florio. A pugnacious lawyer and former Golden Gloves boxer, Florio had won the governor's office in 1989 on a promise not to raise taxes. Nevertheless, he promptly rammed a $2.6 billion tax increase through the legislature. Angry voters reacted by giving the GOP a veto-proof majority in the state legislature. In 1993, they also replaced Florio with Republican Christine Todd Whitman.

Come 1999, U.S. Senator Frank Lautenberg, our former client, announced he would not seek reelection. Seeing his chance for political vindication, Florio wanted the job—much to the horror of Democratic leaders. Gov. Whitman was widely expected to be the Republican candidate and the likely winner of a Whitman-Florio rematch. Unless . . . another Democrat stepped in. The party's leaders set out to find that candidate.

One evening at a Newark dinner headlined by President Bill Clinton, Orin Kramer, a prominent New Jersey fundraiser, turned to me and asked, "What about Jon Corzine?"

It was an intriguing suggestion. I'd heard Corzine might be ready to step down as chairman of Goldman Sachs. Plus, he was a major Democratic donor. New Jersey senator Bob Torricelli asked if I'd sound him out.

When I gave Corzine a call, he was genial but decidedly uncommitted. Still, he agreed to meet. We had breakfast at the Three Guys coffee shop on Madison. For a Wall Street "master of the universe," Corzine was pleasantly low-key. At the same time, he still had the bounce he'd shown on the University of Illinois basketball team. His personal history was appealing. He'd grown up on a farm, served in the Marine Reserves, and, by dint of hard work, had come to run one of the world's most powerful investment banks. He'd been philanthropically generous. Best of all, he had the resources to fund his own campaign. But would he be willing and able to brave the humbling and ruthless world of politics?

In late April, we queried 1,038 New Jerseyites to find out how a hypothetical candidate resembling Corzine might fare against candidates resembling Florio and Gov. Whitman. Corzine matched up well against Whitman in the general election. But in the Democratic primary, Florio won by a margin of roughly 25 percent. It was discouraging news. Another strategist might have fudged the numbers or soft-pedaled them. After all, a rich candidate means a big payday for a consultant. But I've found that, **long term, telling the truth is better for business.** So, when I met Corzine at the Harmonie Club in midtown, I put it to him straight: his odds of a victory weren't good.

Rather than being distressed, he seemed to appreciate my candor. He also didn't accept my grim prognosis.

"Go back to the drawing board," he said.

I turned to strategist Bob Shrum. Even though Bob's politics tilt to my left, I have huge respect for his talents. True to form, Bob proposed that Corzine run, not as a Clintonesque New Democrat, but as an unabashed liberal. I did another poll. It corroborated that leaning left could flay Florio in the primary. We told Corzine that, to win, he'd need to position himself as a progressive. Corzine went for it without hesitation. He was comfortable calling for dramatically increased funding for key social programs. He did have a couple of caveats. He would not relinquish his un-liberal belief that part of the Social Security Trust Fund should be invested in the stock market. His other winking ultimatum: he would not shave his salt-and-pepper beard.

Then he turned to a more serious subject.

"I hate to talk about money," he said, "but what would I need to spend?"

No one was eager to answer his question, so I spoke up.

"Seven, eight million dollars in the primary, and another seven million dollars in the general," I said.

It seemed like a reasonable estimate, considering the cost of commercials in the tri-state media market. Corzine, however, turned as white as an Ocean City seagull.

"I can't even imagine spending $15 million," he said.

144

Despite his sticker shock, he agreed to move forward. By July, our small team had gathered at his East Hampton beach house to finalize our strategy. Arriving late, I ended up getting a kid's bunk bed in Corzine's attic. So much for the glamour of political consulting.

We'd done a poll asking voters how they'd feel about a candidate who promised universal health insurance, universal long-term care, universal college education, and universal gun registration. The "universal everything" strategy tested extremely well—at least among New Jersey Democrats. Of course, this strategy posed problems in the general election, where the Republican candidate was sure to brand Corzine a tax-and-spend liberal. Then again, if he didn't outpromise the liberal Florio in the primary, he'd never make it to the general election.

Corzine still had to sell himself to the state party. Many county leaders no doubt expected him to be a haughty financier or a sleazy shark. Instead, he came across as earnest, down-to-earth, solicitous of their opinions. His willingness to contribute to their political organizations didn't hurt either. By midsummer, we'd lined up the support of some of the state's most powerful Dems, including power brokers in the Black and Latino communities.

Florio accused Corzine of mounting "the equivalent of a hostile Wall Street takeover of the Democratic Party." Just to show he wasn't cowed, Florio crowed that he'd raised $175,000 more than Corzine for his exploratory committee. He'd also hired our competition, James Carville. Now I tip my hat to James as a tactician and showman. You can't minimize his role in shaping Bill Clinton's 1992 presidential success. But, by 2000, I knew James had lost his taste for the grinding work of American campaigns. He told me so when, during Clinton's first term, I asked if he'd be working on the president's reelection.

"Hell, no!" said the "Ragin' Cajun." "Right now, I'm a celebrity. I enjoy it. A company or organization invites me to lunch, I tell some jokes, I get $10,000. I go to dinner, I tell more jokes, I get $15,000 or $20,000. You can't fuck up lunch or dinner!"

When James did take on a campaign, he preferred foreign candidates. One, they paid better. Two, defeats didn't matter as much. "If you go to Peru and you run a presidential race and you lose, no one knows or cares," he told *Politico*. "So why go to New Jersey and lose for 100 grand when you can go to Peru and lose for a million?"

I can't say whether Florio was getting his money's worth from James Carville but, by the end of the summer, we'd helped Corzine win the support of most of the party establishment. Then, in September 1999, we received an unexpected gift. Governor Christine Todd Whitman, our most formidable Republican opponent, announced she would not run for the U.S. Senate. Most pundits reckoned she didn't have the will to take on an opponent with unlimited money. As a result, whoever won the Democratic primary would face a less well-known Republican.

The campaign got underway in earnest in the first weeks of 2000. In their first debate, Florio rattled off detailed policy proposals; Corzine haltingly delivered hazier ideas. Clearly, Corzine needed to improve his speaking style. But he still had the edge financially. By April, when the Corzine campaign had gone through more than $10 million, Florio had raised only $1.38 million. In late April, we started to air ads reminding voters of Florio's 1990 tax increase. Polls soon showed us with a 16-point lead over Florio.

To get out the vote, the campaign doled out approximately $850,000 to local organizations and important state politicians. By late spring, virtually every political operative in New Jersey seemed to be on our payroll. The weekend before the primary, I met with Corey Booker, a talented young African American lawyer who'd go on to become the mayor of Newark, a U.S. Senator, and a 2020 presidential candidate. I asked Booker and his advisers what he thought was going to happen in the primary. Booker predicted Corzine would win more than 90 percent of the African American vote.

"Just watch," Booker said.

By mid-May, Corzine had spent nearly $25 million—well beyond my initial estimate. At first, he'd written big checks and watched his numbers rise. When his lead started to decline in the late spring, he understandably became more anxious. I tried to allay his concerns. But there were no guarantees. Corzine did not take naturally to the campaign trail. But he was one of the hardest working candidates I'd ever seen. By the end of the primary, I understood why he'd risen so high on Wall Street.

June 6 was primary Election Day. That morning our phone banks began calling voters across the state. The main action was in cities like Newark and Trenton. As Corey Booker predicted, African American voters turned out in disproportionate numbers and voted overwhelmingly for Corzine. He ended up trouncing Florio, 58 percent to 42 percent.

That evening at campaign headquarters, I congratulated Corzine on his win and asked if I could peek at his victory speech. He silently handed it to me. Reading it, I saw that he showed no indication of curbing his enthusiasm for "universal everything." His agenda was unapologetically liberal. As a hard-core moderate, I was a little alarmed. Had I created a monster? A Frankenkennedy?

I reminded Corzine that independent voters outnumbered Democrats and Republicans and tended to be more fiscally conservative.

"Look, Jon," I said, "you need to tack back to the center on fiscal prudence for the reasons we discussed."

Corzine shook his head. I realized that, while I'd viewed liberalism as a strategy, Jon embraced it as a belief. The GOP is commonly seen as the party of the wealthy—a bastion of conservatives who want to conserve their fortune. But, in my experience, self-made people, like Corzine, are more likely to be progressive. The richer they are, the more liberal they are. Paying taxes doesn't matter as much to them. They have more money than they can spend, and they often feel they owe something to people who are still struggling.

Corzine showed no intention of accommodating the first political consultant he'd ever hired. This is who he was. That night, listening to him passionately articulate his vision for New Jersey, I wondered what I had gotten myself into. **Winning can be just as perplexing as losing.**

★ ★ ★

The man who moved onto the Republican ticket was Rep. Bob Franks. Many on the Corzine campaign looked at Jon's 14-point lead over Franks and concluded the election was effectively over. I had my doubts. I was focused on a different number—the 20 percent of the electorate that was still undecided.

Meanwhile, the *New York Times* was running article after critical article on Corzine's campaign spending. The stories started to undermine Corzine's image. During the primary campaign, he'd been the underdog. Now he risked being seen as someone who regarded a Senate seat like a new Porsche. The attacks also took a personal toll. Corzine wasn't a battle-hardened politician. He thought of himself as a noble philanthropist who, in this race, was putting his money where his mouth was. He craved the respect of New York's paper of record. More important to me was the downward slide in the polls. By late August, his 14-point lead over Franks had shrunk to 8 points.

Most front-runners experience slippage as the election draws near. Corzine's insistence on running as a liberal hadn't made things easier. Still, I believed we could win—if we went negative.

Franks was a moderate, pro-choice Republican who might appeal to centrist Democrats. We needed to remind those voters that he was complicit in GOP efforts to cut spending on health care, education, the environment, and the elderly. Initially, the Corzine campaign wouldn't listen. Finally, in late September, they came around. We rolled out grainy, black-and-white ads that tied Franks to former Speaker Newt Gingrich. The effect was immediate: Franks's approval ratings fell sharply.

Franks only had $2.5 million in the bank. But two weeks before the general election, he started using it on ads attacking Corzine's campaign spending. "There are some things you can't buy" declared one commercial. The national Republican Senatorial Campaign Committee also opened its coffers. The race narrowed further.

The Thursday before the election, I dined with Corzine, his wife, Joanne, and his campaign finance chair. I told Jon I thought he had a narrow but durable three- to four-point lead.

"New Jersey is basically a Democratic state," I said. "Vice President Gore has opened a wide lead over Governor Bush, and you'll benefit from Gore's coattails."

The day before the election I spoke to Corzine's no-nonsense lawyer and check-writer, Nancy Dunlap.

"Quinnipiac [University] just reported that Bob Franks is a point or two ahead," Dunlap said sternly.

"I think you will see Jon win by a few points tomorrow," I assured her.

"We'll see," she said. Clearly, I would be held accountable if I was wrong.

I wasn't. On Election Day, Corzine won 50 percent to 47 percent. The margin of victory was narrower than I would have liked in a state that Al Gore carried by 16 points. But Jon Corzine had stayed true to his principles and still prevailed. Of course, it hadn't come cheap. All told, he'd spent more than $62 million of his own money—at the time the most expensive Senate campaign in U.S. history.

During the tense last week of Corzine's race, Bill Clinton called me. The Gore campaign had told him he wasn't needed in New Jersey and other states. I could tell Clinton was surprised and hurt that his old pollster, Stanley Greenberg, would have given Gore such advice. I told the president the truth: Corzine could use his support. Clinton chose to respect Gore's wishes and stay away from New Jersey. (Five years later when Corzine successfully ran for governor, he insisted we prominently feature Clinton's endorsement in a much-aired campaign commercial.)

It was excruciating for me to watch from the sidelines as Texas Governor George W. Bush adapt the strategy we'd pioneered for Clinton. Bush sold "compassionate conservatism" as the smart alternative to Gore's big liberal government. We all know how the 2000 election turned out. Yes, Gore won the popular vote. Yes, the Supreme Court decision in Gore v. Bush was, in my view, wrong. But the way many Democrats reacted was even worse. By insisting Gore's victory had been stolen, they failed to grasp the acumen of their opponents.

Fortunately, some people still thought I knew what I was talking about. Across the river from New Jersey, the Corzine win impressed another mogul with a secret dream of holding office.

17

CONFIDENCE GAME

Back in 1998, Kevin Sheekey, a former aide to my old mentor Daniel Patrick Moynihan, dropped by our office. Looking around, Sheekey cheekily observed that no one would guess our business was a success—judging by our spartan workspace. If only we worked for *his* current boss, Michael Bloomberg, he said, perhaps we could afford some décor. I told Kevin we'd love to have Bloomberg LP as a client—and not because I wanted to redecorate. Bloomberg was a true media and financial services visionary. He'd revolutionized the way Wall Street processed information. Happily, I got an invitation to lunch with the man himself. We met at Paper Moon, a Milanese place on East 58th Street. Joining us was Bloomberg's longtime lieutenant, Patti Harris. I wasted no time in pitching him on the services we could provide to his company. Bloomberg didn't seem too interested. Instead, he peppered me with questions about New York politics. I quickly realized that he was considering a run for mayor.

Bloomberg had an evolving vision of a better managed city government that served citizens of all races and incomes. As I listened to him, I recalled my earliest days as a political operative, when the postwar New Deal coalition was falling apart. Bloomberg seemed to have the ambition to create an updated version of that coalition. It was an enticing prospect. Once again, though, I undercut my potential payday with the hard truth. Walking back toward his office, I told him that a campaign would expose him to extraordinary media scrutiny. A lot of people would be eager to take him down. And it would be expensive.

"That's never stopped me before," he said, "and it's not going to stop me now."

We agreed to stay in touch. Two years later, during the New Jersey senate race, I ran into him again.

"How is Corzine doing?" Bloomberg asked.

It was a natural question for a fellow Wall Streeter looking to dip his toe into the political cesspool.

"He's going to win," I replied.

Several weeks later, I saw Bloomberg at an Election Night party. In one room, celebrities were mingling; in another, politicos were nervously watching the returns. Early on, the major television networks had called Florida for Gore. If true, the vice president would almost certainly win the nation. Several hours later, however, the call was reversed; Florida was back in the undecided column. My gut said Bush would claim it. Bloomberg sidled up to me and asked who was going to win.

"George Bush will be the next president of the United States," I said.

Later that evening, as the uncertainty deepened, Bloomberg came back again.

"So, what do you think?" he asked.

"Bush is going to win," I repeated.

Even with Bush leading by only a few hundred votes, I knew it would be hard to dislodge the presumptive winner. Over the next few weeks, Bloomberg would call, half-playfully, to ask if my opinion had changed. It never did. One thing I'd learned by then: **Clients want a firm recommendation. They don't want you to give them a bunch of pros and cons and let them decide. They**

pay for an informed opinion. It helps if the opinion is correct. But first, it should sound convincing.

Anyway, Bloomberg apparently was impressed, if not by my judgment, then by my steadfastness. Soon thereafter, Patti Harris asked me to help find someone to start briefing Bloomberg on the issues facing the city. By January 2001, the gleaming Bloomberg campaign train was on the tracks, and I was on board.

★   ★   ★

It had been a decade since I'd been involved in a mayor's race. New York City had changed dramatically. Ed Koch's 1977 campaign had succeeded by identifying Jews as the swing voters; by 1999, the number of outer-borough Jewish voters had declined. The new swing voters were African Americans and Hispanics. Together, they accounted for more than half the electorate. While many New Yorkers believed outgoing mayor Rudolph Giuliani had reduced crime, minority leaders reviled him. One of our earliest polls found that people were seeking "Giuliani without the divisiveness." The timing was ideal for a candidate who married centrist ideas and managerial know-how with a passion for unifying the city. But first, we had to get him onto the ballot.

Bloomberg was a registered Democrat. However, he deduced on his own that running as a Republican would give him a better shot. Laying the groundwork for that run, he'd switched parties before the 2000 presidential election. Bloomberg was not an ideologue. Rather, he was a problem-solver. As fabled New York mayor Fiorello LaGuardia—himself a member of the GOP—once noted, "There is no Democrat or Republican way to clean the streets."

I was comfortable with Bloomberg's party-switch. Our benchmark polling corroborated that he had little chance of overcoming better-known Democrats. We still had the challenge of explaining: "Who is Michael Bloomberg?" Despite the media empire that bore his name, few voters knew much about him personally. We had to put him in a favorable light, and quickly. As we had with Corzine, we decided to play up Bloomberg's working-class background, his rise as a self-made man, his generosity as philanthropist. Next, we had to address his lack of political experience. We had to connect his business experience with city issues. We also had to preempt criticism that another billionaire was buying an election. My early tutor, David Garth, who'd joined the campaign, hit on a brilliant strategy to **turn a liability into an asset**: *Bloomberg's riches made him un-buyable.* An early commercial highlighted Bloomberg's wealth with a pledge to refuse funding from either private or public sources. Instead of sounding defensive about his fortune, we trumpeted the fact that Bloomberg would be his own man, without obligations to outside donors. We also ran a series of ads that sought to humanize "Mike," as we now began to call him. One ad showed the bookkeeper's son painting schools. These commercials worked spectacularly well. It was now time to find Mike's voters.

Traditional polls identified voters based on party affiliation, race, or other socioeconomic factors. My partner Mike Berland and I started to work on a new kind of poll that expanded on our previous efforts to map lifestyle choices. Our "unification model" would look for connections based on attitudes, beliefs, and values. Together, we worked on it for several months. We showed Bloomberg and his advisers our preliminary findings.

"New York City has 3.6 million voters," I began. "We know how they vote. Unfortunately, the way they vote is overwhelmingly Democratic, so voting history doesn't tell us very much. That's why we've set out to segment the electorate—to place every voter in New York City—into one of six distinct groups—Liberals, Traditional Democrats, Former Archie Bunkers, Traditionalist

Republicans, Middle-Middle Democrats, or Successful and Happy Moderates."

Middle-Middle Democrats were the swing voters who would decide the election. They were low-to-middle-income Democrats, mainly Jews and Catholics, with mid- to low-levels of education; they lived primarily in the Bronx and Brooklyn.

"These voters don't know who you are yet," I told Bloomberg. "But when we told them your story, they loved it."

One of our first surprises about Middle-Middle Dems was that a sizable portion of the group were Hispanics not from Puerto Rico. These voters had attitudes like those of long-established white ethnic groups like Italian and Irish New Yorkers. They thought New York was the greatest city in the world and were passionate about living here; they often owned their homes and sent their kids to public schools. These voters wanted a mayor who'd protect and enhance these vital public services. Much of our advertising would target these Middle-Middle Democrats.

Other segments would be easier to reach. "Successful and Happy Moderates," who made up 19 percent of the electorate, were Bloomberg's base—white, often Jewish, voters with high incomes. Other potential supporters included the "former Archie Bunkers"—hardcore conservatives who were older, with slightly higher incomes than the "Traditional Republicans." On the left were the Liberals and Traditional Democrats, representing approximately one-third of the electorate. While members of these groups voted in a nearly identical fashion, they had little in common personally. Liberals were generally white, secular, middle income but highly educated, and lived mainly in Manhattan. Traditional Democrats were younger, predominately Black, more female, more Baptist, lower income, and more likely to live in the outer boroughs. They were least likely to vote for Bloomberg.

To figure out exactly where all these voters lived, we developed an algorithm that classified each of the city's 5,000 election

THE POLITICS OF LIFE

districts. As soon as we geo-coded these districts, we noticed something startling: neighborhoods that were different demographically had the same attitudes and political orientation. Many upper-middle-class Jewish voters in Manhattan and Queens had priorities strikingly like, say, Italian Catholic homeowners in Brooklyn or middle-class African American homeowners in Queens. Some in the Bloomberg campaign were skeptical. However, I argued strongly for targeting voters with such attitudes with similar messages. Core beliefs bested old demographic demarcations. For a candidate committed to unifying the city, it was a welcome message.

Past targeting campaigns had been crude. Campaigns would buy voter lists and make informed guesses about voters' genders, ethnicity (based on last names), and ages (based on when they'd first registered to vote). Likewise, traditional polls used a small, random sample of people to project what a large number were thinking. We believed that, by buying marketing information and using phone banks, we could build a profile of every swing voter—a profile that combined demographic, voting history, and consumer data. We could tag every voter as a member of one of the groups and develop a dialog with him or her. Every piece of mail and every phone call would be targeted precisely at them.

It had never been done. It wouldn't be cheap. But Bloomberg immediately said, "Let's do it."

Assembling the actual database was enormously complex; it was not uncommon to have as many as 250 variables per voter. Multiply that by four million adult voters, and you start to get a very large database indeed. Nonetheless, by midsummer our database was up and running. We supplemented mail and commercials with something that at the time was quite new—prerecorded phone calls. Traditionalist Republicans heard from George W. Bush. Former Mayor Ed Koch called voters in four different segments, with different messages for each. Black Entertainment

Television co-founder Robert Johnson called minority voters whose lifestyles suggested they might be open to Bloomberg. Our efforts went virtually undetected by the city's media.

By late August, Bloomberg's positives were high, and we had largely minimized his negatives. However, polls showed him still trailing the Democrats' likely pick, Mark Green, by a double-digit margin. Mike was understandably concerned. During one meeting, he pulled me aside and plaintively said, "I'm already in this race for $20 million; when do I start to move?"

★   ★   ★

September 11, 2001, was the day of the Democratic and Republican primaries. Polls showed Bloomberg with a sizable lead over his sole GOP opponent, former Congressman Herman Badillo. I awoke early and headed down to the polling station on 88th Street and Park Avenue. I found Bloomberg's campaign manager, Patti Harris, handing out literature. She asked for reassurance that Bloomberg would prevail. I said I was confident, but that she shouldn't abandon her post. Later that morning, I had breakfast with the *Daily News'* Mike Kramer. Afterward, we noticed that our cell phones weren't working. We wandered into a phone store to try to fix the problem. Suddenly, a woman came in screaming, "They've hit the Trade Center!"

Kramer and I hurried over to his apartment to figure out what was happening. Nothing prepared me for the shock of turning on the television and seeing the twin towers in flames. Black smoke billowed out of two jagged gashes in the buildings. Kramer and I watched in dazed disbelief as the South Tower crumbled, followed by the North. As a lifelong New Yorker, it was one of the most painful moments of my life.

For Bloomberg, 9/11 was especially traumatic. He lost several employees and friends in the WTC attack. He refused to even talk about politics until the primary was rescheduled. Frankly, all of us were so numb we could barely say the word "election."

And yet the 9/11 tragedy presented Bloomberg with an opportunity. The ravaged site of the Trade Center and the surrounding blocks needed to be rebuilt. The fear of future terrorists spilled far outside that neighborhood. Residents were abandoning the city. Uncertainty infected Wall Street. The city's already jittery economy felt like it was on the verge of a nervous breakdown. In the weeks after the attack, Bloomberg concentrated on his ambitious five-borough economic plan. I saw the anguish on his face as he tried to figure out how it would work. It was clear that, for Mike, this was about more than politics. If only we could convince voters that he was the man to do the job.

Both party primaries were rescheduled for September 25. Bloomberg easily won the GOP contest. However, no candidate broke out of the crowded Democratic field with more than 50 percent of the vote. The top two vote getters, Public Advocate Mark Green and Bronx Borough President Fernando Ferrer, traded punches for two weeks before the runoff. Finally, Green was the last man standing.

He wasted no time accusing Bloomberg of "trying to buy the election." In his primary victory speech, he chanted, "Message beats money!" We responded by labeling Green as a "professional politician" who'd issued "more than 12,000 press releases" but accomplished little. We played up the public's embrace of Bloomberg as an outsider beholden to no one. Nonetheless, in a city where there are five Democrats to every Republican, Green sprang ahead by double digits. Then came a frustrating *New York Times* article claiming that Bloomberg's campaign was falling apart. It wasn't true, but the article itself threatened to sow dissension in our ranks. Ten days before the election, we were still 8 points behind. Several seasoned observers pronounced us dead.

But this race had X factor—or, should I say, a G factor—
Rudolph Giuliani. In the months before 9/11, Giuliani's reputation had been in tatters. Many minority voters detested him. His
run for the U.S. Senate against Hillary Clinton had ended with
him pulling out amid the exposure of his extramarital affair. And
yet, on 9/11 and during the weeks after, Rudy showed a steady
hand. He turned into a national hero. The media proclaimed him
"America's Mayor." Voters now looked to see whom he would
bless as his successor. But Rudy was in no hurry to leave Gracie
Mansion. There was talk that the terrorist crisis might warrant
him having a third term or extending his second term into the
spring. Giuliani and Bloomberg had not been particularly close.
Even though Giuliani was a Republican, no one on our campaign
knew when—or if—he would bestow his new popularity upon
Bloomberg. Rudy was playing coy. By early October, some on
our team worried that his endorsement, should it come, would
be too late to do much good. Fortunately, David Garth had been
doing some back-channel diplomacy. Garth had helped Rudy win
the mayoralty in 1993. After months of Garth's courting, Giuliani
finally agreed to dine with Bloomberg at the Palm West steakhouse. The sit-down went well. By dessert, Giuliani had agreed
to endorse Bloomberg.

Our next challenge was to get his endorsement on the air, and
fast. City law forbade us from filming Giuliani in the mayor's
office. So, the campaign precisely re-created the office in a suite
at the Waldorf Astoria. There, on camera, Giuliani urged voters
to let Michael Bloomberg carry on his work. The Bloomberg
campaign splashed the endorsement everywhere. Bloomberg's
numbers shot up. By November 4, our polls showed him leading
for the first time. I dared to feel optimistic. Then, on Election
Day, around 2:00 p.m., media exit polls showed Bloomberg trailing by 2 points. I immediately got on a conference call with Kevin
Sheekey, Patti Harris, Mike Berland, and Bloomberg.

"I don't need detailed explanations of what is happening," Bloomberg said. "I want to know what we do to change things."

Mike Berland and I recommended sending recorded calls to supporters and undecided voters in our strongest areas. One call would come from Bloomberg, the other from Giuliani; both would implore the voter to get to the poll before it was too late. Sheekey dispatched thousands of volunteers to Bloomberg strongholds. In the final seven hours of the campaign, almost one million recorded phone calls got sent; tens of thousands of doors got knocked on.

It was a different sort of Election Night. There I was at the Hilton Hotel in Times Square watching returns with . . . Republicans! As a lifelong Democrat I felt slightly disoriented standing with Governor George Pataki and Mayor Giuliani as, together, we pulled for Bloomberg to win. Bloomberg himself seemed a bit stunned. He'd been behind virtually every day of the race. Not until the final forty-eight hours had he taken the lead. In the end, he won by a slim 3 points. Mark Green later complimented me, ruefully, on our well-concealed micro-targeting campaign. Thankfully, we'd been able to keep a lid on it.

Don't talk about your innovation until you know it works.

★   ★   ★

Bloomberg's self-financed victory came with plusses and minuses. The new mayor wouldn't be indebted to any special interest groups. On the other hand, he would have no supporters with skin in his game. As expected, the city's economy stalled after 9/11. Rather than working with Bloomberg, the city's powerful Democratic establishment was eager to see him fail. Reconstructing of the Ground Zero site, implementing the five-borough economic plan, and reforming the city's schools would be, to a considerable extent, Bloomberg's problems.

Faced with a $7 billion budget deficit, Bloomberg made the politically difficult decision to slash programs and raise property taxes. Many who voted for him were outraged. The mayor also had the audacious idea of wanting to save New Yorkers from lung cancer and heart disease. When he pressed ahead with an initiative to ban smoking in all bars and restaurants, the press fumed that he was turning the city into a "nanny state." He also made some influential enemies when he proposed the construction of a new football stadium for the New York Jets on the West Side of Manhattan. Many New Yorkers saw this as a taxpayer-subsidized gift for another billionaire, Jets owner Woody Johnson, rather than a piece of a broader economic development strategy. Cablevision, which owns Madison Square Garden, feared that the proposed stadium would provide too much competition for the Knicks and Rangers. The company spent millions on a campaign to kill the stadium. Speaking of the Garden, you might think it was an economic win for Bloomberg to have the Republican party hold its 2004 nominating convention there. But his Democratic rivals used the GOP gathering to remind voters the mayor was a Republican (even if in name only).

As the 2005 mayoral election approached, Mike Bloomberg appeared to be in deep trouble. A *New York Times* poll put his approval rating at 28 percent, the lowest of any modern mayor. Bloomberg was remarkably unconcerned by these numbers. He wanted us to do our best to market his programs, but he insisted that they be legitimate programs—not poll-driven ideas concocted to shore up his popularity. He seemed confident that the public would eventually come to appreciate what he was doing. And he was eager to get their reaction, in person. He regularly rode the subway to City Hall. He took Spanish lessons so he could speak with his Hispanic constituents.

He showed me: **If you do what you think is right, things will resolve themselves to your benefit and the greater good.**

That's not to say that I and others on Team Bloomberg had attained our boss's sanguinity. In fact, his numbers had us worried. On this campaign, I was again in the good company of Patti Harris and Kevin Sheekey. Kevin was never one for small ideas. Having managed the Republican convention for Bloomberg, he'd been impressed by the RNC's turn-out-the-vote operation, which had kept George W. Bush in office. That operation relied on a database like the one we'd developed for Bloomberg's 2001 race. Sheekey thought we could do even better. He proposed that we use our trove of data to recruit 50,000 volunteers who could carry Bloomberg's message across New York. I agreed and suggested we could improve the data with personal interaction—calling voters and asking them what they thought about the mayor's job performance.

Toward the end of November, we quietly began to call every voter in New York outside of Manhattan. We also set up an interactive website and bought email lists. That spring, the Bloomberg campaign opened eight offices across the city. By late March, we had 25,000 volunteers. It was kind of incredible that so many people would work for the city's wealthiest man *for free*. But they believed he was on the right track. And, after all, he was working for them for free—well almost; he took an annual salary of $1. In the first five months of the campaign, those volunteers— along with union workers and paid canvassers—would knock on 700,000 doors and speak with 350,000 voters. We also began knitting together a network of 2,500 "validators" to spread the word. A validator could be a politician, a community leader, or just a trusted neighbor.

By the end of the summer, public polls gave Bloomberg a lead as high as 30 percent. I warned the team that some Democratic challenger would chip away at that lead. Fortunately for us, the Democrats had another fractious primary. While Freddy Ferrer narrowly avoided a runoff, almost 60 percent of primary voters had voted for a different Democrat.

We continued to discover surprising convergences in the political attitudes among voters. For instance, Italian-American moderates in Bay Ridge, Brooklyn, were on the same page about schools as middle-class African-American Democrats in St. Albans, Queens. It was a hopeful discovery in a city often seen as deeply divided. In the last eleven days of the campaign, our greatest challenge was not Ferrer but an apathetic electorate not showing up to vote. Many in the media were now calling Bloomberg a shoo-in. We shifted the campaign into an even higher gear. We opened another nine offices. Approximately 20,000 Bloomberg foot soldiers hit the streets every day. As a guy who got his start leafletting subway cars, I was impressed that we had volunteers at every subway stop in the city. By Election Day, Bloomberg workers had knocked on over one million doors.

It all paid off. Mayor Bloomberg captured 59 percent of the vote, Ferrer 39 percent. Against a Hispanic opponent, Mike won a third of the Hispanic vote. He also won 46 percent of the African American vote—a striking validation of his efforts to unify the city. With Bloomberg's willingness to invest in technology, we'd been able to develop a novel and, I believe, revolutionary approach to politics. For decades, politicians—and, yes, political strategists—have won elections by inflaming political division. What Clinton started to do in 1996—and what Bloomberg did do in 2005—was find a more honest and hopeful way of communicating with the public. Instead of targeting Democrats, Republicans, or Independents, we spoke to people as individuals.

Again, it hadn't been cheap. By the end of the race, Bloomberg had shelled out $85 million (about $112 per vote)—$38 million more than he'd spent in 2001. But, as they say, in for a dime . . . Or, as Bloomberg used to jest, **"If you're going to a knife fight, bring an AK-47."** The tireless gun control crusader was of course speaking metaphorically. Or, as Foghorn Leghorn might put it, "I say, that's a joke, son!"

18

BAMBOO, SOCCER, AND DEAR LEADER

Long before it became a world power in business through companies like Samsung and Hyundai, and in culture via K-pop princes BTS and Oscar-winner Bong Joon-ho, I became fascinated by South Korea. I first visited the country in 1983 with then-Congressman Stephen Solarz. Back then, I saw an industrious but poor nation run by an iron-fisted military junta supported by the United States. Casting a long shadow over the peninsula was North Korea, a brutal dictatorship with a growing atomic armory.

On a trip there in the spring of 1997, I was pleased to see that South Korea had taken a great leap forward economically. Now a member of the United Nations, it had evicted its junta and was preparing for its first legal transfer of power under a new constitution. In many ways, though, it was like America 200 years earlier—a young democracy with infant political parties.

I didn't know then that I was about to embark on two South Korean campaigns where I'd see nuclear blackmail, the next generation of high-tech political warfare, and a cast of candidates as wily as the players on *Squid Game*.

A few weeks after returning to New York, I got a call from Sukhan Kim, a U.S.-educated South Korean who'd become a partner in a prominent American law firm. Sukhan, a champion weightlifter, had close ties to the New Korea Party of President

Kim Young-sam, the first civilian to hold the office in over thirty years. Impressed by my role in Bill Clinton's reelection, Sukhan asked if I'd help the party retain power. Thanks to my recent trip to Seoul, I knew the general landscape of the election. That September, I sealed the deal over lunch in New York with Sukhan and Chin Kim, a high-tech investor, martial arts master, and evangelical Presbyterian who couldn't resist trying to save people he liked, including Jews like me. Chin agreed to pay for my services. I agreed to develop a strategy for the campaign, based on a comprehensive poll.

★   ★   ★

The New Korea Party was conservative—meaning it was a good friend of business and fierce foe of North Korea's dictator. The party's nominee was Chin's uncle, Lee Hoi-chang. Lee appeared to be that rarest of political animals—a politician who was popular, honest, and qualified. He'd become a judge at the tender age of twenty-five. At forty-six, he became the youngest Supreme Court justice in South Korean history. He'd even served briefly as prime minister before his criticisms of President Kim led to a hasty resignation. As a young judge, Lee was so upright that people nicknamed him "Bamboo." It was common knowledge that Lee regarded President Kim as crooked and immoral. But now that the president was ending his mandated single term, leaders of the New Korea Party recognized that Lee's corruption-fighting played well with the public. They, therefore, chose Lee as their candidate. Almost at once, Lee's lead over his closest rivals soared to over 20 percent.

Unfortunately, Bamboo had a hidden weakness—his seedlings. Just days after Lee's nomination, it came out that his two sons had avoided mandatory military service—the bane of every young Korean male—by showing up for induction having each

166

lost twenty-two pounds since their initial physical examinations. The Korean public branded them draft dodgers and turned on Lee. Few seemed to buy his claim that his sons had always been slight. Nothing could appease the angry electorate—even when the older son volunteered in a leper colony. By September, the candidate who'd once had a virtual lock on the presidency looked headed for defeat.

Turning around his campaign wouldn't be easy. You can make someone unlikable. It's much harder to convince voters to reassess someone they've written off. Worse still, I had to deal with Lee's revered opponent. Kim Dae-jung—known to Koreans as D. J.—was sometimes called the "Nelson Mandela of Asia." In 1971, he had challenged military strongman Park Chung-hee by running for president. D. J.'s loss didn't deter the government from throwing him in prison, several times. In 1973, South Korean agents kidnapped him. Taking him out to sea on a fishing boat, his kidnappers had him chained to concrete blocks and were preparing to throw him overboard when U.S. Ambassador Philip Habib intervened—saving his life, for a while. In 1980, a military tribunal sentenced Kim to death for purported sedition. Once again, international protests got him off the hook. In 1987, he ran in the first free elections. Kim lost that one—and then lost again in 1992. The 1997 election would be his last shot at the Blue House, the presidential mansion.

D. J. was undoubtedly a heroic figure, but his virtues were those of a dissident. Not only was he beholden to Korea's militant labor unions, but his views toward North Korea struck me as naive, if not dangerous. Just one year earlier, North Korea had announced its decision to disregard the 1953 armistice that ended the Korean War. It had sent soldiers into the demilitarized zone, violated South Korean waters, urged South Koreans to overthrow their government, assassinated a prominent defector, and probably killed a South Korean diplomat. D. J. brushed it all off. He yearned for a détente with "Great Leader" Kim Jong-il, regardless of his behavior.

In mid-October, I flew to Seoul to present my polling results to Lee and his top advisers. The numbers were far from encouraging. Rather than rebounding from his sons' scandal, Lee seemed to have settled into a permanently lower level of popularity. He was stuck in third place, behind Kim Dae-jung and a maverick governor, Rhee In-je, who was also chasing the conservative vote.

Our strategy session took place at the Lotte Hotel, a downtown palace that seemed to be Seoul's center of intrigue. My audience was small but eminent. It included former Foreign Minister Han Sung-joo and Hyun Hong-choo, former ambassador to the U.S. Everyone seemed interested in my findings—except the candidate. Lee was so inattentive that I began to wonder if he even understood English. I sensed he might be feigning nonchalance. But there is no ignoring hard numbers.

Data can tell you what people are thinking and how to change their thinking.

Provocatively, Ambassador Hyun asked, "Mr. Schoen, you've had a great deal of experience. Have you ever seen a situation this bad turn into victory?"

He seemed to be asking if I thought Lee should drop out of the race. As a newcomer to Korean politics, I politely ducked the question. But it was clear that, even within his own party, Lee faced an uphill race.

I pressed on. I told the group that Lee must put as much distance as possible between himself and the graft-tarred incumbent, President Kim. This would be awkward since Lee and the president belonged to the same party. I also recommended that Lee emulate President Clinton and put forward a comprehensive economic plan—in the most dramatic way possible. I suggested that the New Korea Party merge with the Democratic Party of former Seoul mayor and finance minister Cho Soon. A rebranded party would shore up Lee's economic credentials and garner support in the Seoul region. It would also head off a possible alliance between Cho and candidate Rhee. One problem: Lee and Cho weren't exactly fond of one another.

Despite his apparent indifference, Lee agreed to the merger. The move succeeded beyond my expectations. The resulting Grand National Party (GNP) was an immediate hit with the electorate. Within just days of the announcement, Lee moved from last place to a position where he was essentially tied for the lead. Lee and his aides were now interested in hearing more of my ideas. But there was only so much I could do. I was technically working for Chin Kim and Sukhan Kim, not the campaign. I also knew that the South Korean electorate was wary of American meddling. As a result, I kept our monthly meetings on the down-low.

When I did meet with Chairman Lee, it was hard to tell if I was getting through. He was unfailingly polite, nodding his head and saying, "Yes, yes." He was a shy person. In private, he often displayed a wry sense of humor. In public, even when he dressed informally, he had the rectitude of a judge. By contrast, his opponent, the seventy-one-year-old D. J., had the relaxed demeanor of a seasoned actor. In November, the two candidates met in the first live televised presidential debate in Korean history. Living up to his nickname, Lee was as stiff as bamboo. D. J. was as suave as James Bond. D. J. went on to invade Lee's right-wing base by forming an alliance with ultra-conservative Kim Jong-pil—the same man who'd founded the secret intelligence force that had twice tried to kill D. J. Evidentially, the fact that D. J.'s positions on North Korea were much softer than Lee's didn't bother the ruthless old spymaster. In South Korea, political parties were first and foremost vehicles for personal power. Both men had followed my maxim: **make the deal.**

For months I'd been telling Lee's campaign it should play up *his* alliance with Cho Soon by making some commercials. At first, I was told that Lee "didn't want to deal with Cho." Finally, party leaders made him. I emphasized that the ad needed to be upbeat and inspire confidence in Lee's economic plan. Instead, the media team produced a commercial so poorly lit that you could barely see Cho. The music was funereal. The whole thing reminded me of a Kremlin death announcement.

Commercials soon became the least of our problems. With the onset of the Asian economic crisis that summer, stock markets across the region were collapsing. South Korea's currency was falling sharply against the dollar. At first, the politicians seemed paralyzed by this unfolding catastrophe. President Kim denounced "speculative foreign press reports" for creating an atmosphere of panic. He insisted that an International Monetary Fund bailout was "unthinkable." At first, Lee hesitated to contradict him. By contrast, D. J. had been the first candidate to raise the possibility of an IMF bailout. But once negotiations with the IMF began, D. J. shifted, striking an angry, nationalistic posture, designed to tap into Korean resentment that lingered after a century of war, occupation, and division. D. J.'s stance initially played well with the public. However, as Koreans realized the depth of crisis, even President Kim changed his tune. Now he was for an IMF bailout.

This was our opening. At my recommendation, the Lee campaign made the most of D. J.'s flip-flops. Lee called him an untrustworthy figure who would bungle South Korea's recovery. On November 21, President Kim's government announced it would seek the largest bailout in IMF history—a credit line of more than $60 billion. As voters got real, their support shifted from D. J. to Lee. Our message (Lee equals stability) was working. By the end of the month, Lee had fought back to a virtual draw with D. J. in what the *Financial Times* called "one of the most remarkable comebacks in South Korean politics."

Lee kept pounding D. J. for recklessly vacillating on the IMF agreement. One week from Election Day, Lee was only a point or two behind him. Then President Kim threw a curve—summoning candidates Lee, Rhee, and D. J. to the Blue House for a "unity luncheon." I sensed a trap. The evening before the meeting, I shared my concerns with Lee's nephew, Chin Kim.

"This unity lunch is a terrible track for us to take," I told him. "If you come out and say, 'The country is united. We're all in this together,' then the loser is Chairman Lee because it takes the issue of D. J. off the table."

Don't dicker with people who have more to gain than you do. Stay attuned to your own needs. Deal only with those who can help you.

Chin promised to convey my worries to his uncle. After the luncheon, I asked Lee how it had gone. He replied, in fluent English, that all the candidates had agreed to issue a joint statement of support for the IMF bailout deal. I was stunned. By agreeing to the joint statement, Lee had at once aligned himself with the unpopular incumbent president and removed our best argument—that a vote for D. J. would jeopardize the IMF deal and by extension the future of the country. Lee proceeded with his leisurely lunch report, not grasping his mistake. I saw no way to correct it, so I bit my tongue and listened politely. Later that evening, I told Chin Kim, "That's it; we're going to lose."

Little did I know that other Lee supporters were cooking up their own plan to get our candidate elected. At least that was the claim of Park Chae-seo, a South Korean spy code-named "Black Venus." The double (or triple) agent alleged that three members of Lee's GNP met with North Korean agents in a Beijing hotel. Black Venus claimed he saw the GNP trio offer the North Koreans $3.6 million in cash. In return, he said, North Korea was to instigate a military skirmish in the DMZ. The incursion, right before the election, was intended to scare South Koreans into voting for Lee and not for the dovish D. J.

Lee's three supporters denied Black Venus's claim and there was no DMZ skirmish. In any case, D. J. ended up edging out Lee, 40.4 percent to 38.6 percent. Rhee received 19.2 percent of the vote.

★ ★ ★

I believed my advice to Lee was correct. I didn't expect him or his team to recognize that. That's what losing candidates usually do. **Expect to be blamed, even when your predictions come true.** To my surprise, though, Lee had been sufficiently impressed by my insights that, five years later, I got a second chance to put him into the Blue House.

I returned to South Korea confident that, if we could keep the conservative party united and run a better media campaign, Lee could win. This time, he wouldn't have to face the crafty D. J., since as mandated by law, the incumbent must step down after one term. Like most observers, I expected D. J.'s Millennium Democratic Party to nominate Rhee In-je, the upstart governor who had probably cost Lee the last election. However, in the party primary, Millennial Democrats chose Roh Moo-hyun. Roh (pronounced "No") was even more of a maverick than Rhee. A former labor lawyer, Roh had bucked the political system at every turn. He was the son of a poor farmer. His only previous national experience had been as head of the Fisheries Ministry for a short time. He'd never been to the U.S. For a country that valued expertise and education, he was a startling choice.

Roh had one qualification that was important to the outgoing president: he strongly supported D. J.'s "Sunshine Policy" toward North Korea. D. J. had long sought sunnier relations with the North. It wasn't so much that he wanted to ease the misery of ordinary North Koreans or hasten the collapse of Kim Jong-il's regime. In fact, D. J. and his circle wanted "Dear Leader" to stay in power. They feared that, if he lost his grip, the gulag might disintegrate, and millions of impoverished North Koreans would stream into the prosperous South. Of course, D. J. didn't present it to the South Korean public in quite those terms. The purported rationale for the Sunshine Policy was that it would let light into North Korea and encourage the hermit state to abandon such unpleasant habits as attacking South Korean vessels and soldiers, smuggling drugs, building nuclear weapons, and threatening Seoul with "unspeakable disaster."

Appeasement was a dubious strategy. Nevertheless, D. J.'s Sunshine Policy produced what looked like a historic break-through. In the summer of 2000, he traveled to Pyongyang for a summit with Kim Jong-il. Children sang. The two leaders held hands. Sweden's Nobel committee was so impressed with D. J. that it gave him its 2000 Peace Prize.

When it came to coddling North Korea's madman, Roh made D. J. seem like a hawk. Roh argued that Kim Jong-il would behave better if only the South was nicer to the North. Moreover, unlike D. J., Roh was an outspoken critic of the United States—even questioning why American troops should be on South Korean soil.

Our first step to victory was linking Roh to D. J., who had his share of kickback scandals. I was relieved to find that Lee's current media team could make effective attack ads. But Roh didn't take our attacks lying down. Indeed, he was a shrewd tactician. While we pounded him on TV and radio, the Roh campaign struck back on something called "the Internet."

South Korea is a nation of tech-savvy early adopters. At the time of the race, it had the highest broadband penetration of any place in the world. Roh used the Internet as no politician ever had. Two years earlier, he'd lost a hard-fought campaign for parliament. After his loss, Roh supporters had flooded his campaign website with emails pledging their continuing support. Some supporters even started a cyber fan club, which they dubbed "NOSAMO" (an acronym for "People Who Love Roh"). The club now had 37,000 members; by election day, that number would swell to the hundreds of thousands.

Still, the momentum was on our side. Roh was sinking, and we were moving up. Unfortunately, I had the classic blind spot of an American abroad. I forgot about soccer.

That summer, for the first time, the World Cup was being played in Asia. I knew that South Koreans were proud to be hosting soccer's world championship; I never expected that their team would win a game. Incredibly, it overwhelmed Poland, fought the U.S. to a tie, beat Portugal, and defeated three-time champion Italy to advance to the quarterfinals against Spain. Suddenly, South Korea had a new hero—Chung Mong-joon, the head of the South Korean football association and the man responsible for bringing the World Cup to Korea. The fifty-year-old Chung was handsome, rich (his father was the billionaire founder of Hyundai), and a member of parliament.

As soon as Chung made it known that he was considering entering the race for the presidency as an Independent, he shot to the front of the opinion polls. (It was rumored that my old compadre, Dick Morris, was masterminding Chung's candidacy. True or not, Chung's "outsider" rhetoric certainly had a Morrisonian touch.) Chung's entry most hurt Roh. I began to worry about the members of Roh's party who were agitating to replace Roh with Chung. If they got their way, the popular Chung would almost certainly beat Lee. If, however, Chung ran as an independent, he would split Roh's vote and potentially ensure Lee's election.

Fortunately for us, Roh stubbornly refused to give up the fight. All the conditions for a divided election seemed to be falling into place. But too slowly. Lee's favorable/unfavorable ratings

174

were 29/56. Even Lee's supporters didn't like him so much as hate D. J. Lee's most serious problem was the "386 generation"—people born in the 1960s. They had no personal recollection of the devastation wrought by the North's invasion of the South in 1950. They'd spent their student years protesting South Korea's military dictatorship and its American supporters. They were deeply skeptical of the conservative establishment. We knew Lee would have a hard time connecting with them.

★   ★   ★

By this point in our relationship, Lee and I were speaking more freely. I pushed for him to promote other ideas that would prove his commitment to the younger generation.

"You've got to talk about closing the gap between the rich and poor," I told him. "Propose programs that will address people's concerns about affordable housing, day care, and health care."

Lee agreed with me in principle. But he had a touch of the fatalism I'd seen in the Serbs fighting Milošević.

"Mr. Schoen," Lee would say, "solve this problem for me. You tell me I must appeal to young people, yet the media only wants to report on my fights in parliament. What use is it to propose initiatives when the press only covers controversies?"

Lee also remained hesitant about making strategic alliances. **Managing the competition is the key to victory.** In this race, I saw that Lee should reach an understanding with Assemblywoman Park Geun-hye. Park was the daughter of General Park Chung-hee, one of the most controversial leaders in South Korean history. In 1961, General Park had seized control of the government in a coup d'etat. Once in charge, however, his reforms laid the foundation for South Korea's economic miracle. The reforms didn't prevent assassins from killing Park and his wife. Even four decades later, he remained a polarizing figure. Ideologically, supporters of the young Ms. Park should have been Lee backers. Like all Korean politicians, however, Park wanted to negotiate the best possible deal for herself. She was holding out for nothing less than the position of prime minister. (She later became South Korea's first female president.) It was a high price, but I thought Lee should pay it. He refused.

"She's not qualified," he told me firmly. "I won't do it."

Don't mistake confidence for stubbornness. Don't refuse help when you need it.

With his unbending righteousness, Lee had chased away nearly every ally he needed.

Fortunately, we caught a break when soccer mogul Chung Mong-joon finally entered the race. If the Hyundai heir split the vote with Roh and other candidates, Lee might eke out a narrow win. Former Hyundai executives were alleging that Chung had illegally manipulated Hyundai share prices. For all his flash, I foresaw that Chung was vulnerable. What I didn't anticipate was a terrible accident, an orchestrated anti-American campaign, and one of the most bizarre uses of a political poll in the history of electoral politics.

The accident came first. In June, an American armored personnel carrier, out on a training exercise, ran over and killed two Korean girls on their way to a friend's birthday party. The tragedy occurred at the height of World Cup fever, when South Koreans were flush with national pride. The accident turned pride into outrage. The presence of American forces in South Korea had long been a sore point. Gratitude for U.S. support had given way to resentment—particularly when it came out that the soldiers who'd killed the two girls would be tried before an American military tribunal instead of before a Korean court.

In October, American officials revealed that North Korean negotiators had admitted the existence of a secret weapons program. As Koreans of all ages worried again about the nuclear specter, the anti-American Roh fell in the polls. But then the two American soldiers were acquitted of negligent homicide and quickly flown out of the country. The verdict convulsed South Korean society and resurrected Roh's campaign. By late November, he was neck and neck with Chung. Roh and Chung recognized that if they both stayed in the race, Lee would win. So, Chung and Roh struck the strangest of bargains. Chung and Roh would face off in a televised debate. Afterward, a Korean research company would poll 2,000 viewers. Whoever came out ahead would then become "the unified candidate" who'd run against Lee.

I was astonished. It was like the presidential election had turned into the recently launched *American Idol* show, where viewers voted for their favorite pop star. I was surprised Chung had taken the bait. He might know about soccer and shipbuilding, but when it came to a live debate on politics, he was clearly out to sea. He would've been better off making a deal with Roh and the Millennial Democrats. No doubt, they would have promised him the prime ministership. Instead, he was ready to step before the cameras and let whoever tuned in decide his political fate and the future of the country.

When Chung and Roh met for this high-stakes showdown, Chung arrived unprepared. He needed to present a coherent rationale for his candidacy. Clearly, he had none. Polling gave Roh a slim 6.4 percent edge. Chung agreed to end his candidacy.

The debate experiment begged a troubling question: if polls are accurate, why bother with elections anyway? I'd never thought of polls as a substitute for an election. I view polls as a starting point, a way to understand the public and move them in the direction of my candidate. Chung had let polling replace voting.

It was a major mistake for him, and yet I wonder if it's a mistake that won't be repeated in the future.

Our first polling after this bizarre reality show gave Roh a startling 20-point lead over our candidate. In the final weeks of the campaign, we targeted Roh's embrace of the Sunshine Policy even while North Korea had been secretly pursuing atomic bombs. Still, the anti-American protests continued. A mob broke through police barricades in front of the U.S. embassy. Three Korean men attacked and stabbed an American soldier on the way to his post.

One afternoon about four days before the election I was walking through the Lotte Hotel when I heard someone shout, "Hey, Doug!" It was David Morey, an American consultant who seemed to be something of a fixture in quasi-authoritarian East Asian countries. He was with his business partner, Bob Armao, former personal adviser to the Shah of Iran. Morey and Armao seemed happy to see me, and frankly, I was glad to see a couple of Yanks. After the South Korean press had identified me as an American "smear master," Lee's advisers had asked me to stay away from campaign headquarters. So, when Morey proposed dinner for the night before the election, I accepted.

The three of us met at the Hyatt Hotel. Back in the fall, I'd had lunch with Morey. He'd claimed then that he wasn't involved in the South Korean election. Now, over drinks, he told me he'd been in Seoul for about two weeks. He said he'd been advising his longtime client, D. J. The president was theoretically neutral in this race, but it was obvious that he was pulling for Roh. What Morey and Armao were doing for D. J. was unclear. I couldn't help but wonder if they might be helping D. J.'s preferred candidate by orchestrating the anti-American demonstrations. Yes, the Koreans had historical grievances. But could American consultants have stage-managed the apparently spontaneous protests?

That wasn't the only surprise of the evening. That same night in another part of town, ex-candidate Chung announced that he was withdrawing his support for Roh and coming out in favor of Lee. If only he'd made the announcement a few days earlier when it might have given an important boost to Lee's campaign. Lee also had an eleventh-hour change of heart. Months before he'd flatly dismissed my suggestion that he promise Assemblywoman Park Geun-hye the prime minister's job in exchange for her endorsement. Now, in desperate straits, he agreed to her demand. But, again, the support came too late.

On Election Day, morning voters were leaning toward Lee. Many of these voters were undoubtedly older Lee supporters. Still, it was a hopeful sign. If Roh's younger supporters turned out in light numbers, Lee just might squeak by. But Roh's strategists also saw the pro-Lee trend. That afternoon, they unholstered a secret weapon. They sent out one million text messages urging young People Who Love Roh to go to the polls. The last-minute digital counterpunch must have helped. Lee lost again, this time by just 2.3 percent.

★　★　★

We had gone up against a generational divide and an opponent who'd skillfully manipulated anti-American rage. I was disappointed. My job was to win, no matter the sociological forces. **Every loss is a lesson.** This one was a master class.

With all the sixteen-hour flights back and forth to Seoul, the campaign had tested my endurance. And Internet and mobile messaging would become part of my arsenal.

I did find some cold comfort after the election. The Millennial Democrats turned out to be even more duplicitous than I'd suspected. A few months after Roh took office, it emerged that his mentor, D. J., had essentially paid for the privilege of holding hands with Kim Jong-il. D. J.'s chief aide was convicted of orchestrating covert money transfers by Hyundai to North Korea just before the summit. The carmaker was alleged to have paid as much as $500 million. The company claimed it was for exclusive business rights. Facing prison for his role in the transfers, Hyundai Asan chairman Chung Mong-hun leapt to his death from his office.

Despite new campaign finance limits, bribery is deeply ingrained in Korean culture. *Tokgap*, or "rice cake expenses," are cash envelopes doled out on holidays to anyone from your child's teacher to your local representative. Roh's first year in office also saw the indictment of eight aides and donors for bribery and illegal fundraising during his presidential campaign. Prosecutors charged that the country's *chaebol*—family-owned conglomerates—had made under-the-table payments of about $5 million. The prosecution did not pursue Roh, citing a constitutional law exempting sitting presidents from being charged with offenses other than national security crimes.

The same investigation found that the *chaebol* had given even more generously to the party of my client. The problem was that South Korean currency comes in small denominations. At first the cash came in apple crates. When those weren't big enough, the LG Corp. allegedly stuffed billions of *won* into a truck left at a highway rest stop—the keys given to one of Chairman Lee's aides. The Hyundai Group allegedly delivered cash in a sedan packed so tightly it could barely be driven. All told, the GNP was said to have received $42 million for the benefit of Lee, the corruption-fighter. Requesting leniency for his staff, Lee said, "I will shoulder the entire burden and go to prison." Some of his aides did do time. Lee was eventually cleared. He ran again for president in 2007 and once again lost, without my help.

19

SUNNY PLACES
AND SHADY PEOPLE

Penn, Schoen & Berland continued to attract clients on almost every continent. Working on a campaign abroad, I'd sometimes visit the nation on my own. Other times, we'd send a small team of operators—sort of a political Delta Force—to work in-country with local partners. Foreign elections were a "wilderness of mirrors"—to borrow the phrase CIA counterintelligence chief James Jesus Angleton borrowed from T. S. Eliot. Things were never quite how they appeared. I did my due diligence to learn who was paying us and what their agenda was. But invariably, after I'd spent time in the country, I detected the smell of fish—even when I was nowhere near the sea.

In 1997, a wealthy Filipino businessman hired us to advise defense minister Renato de Villa. De Villa wanted to succeed Fidel Ramos (another former defense minister) as president. When I arrived in Manila, I saw that De Villa was going nowhere fast. His name recognition hovered around 4 percent. Television ads were not allowed during the campaign, so there was no way to make voters aware of my candidate unless President Ramos endorsed him. But Ramos wasn't showing his cards. Ramos's vice president, former movie star Joseph Estrada, was a much stronger candidate. I was also getting the sense that even De Villa's supposed supporters were iffy about him. I spent most of the week

181

in my hotel room waiting for phone calls. Occasionally, when I was summoned to meet with De Villa or his adviser, it was at an odd hour under cover of darkness. After a week in limbo, I left. Ramos ended up endorsing someone else. De Villa started his own party. Estrada won.

★ ★ ★

Working in Mexico for presidential candidate Roberto Madrazo in 2000 was even more baffling. Madrazo was the Governor of Tabasco (the state, *not* the hot sauce). He was running in the primary, aiming to be the candidate of the Institutional Revolutionary Party (PRI), the world's longest ruling political party. At the time, PRI had held power for seventy-one years. Early polling showed Madrazo well ahead. But the PRI had a tradition of letting the sitting president—in this case, Ernesto Zedillo—pick the party's candidate. The tradition was known as the *dedazo* ("the finger"). Zedillo decided to tap his former Interior secretary, Francisco Labastida, rather than Madrazo. Instead of folding, Madrazo assailed the imperial practice. Playing on his surname (*madrazo* is Mexican slang for a severe blow), his campaign posters implored voters to "dale un Madrazo al dedazo" ("smash the finger").

I welcomed the challenge of disrupting Mexico's backroom politics. But I began to wonder whether Madrazo was as keen as I was about winning. Bad poll numbers didn't bother him. The race seemed almost like a *lucha libre* wrestling match. Madrazo was the masked mauler due to take the fall, but he and other insiders seemed to know the fight was a farce. The ringside promoter who oversaw the PRI bouts was Carlos Hank González. González had started life as a humble teacher—people still called him *El Profesor.* Now he was the billionaire magnate of a transport and banking empire. González had served as a congressman and the governor of the State of Mexico. But Mexican law barred him from running for president because his father was German. His real power was as a kingmaker in the PRI. He readily acknowledged there was money to be made in public service—famously quipping, "A politician who is poor is a poor politician." González was more sensitive to a U.S. Justice Department report linking him to drug cartels. After he denounced the allegation, U.S. Attorney General Janet Reno retracted the memorandum.

I found González to be a delightful gentleman when we met. But I didn't trust him. Perhaps Madrazo was a ringer recruited by the PRI to give the appearance that the primary was competitive. If Madrazo had won, he probably would've demanded a recount. (My doubts about his character were reinforced in 2007 when he was disqualified as a runner in the Berlin Marathon for alleged cheating.)

Doing business with mysterious strangers can be profitable. But, before you get into bed with them, check the sheets for scorpions. And be ready to get out of bed quickly.

By intention or accident, Madrazo's candidacy did injure the PRI and its candidate, Labastida. For the first time, all registered voters—not just PRI members—had been able to cast ballots in a primary. Many of them recognized President Zedillo's "finger"-print on Labastida and didn't like it. Opposition candidates were eager to exploit the issue in the general election.

Cutting ties with Madrazo, we went to work for Alliance for Change candidate Vicente Fox. Fox was a towering rancher who had gone, in nine years, from driving a Coke truck to serving as chief executive of Coca-Cola Mexico. He was sure that the PRI would try to steal the election again. Our task was to expose possible fraud. We saw the so-called "New PRI" greasing the usual palms—giving voters tortillas and chickens and free rides to rallies. On Election Day, we conducted exit polls across Mexico. Various civic organizations fielded more than 80,000 trained observers to validate the official count. In the end, Fox claimed 43 percent of the vote, becoming the first opposition party winner since 1910. Since most polls had failed to predict Fox's victory, some observers posited that many respondents lied about their preferences out of fear that the PRI might strip them of their government benefits. In any case, the monitoring techniques we'd developed in Serbia had worked again.

★　★　★

Africa was tougher to crack. In 1999, I advised South Africa's Democratic Alliance, a multiracial party that traced its roots back to white progressives opposed to apartheid. Tony Leon, our candidate to succeed Nelson Mandela as president, placed second in a field of six. The fact that Leon was almost 57 points behind winner Thabo Mbeki testified to the dominance of Mandela's African National Congress.

Two years later, I helped Zimbabwe's Movement for Democratic Change (MDC), co-founded by Morgan Tsvangirai, the brave opposition leader who risked his life to unseat President Robert Mugabe. Given that Tsvangirai had been arrested the year before for alleged treason, MDC leadership thought it would be safer if we met in South Africa at a game reserve. As elephants foraged in the distance, we strategized about how to defeat "Bob," as the dictator was colloquially known. The campaign was one of the deadliest I'd ever worked on. I wasn't personally in danger. But police and soldiers routinely detained, beat, and tortured opposition party members, including parliamentarians, who spoke out against Mugabe. MDC leaders reported that several of its members were murdered in state-sanctioned assassinations. Mugabe's methods were sometimes more clandestine. Much later, an American professor who met with Mugabe heard recordings of our strategy session. Obviously, one or more of our attendees was a spy. Mugabe won with 56.2 percent of the vote. Despite his vicious intimidation, 41.96 percent of the electorate dared to vote for Tsvangirai—the closest presidential election to date. No doubt Tsvangirai's true support was much higher.

★ ★ ★

One risk of working with clients abroad is not getting paid. In 2004, Indonesian president Megawati Sukarnoputri was hoping to be reelected. Megawati ascended from vice president to president in 2001 after the legislature impeached and ousted her predecessor, Abdurrahman Wahid. Now Indonesia's first female president hoped to win on her own merits. One of her backers had hired Penn, Schoen & Berland to import our strategies. He'd made a down payment. But after our team had been working on the campaign for several weeks, Mark and I agreed that another payment was in order. Raj Kumar, the young head of our team, was a proficient pollster. But he didn't have the seniority to extract the required *rupiah* from Megwati's backer.

"This is a big investment," Mark reminded me. "We've got to get paid. Can you go over there?"

I boarded a Singapore Air flight. Almost twenty-four hours later, I arrived in Jakarta. Bleary with jet lag, I promptly collapsed in my hotel. I woke up in time to have lunch with Raj and our candidate's contributor. The lunch took some time. With forty or more dishes and side dishes, the traditional Indonesian *rijsttafel* is the gastronomic equivalent of waterboarding. By the end of the feast, I would've confessed to anything. Fortunately, the meal elicited a promise from Megawati's moneyman that he'd wire the funds. Stuffed with satays and gado-gado, I returned to my hotel to collapse again. The next day, I got on a plane back to New York.

Another payment did come through. But as the campaign wore on, our polls showed Megawati's odds of winning weren't good. It was the first time that Indonesians would vote directly, rather than through electors. As the daughter of Sukarno, Indonesia's mighty first president, Megawati certainly had name recognition. But, as one report observed, she also had the "unique burden of being the only candidate in the race who is held responsible for the current situation most voters are unhappy with." Our team did our best to tell her advisers how to accentuate her achievements. But we were dealing with a nation of over 17,000 islands, where people spoke over 400 regional languages, and where technology was so basic that citizens voted by poking a nail-hole above a photo of their preferred candidate. It was also the most populous Muslim majority nation in the world; research showed that even some women didn't think a woman was qualified to be president. Mark and I had learned that getting paid becomes harder as the voters' handwriting becomes clearer on the wall. Thus, I made another day-long trip to the other side of the world—again, simply to act as a bill collector. In the end, after 113 million ballots were cast across the archipelago, Megawati Sukarnoputri came in second (with 26 percent) after former security minister Susilo Bambang Yudhoyono (with 33 percent). Still, she'd done better than we'd expected—well enough for her backer to pay our invoice.

★　★　★

Our expertise in fielding exit polls in tense, high-stakes elections brought us many customers from Central and South America. Over the course of twenty-five years, we'd helped elect more than half-a-dozen heads of state in Latin America. In 2004, we heard from some Dominican businessmen. The Dominican Republic had a long history of poverty, corruption, and rule by brutal *caudillos* like presidents Rafael Trujillo and Joaquín Balaguer. In 1996, candidate Leonel Fernández had broken the cycle. As president, Fernández oversaw an economy whose growth averaged 7.7 percent per year. His administration had reformed the judicial system. Fernandez's successor, Hipolito Mejia, had squandered these achievements—presiding over a period of high inflation and renewed graft. Fernandez believed he needed to return to office. Early polls put him in the lead. However, the campaign had become so heated that many Dominicans feared that the Mejia government might tamper with the process.

The businessmen who approached us hoped that our presence would deter Mejia from trying to manipulate the results. Accepting the offer, we dispatched Raj Kumar and my partner Michael Berland's wife, Marcela, a specialist in Latin American politics.

When the polls closed, we were able to predict with confidence that Fernandez had won an overwhelming 20-point victory. It was a prediction that clearly unnerved the incumbent. In the last election, he'd been far enough ahead to persuade his two opponents to concede. For three hours after this year's voting had ended, President Mejia was silent.

Raj called me in the U.S. to say Mejia's henchmen were rumored to be sending thugs to steal the ballot boxes. Fernandez was worried. Complicating matters were Mejia's good relations with the Bush administration. Would our exit poll numbers be enough for Washington to confront a close ally?

As the evening stretched on, I was relieved to hear that the U.S. State Department accepted our poll's legitimacy. Meanwhile, the Organization of American States (OAS) was urging the Mejia government to cooperate with the vote tally. Later that night, the government finally posted numbers showing Fernandez ahead, but only slightly. Instead of our predicted 20-point win, the election commission showed a mere 7- or 8-point lead. I worried that, by claiming Mejia was only narrowly behind, the government was preserving the options of a runoff or a recount.

Then, just as it looked as though Mejia was hunkering down for a long stalemate, he conceded. OAS Secretary-General César Gaviria later told reporters that we'd played in important role in keeping him honest. We'd helped cultivate democracy in a climate where some doubted it could take root. People with a stake in the status quo frequently discount the possibility of change. They say it's pointless to challenge "conventional wisdom."

Never accept conventional wisdom.

20

HUGO & JIMMY

If you were going to map Penn, Schoen & Berland's journey around the world, the departure point would have to be Venezuela. Back in 1979, David Garth asked Mark if he wanted to do some polling there for presidential candidate Luis Herrera Campíns. The proposal at first seemed preposterous. How would Mark overcome the language barrier? How would he learn enough about Venezuelan politics to frame questions? And yet . . . Mark flew to Caracas. There, he saw some familiar faces. The ruling Democratic Action party had hired Joseph Napolitan, the man who coined the phrase "political consultant" during John F. Kennedy's 1960 presidential campaign. A smaller, independent party had hired our former rivals Pat Caddell and John Deardourff. Despite this competition, Mark, working with local partners, went door-to-door, asking Venezuelans for their opinions. He helped Herrera come up with a campaign slogan that expressed popular discontent with President Carlos Andrés Pérez: "Ya Basta," meaning, "Enough!" Herrera won by a healthy margin.

A quarter century later, Venezuela beckoned again. One day, Diego Arria, the country's former ambassador to the United Nations, asked me if we could talk about his nation's current president, Hugo Chavez.

I'd been following Chavez. His politics were a bizarre blend of cult-of-personality authoritarianism and retro socialism. As a young lieutenant colonel in 1992, he had attempted to seize power through a military coup. The effort failed and Chavez was arrested. Before he was thrown into prison, Chavez was allowed to go on national television to urge his co-conspirators to abort the coup. His brief address made him a hero to Venezuela's most disaffected citizens, particularly the rural poor who felt neglected by the moderate, two-party political system. After serving a two-year sentence Chavez returned in 1998 to announce he was running for president. His far-left anticorruption, antigovernment platform won him a landslide victory. Chavez's increasingly authoritarian policies, his open admiration for Cuban dictator Fidel Castro, his delusional association with the great liberator Simon Bolivar, and his strange penchant for spontaneously bursting into poetry and song—often on national television— disturbed a broad swath of Venezuelan society. In early 2002, Chavez tried to install loyalists in the corporate suites of the state oil corporation, PVSA, the country's single largest source of hard currency. Unions staged massive demonstrations. When the demonstrations took a violent turn, the army sided with the protestors and took Chavez into custody. The provisional government that replaced him soon collapsed, and Chavez returned to office, stronger than ever. He soon purged the armed forces and took complete control of PVSA. By 2004, Venezuela was firmly under Chavez's control.

Over lunch, Arria told me that an anti-Chavez coalition had gathered enough petitions to force a nationwide referendum on whether Chavez should step down. Arria was nervous. He believed that Chavez wouldn't hesitate to steal the recall election. What, Arria asked me, could be done to prevent that?

"If there isn't an exit poll," I said, "you will lose."

We got the job. Chavez was clearly a formidable—and unscrupulous—character. However, I was confident that, with our firm's experience, we could take him on.

★ ★ ★

The first sign of trouble came when Raj began phoning potential partners in Venezuela to conduct our exit poll. Raj called twelve vendors. Ten said no, without even bothering to ask a standard question like, "How much would it pay?" It was clear that all these people were afraid. At the time I thought they were being paranoid. I moved onto the possibility of training Venezuelans to do polling. But we could find just one group willing to team up with us. Súmate (which means "join up") had been instrumental in organizing the recall election. Its leaders were already planning to conduct an exit poll of their own. Raj suggested we piggyback on Súmate's efforts—using their volunteers to conduct our poll. At a meeting with María Corina Machado, one of Súmate's founders, I insisted that we develop the procedures and have the final say on polling decisions. The exit poll must be beyond reproach. María agreed. Of course, I knew that. by using Súmate, we were opening ourselves up to enormous scrutiny. Chavez and others could accuse us of bias. But we had no better options.

A few days before the election, I learned why local pollsters wanted no part of this. Chavez went on television to accuse Súmate's leadership of treason. He then gave out the names and home addresses of key Súmate members—whom, he warned, might face potential "action." He made no mention of Penn, Schoen & Berland. But I worried about my people on the ground. Marcela and Raj had just flown into Caracas. We were speaking on the phone daily, and I didn't like what I was hearing. Raj reported that, during a meeting at his hotel, some beefy men wearing wraparound sunglasses and earpieces had sat at the next table. Raj sensed they were trying to eavesdrop. Raj and Marcela spotted other men shadowing them around the city. I hoped this was just an attempt at intimidation. But who really knew what Chavez might do if his power was at risk.

The turnout on Election Day surpassed all expectations. Across the country, Venezuelans lined up for hours to vote. Despite the gridlock at many polling stations, the mood of the electorate seemed upbeat. In many areas, residents supplied drinks and sandwiches to those waiting. Turnout like this is almost always inspired by dissatisfaction with the incumbent. Our early exit poll results confirmed that Chavez was in serious trouble—59 percent of voters wanted him out; 41 percent still supported him. I called Diego Arria. He agreed that the earlier we released our findings, the more pressure Chavez would be under to respect the will of the public.

That afternoon, I asked Raj to draft a press release spelling out the results. At 7:30 p.m., we faxed the release to Western media outlets. The document was clearly marked, "Embargoed till 8:00 p.m."—the time when polls closed. In Venezuela, as in many countries, it is illegal to publish exit poll results before voting has ended. Nonetheless, it's standard to send out embargoed results. However, due to higher-than-expected turnout, the election commission kept the polls open until midnight. By then, it was too late to retract or delay our press release. Our results were out and circulating fast. Strategically, this helped keep the government honest. At the same time, our people were now vulnerable to retribution. It wasn't long in coming.

In the Dominican Republic, authorities had reacted to our poll in two stages: first, confused silence; then, reluctant acceptance. Chavez took a different approach. Word was spreading that the government was preparing to declare victory. Considering our poll, we didn't know how that was possible. The only way

Chavez could win would be if he ignored the official results and invented his own. Such a brazen play seemed unlikely considering the presence of international election observers. And yet, Chavez's mouthpieces were already attacking our poll numbers. Police were arresting anti-Chavez protesters.

As the night wore on, I was in constant contact with Raj. He'd been meeting with international observers at his hotel. At about 2:00 a.m., Raj and the rest of our team headed over to the Súmate headquarters. As they approached their destination, they saw a van parked in the middle of the road, just ahead. In front of the van were four plain-clothed men with machine guns. Our team's driver made a quick turn and headed the wrong way down a one-way street. When the team reached Súmate's offices, people there were panicked. They'd heard that vigilante militias were hunting down anti-Chavez forces. Súmate's leaders believed they could be assassinated. They decided to abandon the office. Avoiding Súmate's main entrance, everyone slipped out through an adjoining shopping center.

After about an hour, our Súmate partners began to calm down. Raj decided to head back to his hotel. He figured that, as the hub of election observers and Western journalists, it was the safest place in town. On the way there, uniformed police stopped his car. Raj assumed they'd wave him through once they saw he was an American. But one of the officers began asking him pointed questions, almost as though he knew exactly who Raj was. The officer began rifling through Raj's bag. He pulled out Raj's laptop. Raj at first thought that the cop was simply taken with his sleek new computer. Then he asked Raj to turn it on and to pull up every document he'd been working on. As Raj clicked through his recent files, he remembered the press release. Proclaiming that Chavez had lost could give the police a pretext for detaining a foreign agitator. Raj stalled for time. Fortunately, a vanload of TV journalists arrived on the scene, causing the police to make a speedy departure. Amid the confusion, Raj rushed back to the hotel.

★   ★   ★

The next morning, Raj boarded a flight back to the U.S. But for Súmate and the people of Venezuela, the battle was only beginning. The National Electoral Council, headed by a dedicated Chavez supporter, claimed 59 percent of voters wanted Chavez to stay in office; 41 percent wanted him to go. The numbers were almost the exact opposite of our results. Polling by the Primero Justicia party was almost identical to ours. It's one thing for an exit poll to be off by a few points, but for two independently conducted polls to be off by 20 points strained belief. Súmate's volunteers had conducted approximately 20,000 exit interviews at 267 well-chosen voting stations—a huge sample for a country of 25 million people.

Chavez's victory claim was patently absurd—and yet some supposedly sane people were believing it. On the scene in Caracas was former President Jimmy Carter, whose Carter Center was responsible for much of the international election monitoring. Before he left, Raj had met with Jennifer McCoy, the head of the Carter Center's Venezuela mission, and Cesar Gaviria, secretary-general of the OAS. Raj had briefed both on our results and methodology. You'd think that the evidence of irregularities would at least warrant a wait-and-see attitude. Instead, President Carter went on television to hail the election as "free and fair." He even asserted that it was now "the responsibility of all Venezuelans to accept the results and work together for the future."

Back in the United States, the media and our competitors were accusing us of producing a highly flawed poll that relied far too heavily on an anti-Chavez organization. The Associated Press reported: "U.S. Poll Firm in Hot Water in Venezuela."

While our work was being vilified, skepticism about Chavez's victory claim were growing. Votes had been cast on electronic machines provided by an obscure company, Smartmatic, reputed to have close ties with the Chavez government. Election observers also learned that the computer server used to tabulate results had not simply received reports from field stations but also had sent communications to the stations. This suggested that the central computer might have been transmitting vote tallies to the precincts. Two days after the election, both the Carter Center and the OAS demanded that the Chavez government randomly compare the supposed electronic results with actual paper records. After some hesitation, Chavez agreed.

Even as the audit began President Carter downplayed its importance. "There is no evidence of fraud, and any allegations of fraud are completely unwarranted," Carter told the press. He went out of his way to criticize us, telling reporters that our polltakers "deliberately distributed this erroneous exit poll data in order to build up, not only the expectation of victory, but also to influence the people still standing in line."

I hoped for the best. Surely the audit would give an inkling of how Chavez had stolen the election. At the end of the week, OAS Secretary-General César Gaviria announced that the audit confirmed Chavez's victory.

I was speechless. Most media outlets leapt to the conclusion that we'd gotten things wrong. A handful recognized that an unprecedented fraud had somehow been committed. The *Wall Street Journal* ticked off five ways that Chavez had made sure that audit came out the way he wanted. *U.S. News and World Report* correspondent Michael Barone noted the implausibility that our polling teams could have colluded in changing 20,000 written responses. Two academics, Harvard's Ricardo Hausmann and MIT's Roberto Rigobon, did a deep dive. They found that the recall tallies were lowest in areas where you'd expect them to be much higher. It was as if some uniform percentage of the anti-Chavez vote had been systematically shaved away. Chavez, it appeared, had tampered with the thousands of voting machines in a subtle way—through transmissions from the central election computers. The study posited that he had meddled in hundreds of precincts but not all of them. During the audit, he'd directed international observers to those precincts where no fraud had occurred.

The widespread acceptance of the fraudulent election was demoralizing. Just as the Bush (I) and Clinton administrations were unable to do anything about Milošević's stolen election in 1992, the Bush (II) administration shrugged as an avowed anti-American autocrat—who happened to control the largest oil supply in the Western hemisphere—did the same thing.

My frustration didn't stop me from trying to oust Chavez in 2006 when he sought a second term. Once again, Diego Arria brought us in—not just to do exit polling but to advise Chavez's opponent, Manuel Rosales, the governor of Zulia, Venezuela's largest state. Obviously, Chavez had a considerable advantage. He never hesitated to use the state-run media to promote himself and intimidate his enemies. Rosales tried to keep up by offering the electorate even more cash and prizes. He promised the poor a debit card with monthly deposits derived from oil industry profits. But Rosales gave me the same feeling I'd gotten in Mexico from Roberto Madrazo. He was passive and unwilling to directly attack Chavez. He seemed like a straw man just going through the motions.

Chavez ended up winning by the widest margin in the history of Venezuela—62.85 percent to 36.91 percent, according to its National Electoral Council. Initially, the election appeared more transparent than the 2004 referendum. But an investigation by two Venezuelan universities showed that Chavez may have manipulated more than four million votes—casting his victory into doubt.

This, despite four organizations having monitored the voting. Once again, the Carter Center was among the observers. I was disappointed with Jimmy Carter. Here was a Democrat, a man I'd voted for, a Nobel Peace Prize winner, who'd gone to bat for a despot in 2004 and who continued to lend him legitimacy. I couldn't fathom why. Then I learned that one of the Carter Center's biggest benefactors was the Citgo Petroleum Corporation, whose majority owner was the Venezuelan government. At one point, Carter wanted to meet with me. I respectfully—or maybe disrespectfully—declined. Even after all the evidence of fraud, Carter insisted the 2004 referendum was legit. I didn't see any purpose in our meeting.

Don't try to persuade someone who can't be persuaded.

21

WHEN TO LIE

That same year, another populist demagogue provided some lighter moments. Italy's Prime Minister Silvio Berlusconi was facing off with Romano Prodi, head of the center-left coalition known as The Union. Berlusconi, leader of the center-right House of Freedoms coalition, wanted an American firm to do independent polling. So, about a month before the election, I flew to Rome.

It was a Saturday morning. I was sitting with members of Berlusconi's team at his grand residence, Palazzo Grazioli. We were all waiting for the candidate to emerge from his bedroom. As someone accustomed to the notoriously tardy Bill Clinton, I was used to a head-of-state living in his own time zone: **the meeting starts when the boss shows up.** Finally, Berlusconi arrived. Judging by his wet hair, he'd just stepped out of the shower. We were just getting down to business when there appeared a willowy blond. Her damp blond hair suggested she too had just showered. She wore a short, slinky sequined dress, the sort of thing a lady might don for an evening gala or a disco. She also wore a sheepish look.

Berlusconi welcomed her with a kiss and introduced the shimmering *signora* as "my newest member of parliament."

I wondered if he was pulling our legs. I later learned that, indeed, he had appointed or nominated several of his mistresses to be members of the European Parliament or his own cabinet. These beauties tended to have more experience in acting or modeling than in governance. But they each had some expertise the prime minister deemed vital. They served—what's the phrase?—at his pleasure. At least until his wife, Veronica, threatened again to divorce him.

As our meeting resumed, Berlusconi's latest nominee chimed in now and then—no doubt wanting to demonstrate her qualifications for higher office. When we'd wrapped up our discussion, Berlusconi asked us to take the *signora* to lunch while he attended to other business. Obediently, our little group went out to a trattoria. As we sat down, the *signora*, still in sequins, whispered to me, "I look ridiculous, don't I?"

"No, you don't," I lied. I sensed her embarrassment. Many have endured a morning-after "walk of shame." This was the lunch of shame.

Sitting next to me was Berlusconi's right-hand man, Valentino Valentini. Besides serving as head of the office of the prime minister, Valentini was the PM's special adviser for foreign relations. He spoke seven languages. Russian being one, he was Berlusconi's point-man in dealing with Vladimir Putin. The multitasker also happened to be a candidate that year for Italy's Chamber of Deputies.

For some reason, Valentini did not want me talking with the *signora*. Whenever I did, he would kick me under the table.

Continuing to lure me into conversation, the *signora* lamented that she had nothing to wear to that night's dinner with the prime minister.

"Will you go shopping with me and help me pick out a dress?" she asked me.

Another kick to my shins told me the boss's consort should not be picking out a new frock with his American consultant.

"I wish I could," I told her. "But I have some more meetings this afternoon."

Since talking to the *signora* was forbidden, I turned my attention to another woman. She was an English-Italian interpreter who happened to be African American and Jewish. Did you get all that? It took me a minute. She told me that, twenty years earlier, she'd married an Italian and moved to Rome. She'd grown up in New York City. Small world: she'd been confirmed at the synagogue where I'd had my bar mitzvah.

That night, I returned to Berlusconi's residence for the dinner. I immediately ran into the *signora*. She was wearing another dress, also short and tight. But no sequins.

"I look ridiculous again, don't I?" she asked.

"No, you look beautiful," I said. This time, given the occasion, I wasn't lying.

Chatting with Berlusconi, I saw the bravura charm that had won him wealth and power.

"Let me give you some advice," he said. "Succeed, make money, but enjoy your life!" He recalled his youthful days as a cruise ship crooner—entertaining passengers, making sure they were happy. "If they didn't like me, it was a long time till we made land and I could get off," he told me. He saw his current job in much the same way: he must keep voters happy. Living *la dolce vita* was the touchstone of Berlusconism and, as if to prove it, he and the *signora* disappeared from the table after the main course. They returned after about forty-five minutes, looking refreshed.

A few weeks later, I was in Las Vegas, having breakfast when Valentini called. He said the prime minister wanted to speak to me. With Election Day approaching, Berlusconi wanted us to announce that he was going to win. Our latest poll had shown that his House of Freedoms coalition was 2 or 3 points behind Prodi's Union alliance. I told him that the best I could do would be to say that, within the poll's margin of error, the candidates were tied.

In the end, Prodi won by less than 0.1 percent of the vote. Berlusconi alleged there were discrepancies in the counting process. Only after Italy's supreme court confirmed The Union's win, did he resign. I never heard from him again. He'd hired us because he thought Italian surveys were politically biased. I guess he didn't mind bias in his favor. But I couldn't lie. An election is not a sequined dress.

The only thing you have is your integrity. It's more important than any client, even a head of state.

PART THREE

PART THREE

22

UNCOUPLING

During the quarter of a century that Mark Penn and I had worked together, we'd come to appreciate—and, in fact, find strength in—each other's differences. I was more of the rainmaker, willing to do the schmoozing and to get on planes at a moment's notice. Mark remained our tech wiz or, as *Time* magazine described him, "a large and rumpled man with an absent-minded brilliance and a disheveled charm . . . who can work wonders with a laptop so long as he hasn't left it behind in a cab."

We'd developed an intuitive understanding of each other. One example of our teamwork: our pitch to Texaco in 1992. Mark, Mike Berland, and I had flown to Atlanta to present a big, multi-country plan. Mark needed to make some last-minute tweaks to our presentation deck. Not to worry, he said; he'd have the deck ready in the morning. True to his word, Mark stayed up much of the night working on it. Putting our firm's future ahead of personal hygiene, he looked like he'd slept in his clothes. There was a lot riding on this pitch. It was during the economic downturn and our company needed the $600,000 or so that the deal promised. If Mark could work his magic, we'd be set. Walking into the meeting, I sized up the Texaco team. They were some of the straightest-looking execs I'd ever seen: short hair, crisp white shirts, tightly knotted ties. Safe to say, they'd showered. Deciding it would be best to keep Mark downwind of them, Mike and I handled the handshaking. Then Mark went to work—masterfully laying out our vision for their company. Afterward, all the Texaco guys wanted to give Mark their business cards. Nothing doing! Mike and I formed a defensive line around Mark, intercepting the cards, leaving our quarterback free to smile from a distance. We got the deal.

The *New York Times'* James Bennet observed, "While Penn is hulking and nervous, Schoen is small and deft. It is Schoen who sells their 25-year partnership, Schoen who brought in most of the clients, including [Bill] Clinton and [Bill] Gates. Of the two, Schoen is the better day-to-day operative, associates say, but it is Penn who can supply the insights that elect a long shot."

That pretty much summed us up—though I might argue that I've had a couple of insights over the years. We had a friendly competitiveness. Except it had become less friendly. There'd been warning signs. Years earlier we'd had a money beef with our political rabbi David Garth. Yes, Garth could be irascible, but the way Mark handled it led to years of bitterness. When I brought Mark into the White House, I called out Dick Morris for disrespecting my partner. Mark thought I should have done more. Mark ended up winning the war of wills with Morris. Then a strange thing happened. When Dick resigned under pressure, *Time* reported, "Clintonites couldn't help noticing [Penn] taking over not just Morris' responsibilities but his persona as well. Gone was the shambling professor; enter the adviser who brooked no interference, who seemed as confident and quick-tempered as Morris had been. He vetoed a meeting between pollster Stan Greenberg and Clinton. And tensions were building between him and Schoen. Some thought he was excluding Schoen the way Morris had tried to exclude him."

Sometimes I fought back. Bob Squier, whom I'd invited onto the team, called us The Bickersons. Bob said it in a joking way but, coming from a friend I respected, I got the message. Mark and I shouldn't be squabbling in front of the president of the United States, expecting him to referee our spat. He'd hired us to get him out of trouble. We had to keep our eyes on the prize. So, I stood down.

Don't let your personal dignity overpower your professional responsibility. Nothing heals an ego like getting the job done.

The night of Clinton's victory party in Little Rock, Mark and I shared in the satisfaction of getting the president reelected. Penn and Schoen had come a long way together. The campaign had put us under a lot of stress. As if that weren't enough, we'd both been going through divorces.

Having trouble with your business partner and with your spouse at the same time is tough. As someone who was in the business of peddling advice, I knew I could use some. I consulted a therapist. She was trained in Freudian analysis, but she didn't think we needed to plumb my childhood. More of a life coach, she helped me break down my issues with Peggy and with Mark. She said, "Make detailed plans, we'll go over them, and then you're dismissed."

Therapy can work—if you make sure it's solving your problems, not creating new ones.

Around this time, I got a call from a Serbian friend. He said, "Doug, I'm in New York. I desperately need your advice."

I suggested we meet at Donohue's Steak House on Lexington Avenue. Sitting down in a back booth with him, I could see how distressed he was.

"I'm worried," he said.

"What is it?" I asked. "Is it Milošević? Paramilitary groups?"

"No, something far worse," he said.

"What?"

"My wife and I are getting divorced. I need your help. You have unique experience."

I was taken aback. Could news of my own marital difficulties have reached Belgrade? Maybe my friend reasoned that, since I'd witnessed the uncoupling of Yugoslavia, I could help his Balkanized marriage. Did the breakaway husband want me to write his declaration of independence? I'm probably not qualified to give anybody advice on matrimony. But having now lived through a mostly amicable divorce, I do recommend seeing a counselor or arbitrator who can help both sides articulate what's bothering them. I'm not saying you're going to be bosom pals afterward, but you may find an off-ramp with less bitterness and lower legal fees. Even if you're not Serbian.

★ ★ ★

I still wasn't sure if Mark and I could reconcile. Maybe a truce would be good enough. Thankfully, there was enough work to keep us both busy. We now had around seventy employees. It wasn't too hard to stay out of each other's way. I handled my campaigns (Bloomberg, Corzine); Mark handled his (British PM Tony Blair; Hillary Clinton).

By 2001, we had another incentive to get along. WPP plc, a British multinational on its way to becoming the world's largest advertising and public relations company, wanted to add Penn, Schoen & Berland to its portfolio. Part of the deal involved an "earnout" provision that tied our final compensation to performance over the next six years.

The earnout period had its highs and lows.

There was never a better night than October 29, 2006, at New York's Beacon Theater. It was a celebration of Bill Clinton's sixtieth birthday as well as his foundation. The entertainment? A little band called The Rolling Stones. At a meet-and-greet before the show—filmed by Martin Scorsese—there was a receiving line. When my turn came, Bill Clinton threw his arms around me and told Mick Jagger and Keith Richards that I was the "genius" who'd gotten him reelected. He was being too generous, but I couldn't help but feel like a rock star when Mick and Keith high-fived me and said, "You the man!"

Conglomerate life was somewhat less exalting. WPP wanted our company, and wanted me to keep bringing in clients, but its management wasn't particularly welcoming. Once, visiting the WPP offices, I went to the restroom. I must have forgotten to lock the door. As I was exiting, I found myself face-to-face with some executive who had thought the restroom was empty.

"Make sure you lock the door next time!" he snapped. "Close the door fully, okay?"

I felt like a six-year-old who hadn't zipped his fly. The scolding underscored how much I'd been marginalized. That's how it seemed anyway. Mark, who'd pushed for us to get into corporate work years ago, thrived at WPP, moving up in the hierarchy. Mike Berland, who excelled in business strategy, also did well there.

I focused mostly on political campaigns. When I did dip into the corporate side, it wasn't always gratifying. For instance, the National Football League asked for a proposal on its regular survey of players' health issues. In our meeting with NFL execs, I suggested that we could make the survey more incisive by taking a closer look at head trauma. This was before the link between head hits and chronic traumatic encephalopathy had been established. Several of the NFL team seemed to agree. Strangely, the NFL's medical adviser, Dr. Elliot J. Pellman, did not. He maintained that there was no need to depart from the usual survey. I naively insisted that a rigorous study of former players could help protect current ones. The more I argued, the more I talked Dr. Pellman out of hiring us. We never did hear back from the NFL. I did read in 2016 that Dr. Pellman had stepped down from his job there—after more than 5,000 retired players had sued the league, charging that Pellman and others had deliberately hid the dangers of concussions.

More and more, I was nagged by the sense that I was incidental to the company I'd co-founded—which would come to be known simply as PSB. Would anyone remember what the "S" stood for? Under the circumstances, some people might quit. But I wanted a full share of what I'd built. So, I kept coming to work. Six years went by. Due to the hard work of my two brilliant and energetic partners, we walked away with a payout in the millions of dollars. It's safe to say that, thirty years earlier, Mark and I would have been stunned to find such a check when we scrambled for the morning mail. WPP didn't ask me to stay. They did ask me to sign a two-year non-compete agreement. I guess they considered me a potential threat, but I wasn't interested in competing with my old company. I needed to figure out what I was going to do next.

It's not easy to reinvent yourself in middle age. Even if you've been successful, you've been branded. You're a slave to your own achievements.

You may need to make mid-course corrections. When you must reposition, it helps to sit down with trusted friends, your team of advisers.

My team suggested that I build a profile apart from Penn, Schoen & Berland—that I burnish my reputation as a "thought leader." The *Washington Post* once called me "the president's usually press-shy pollster." Staying off-camera and on-background had long been my MO. The candidate was the story, not me. But now I felt freer to step from behind the curtain and share some of my experience. I hadn't written much since the late seventies when my biographies of Pat Moynihan and Enoch Powell were published. But now I started contributing op-eds on current politics for the *Wall Street Journal*, *Forbes*, the *Washington Post*, and other outlets. In a way, it was like returning to my days at the *Harvard*

Crimson. Like Alexander Hamilton in Lin-Manuel Miranda's
musical, I was looking for a way to "write my way out" of my pre-
dicament. I helped produce advisory bulletins on the Balkans and
Kenya for the International Crisis Group, a nonprofit, nonpartisan think tank trying to resolve deadly conflicts. My consigliera,
Judith Regan, publisher of many bestsellers, encouraged me to
write *The Power of the Vote* in 2007. In it, I showed how polling
could protect democracy. It was also my prescription for how the
Democrats could reclaim the White House.

Away from my laptop, I began offering my two cents on television. I became a familiar face to news junkies on Sundays—and
any other day when punditry was needed. Most of these bookings
were last minute, catch-as-catch-can; my only compensation was
a little publicity for my book. Then I heard from Roger Ailes. He
and I had first crossed paths when he was a Republican media
consultant. In 1996, Rupert Murdoch had hired him to launch
Fox News. Since then, the network's ratings had steadily grown—
viewership rising 300 percent during the 2003 Iraq invasion. Fox
News always had a conservative bent. But politics was less polarized then, and Ailes thought it made for better television to have
a right-winger duking it out with a lefty—in the tradition of
William F. Buckley Jr., and Gore Vidal at the 1968 presidential
conventions and James J. Kilpatrick and Shana Alexander on
60 Minutes. Liking that I was a moderate, he offered me a deal
with regular appearances for actual money.

The easier path would have been for me to go on MSNBC,
where Democrats preached to the converted. But rather than sit
comfortably in an air-conditioned echo chamber, I thought Fox
News might offer the chance of changing a few Republican and
independent minds. I believed in talking across the divide.

So, I accepted the offer. The network had had difficulty booking Democratic politicians. They weren't wild about stepping into
the "No Spin Zone" with Bill O'Reilly. I thought these politicians

were shortsighted. On a network where the word "liberal" was often uttered in the same tone as "terrorist," a Democrat might win over a few viewers just by showing up and appearing reasonable. I hoped to move beyond facile "horse-race" election analysis to a more nuanced discussion that demystified what lawmakers do. Ailes apparently liked my approach. He teamed me with Democratic consultant Pat Caddell and former Republican representative John LeBoutillier on a Sunday night prime-time show called *Political Insiders*.

I certainly was raising my profile. But, like a soldier lifting his head up from a trench, I learned that visibility has its risks. Appearing on Murdoch's network was enough for progressive Jacobins to brand me a "Fox News Democrat," a "DINO" (Democrat in Name Only), and a "Liebercrat" (because of my supposed political resemblance to Democrat-turned-Independent Sen. Joe Lieberman). Daily Kos blogger Markos Moulitsas called me "a caricature of the evil DC-based Democratic consultant" when I offered a constructive critique on how Democrats could win in the midterms. His blog post—titled "Piling on Doug Schoen"— applauded others who'd chastised me for my thought crimes.

In 2007, I wrote an op-ed calling for both parties to work together to reform health care. I didn't think it was an incendiary proposal. But it set off future *New York Times* columnist Ezra Klein. "There's this wonderful moment in *The Simpsons*," he began, "where [Mr.] Burns goes into the doctor for a check-up, and the doctor explains that the only reason he's alive is that there are so many diseases trying to kill him that none can get through. They're all crowded at the door, struggling to enter. That sort of describes my reaction to Doug Schoen's health care op-ed. I feel virtually incapable of engaging with it, paralyzed by the infinite expanse of logical holes, self-serving omissions, and political hackery riddling the article." Nevertheless, Klein proceeded with his rant, concluding that I was "almost a parody of the pernicious Democratic consultant."

I took these spitballs in stride. Years earlier, I'd gotten into a feud with John Prescott Ellis, a nephew of former President George H. W. Bush. At the time, Ellis was working for NBC News. I leaked him some polling data. It bit me in the ass. For eight years, I wouldn't talk to Ellis. Then, as part of a 12-step sobriety program, he tried to make amends by inviting me onto *The Today Show*, to do commentary for two straight days. Being angry at Ellis for eight years hurt me more than it hurt him.

Don't waste time on feuds. Grudges sap your strength and hurt you almost as much as the person you're fighting.

My critics' hostility invigorated me. It told me I was hitting my mark.

If you truly believe you're right, take criticism as a compliment.

23

BREAKING RANKS

I didn't set out to piss people off. I was just trying to make a few observations from a weather station overlooking the tornadoes on the left and the wildfires on the right. But that viewpoint came to seem extreme as politics grew more divisive. I felt America was at a treacherous intersection where the traffic lights had stopped working. In 2008, I wrote a book, *Declaring Independence: The Beginning of the End of the Two-Party System*. At the time, polls showed that 60 to 80 percent of registered voters craved an independent presidential candidate. They were fed up with candidates who cynically traded in "hot-button," culture war issues instead of offering practical solutions to urgent problems—such as jobs, the environment, energy independence, and affordable health care. I believed these voters would back a centrist candidate who was also looking for consensus. I called these voters "Restless and Anxious Moderates"—or RAMs. Sure, there'd been third-party candidates before—George Wallace, Ross Perot, John Anderson. They failed for different reasons but, usually, because they lacked money, media, and access to televised debates. I argued that now, with the dawn of the Internet and social media, third-party candidates had the means to raise funds and bypass the traditional gatekeepers.

The year *Declaring Independence* was published, Libertarian, Green, and Constitution party candidates used the presidential election to attract attention to their issues. Ralph Nader, whose runs in 2000 and 2004 had contributed to Democratic defeat, also ran as an independent. But without a plausible centrist, third-party candidate, my RAMs were back to the usual menu—choosing one from Column A or B. That year Sen. John McCain dispatched Republican primary opponents by March. But the grinding battle between Democratic senators Hillary Clinton and Barack Obama dragged on for seventeen months. I'd never met Obama, though I later learned that, as a Columbia student, he'd attended a talk I'd given on surveys. I obviously knew Hillary. Mark Penn was serving as her chief strategist, tangling with other campaign advisers over the right mix of style and substance in her messaging. I was watching from the sidelines as the primaries proceeded. Some of my hecklers claimed I favored Hillary. I never thought Hillary was the inevitable nominee. I called the poll numbers as they came in. When she was up, I said so. When she was down, I said so. That April, in the *Washington Post*, I said it was time for her to abandon her pledge against negative primary ads. "A positive message is simply not enough to alter the race at this point," I wrote. "She must seize the opportunity that Obama's self-acknowledged mistakes last week presented to her campaign; it is almost certainly her last chance."

By June, Obama had clinched the nomination. One writer claimed I was "associated" with the People United Means Action movement of Clinton supporters who refused to support Obama. Not true. As someone who thought the two main parties had too much power, I recognized Obama as the candidate more outside the establishment. I couldn't help but be impressed by his political arc. Four years after losing his 2000 run for Congress, the community organizer had become a U.S. Senator who'd given a soaring keynote address at the Democratic Convention. Four years after that, he had become America's first African American president. I voted for him. I hoped he would be the transformative leader the country needed to build consensus.

★ ★ ★

I was happy to offer him advice. The week that Obama took office, I warned about *The Threat Closer to Home: Hugo Chavez and the War Against America*. Written with Michael Rowan, the book explained why our neighbor to the south was as dangerous as 9/11 mastermind Osama Bin Laden. Drawing on my Venezuela experience, we demonstrated that Chavez was in every sense a terrorist. Our research showed that, besides letting Hezbollah use his country as a basecamp, he financially supported Hamas and the Colombian guerrillas of FARC. He was complicit in drug trafficking, money laundering, even in the development of a dirty bomb. Oil fueled his malevolent ambitions. As the fourth largest supplier of oil to the U.S., he'd helped drive its barrel price from $10 to more than $100. Most insidiously, the Castro fanboy was using his country's wealth to buy off American leaders across the political spectrum.

That same year, I teamed up with my old partner Mike Berland on a more inspirational read. In *What Makes You Tick: How Successful People Do It and What You Can Learn from Them*, we studied fifty people who'd made it big in fashion, sports, entertainment, and business, trying to figure out how they did it. We gleaned that, rather than remodeling your personality, as some self-help gurus prescribed, your better odds were in improving the skills you already had.

The following year, in the run-up to the 2010 midterms, fellow pollster Scott Rasmussen and I explored the rising tide of fiscal conservatism in *Mad as Hell: How the Tea Party Is Fundamentally Remaking Our Two-Party System*. At the time, many in the political, business, and media elite dismissed "teabaggers" as a small gaggle of loons. Scott and I believed they constituted an organically grown movement capable of getting like-minded candidates elected. Digging into the movement's origins, we showed how its organizers had used many of the social networking strategies employed by Obama's campaign. And though they opposed most of Obama's agenda, even he admitted many Tea Partiers were "legitimately concerned about the deficit." We predicted that their hostility toward both major parties was not going away.

The same year, I proposed some bold remedies for stubborn problems in *The Political Fix: Changing the Game of American Democracy from the Grass Roots to the White House*. Some ideas I culled from the local level (Alaska citizens examined their state's checkbook on the Web; NYC residents called a single number for help with any government problem). Most of the other fixes were my own: preserving the Department of Justice's independence by removing the Attorney General from the cabinet and creating a Justice "joint chiefs of staff." Giving free airtime to presidential candidates and tax credits to small donors. Demanding that Congress disclose any contact with lobbyists. Abolishing Senate "holds" on judicial appointments. I considered all of them achievable. Say what you will, I may have written the only book ever to get blurbs from Bill Clinton *and* Fox News' Sean Hannity.

Despite my high hopes for a "post-partisan" America, Obama disappointed me. He didn't defend Israel or combat Putin vigorously enough. The Great Recession offered him an opportunity to bring the country together. Instead, he became aggressively partisan, proclaiming, "We're going to punish our enemies and . . . reward our friends who stand with us on issues." He muscled the Affordable Care Act into law even though his own Chief of Staff, Rahm Emanuel, admitted Obamacare should have been rolled out incrementally.

I certainly didn't hold the Republicans blameless. Their determination not to give Obama any wins had led to the debt-ceiling crisis and hurt us all. This gridlock-glued-to-a-logjam-cemented-in-a-stalemate compelled me to write *Hopelessly Divided: The New Crisis in American Politics and What It Means for 2012 and Beyond.* In it, I tried to figure out how we'd gotten here, and why our lawmakers' paralysis had forged wingnuts on the left and the right. I copped to having been part of this crippled system and to having benefited from it. But my membership in the political class had convinced me that repairs were overdue. Among my proposals: barring lobbyists from making financial contributions during legislative sessions; stripping gerrymandering legislators of the power to redraw districts; and making primaries easier for independent candidates to get on the ballot.

In October of 2011, I wrote a *Wall Street Journal* column about the Occupy Wall Street movement begun by protesters encamped in a park in New York City's financial district. Obama had lauded their protest, saying it "expresses the frustrations of the American people" about income inequality and money in politics. Listen, I believe the rich should pay a higher marginal income-tax rate—including on their investment income. But having interviewed nearly 200 of the Occupy protesters, our pollsters found that their views on violent civil disobedience and radical redistribution of wealth were far to the left of the swing voters Obama needed to get reelected. It was a piece of research that might help the president stay in office. Instead, some saw it as heresy. The same day as my op-ed, one of Rachel Maddow's MSNBC producers called me "actively hostile to Dems and the party's agenda," adding, "[Schoen's] credibility has crumbled. Today's op-ed probably won't help restore his reputation."

Sweeping up the crumbs of my credibility, I floated an audacious recommendation a few weeks later. Writing again in the *Journal* with Pat Caddell, I implored President Obama not to run for reelection in 2012. Our piece argued that, given the president's abysmal poll numbers, he would need to "wage the most negative campaign in history to stand any chance." That campaign would exacerbate division, dooming bipartisan legislation for the remainder of his term. Urging him to preserve what was left of Congressional accord, we pointed to Democratic presidents Harry Truman and Lyndon Johnson, who both recognized they couldn't govern effectively while running for another four years.

"If President Obama is not willing to seize the moral high ground and step aside," we wrote, "then the two Democratic leaders in Congress, Sen. Harry Reid and Rep. Nancy Pelosi, must urge the president not to seek re-election—for the good of the party and most of all for the good of the country."

We went so far as to nominate the "only clear alternative" to Obama—Hillary Clinton. Her 69 percent approval rating at the time far surpassed that of Republican opponents. "Having unique experience in government as first lady, senator and now as Secretary of State," we observed, "Mrs. Clinton is more qualified than any presidential candidate in recent memory, including her husband."

Of course, this was a fanciful proposal. Pat and I knew that the chance of Obama recusing himself was slim. Nevertheless, in a *Politico* piece a few weeks later, we called upon Democratic voters—particularly in New Hampshire—to organize a write-in campaign for Hillary. There was already such a petition online. "We advocate this Draft Hillary movement not because of the desire to make political mischief," we insisted, "but to put the country on the right course."

On cue, the backlash began.

"No one drives President Obama's supporters and progressives more nuts than Doug Schoen," wrote Glenn Thrush in *Politico*. Ticking off other shots I'd taken at Obama, he concluded, "Is it truth in advertising for Schoen to call himself a Democrat?"

I sensed that my opinions had found their way to the president when I attended a White House event. Meeting him on a receiving line, I faced a glare so frosty I should have worn a sweater.

We posed together for a routine photo, but he wasn't interested in any more of my thoughts.

I will say Obama was more civil than Sen. Chuck Schumer. I'd known Chuck since Harvard. He was in law school when I was in college. He'd considered hiring Mark and me for his 1998 senate race. I'd recently criticized some of his positions. Apparently, he'd had his fill of me by the time we ran into each other at a Fourth of July party in the Hamptons. I was digesting a hot dog when he marched over and announced, "You're not a Democrat! You are officially out of the Democratic Party!"

I didn't know anyone had the power to excommunicate someone from an American political party. I guess Chuck thought he did. He didn't go into my specific sins, but he wasn't kidding.

★ ★ ★

Feeling like a man without a party, I had no choice but to invent one. For years, I'd advocated for a third centrist party. During the 2012 election, I joined up with others who had the means to try to launch that dream. Peter Ackerman was a successful financier with a long commitment to democratic movements abroad. We'd gotten to know each other when he funded student dissidents in Serbia. In 2010, Ackerman and entrepreneur Kahlil Byrd incorporated Americans Elect, an organization that aimed to let voters draft and support candidates via a national online primary. To foster bipartisanship, the winning presidential candidate would have to pick a running mate from a different party.

The board of Americans Elect was comprised of serious political veterans from across the spectrum. This was not just a playful exercise. We wanted the Americans Elect ticket to be listed on actual ballots. In fact, fifty states approved an Americans Elect ballot line. Our plan was to have three rounds of online balloting in May to narrow the field of candidates. We planned to choose a final candidate in June through an online convention. In the initial round, hundreds of thousands of "delegates" nominated fifty-two possible candidates—among them Michael Bloomberg, Warren Buffett, Hillary Clinton, Jon Huntsman Jr., Ron Paul, and Condoleezza Rice. Alas, we hit a snag. Depending on their past accomplishments, candidates were required to get between 1,000 to 5,000 clicks in each of ten states. By the end of May, no candidate had enough clicks to qualify for the primary. In July, our board withdrew Americans Elect from most state ballots.

When we proposed the idea, *New York Times* columnist Thomas L. Friedman recognized that "what Amazon.com did to books, what the blogosphere did to newspapers, what the iPod did to music, what drugstore.com did to pharmacies, Americans Elect plans to do to the two-party duopoly that has dominated American political life—remove the barriers to real competition, flatten the incumbents and let the people in." I still think it was a noble experiment. Peter Ackerman and I had seen the ouster of Slobodan Milošević. But America's two-party system proved more impervious to disruption than a dictatorship. The only thing Democratic and Republican leaders can agree on is that they don't like interlopers. That same year I wrote another book, *American Casino: The Rigged Game That's Killing Democracy*. In it, I detailed the election mechanisms—PACs, super PACs, 527s—that rich, anonymous individuals to enhance their power.

I was deeply disillusioned with the system. But as Election Day approached, I still couldn't entirely give up on it. I felt the need to vote. I'd come to see that Obama's opponent, former Massachusetts governor Mitt Romney, held positions closer to my own. And so, though I knew my liberal mother would have my head, I cast my first vote for a Republican.

Don't be afraid to modify your position. It's not a crime to change your mind.

24

A LONG FLIGHT TO KYIV

My mother had the satisfaction of seeing Obama hold on to his job. (Romney lost but later distinguished himself as one of the more courageous members of the GOP.) By now I'd come to doubt the efficacy of either party. In my 2013 book, *The End of Authority: How a Loss of Legitimacy and Broken Trust Are Endangering Our Future*, I noted that Obama and Romney had accused each other of crony capitalism—and that neither of them was wrong. There was a pernicious problem that went beyond debate brickbats, and it wasn't confined to America. In *The End of Authority*, I waded through rebellions, debt crises, rigged elections, and many other examples of how institutions had broken down around the globe. At the time, many people blamed these problems on the world-wide recession. But voters' loss of faith predated the economic downturn. I proposed some solutions. International leadership—at the UN, the European Union, the World Bank, and other institutions—needed to talk less and do more to mediate violent disputes and enforce fair trade and currency practices. At the same time, I believed that local governments had to rely on themselves to solve dilemmas they knew best. The synapse between local need and global wealth was microtargeting technology. I sighted examples of groups that were using it to get resources to students, disaster victims, and others who needed help.

As I broke away from party orthodoxies, I started to ease back into consulting—in a new way. I was looking to do more than polling. I wanted to have a more substantive relationship with clients—to offer them the benefit of the thinking I'd done in my books and op-eds. More than crunching survey numbers, I wanted to help them articulate a philosophy and put it into action. Clients came calling, including some from abroad. In early 2009, I had a long lunch at the Harvard Club with Dr. Ashraf Ghani. Having served as Afghanistan's minister of finance, the Columbia-educated professor planned to run against Hamid Karzai for the presidency. Ghani wanted my campaign expertise. He assured me that, if I signed on, I'd be safe staying in Kabul's top hotel. I was flattered by the offer, and I shared his hope that the benighted tribal land could one day become a technocratic trade hub. But the U.S. had been fighting a guerrilla war there for eight years now. The Pentagon had just acknowledged that the Taliban had "coalesced into a resilient insurgency." Terrorist attacks were up 40 percent for the year. I'd survived some hairy episodes in Serbia and Venezuela. But, at age fifty-six, I was getting too old for magical thinking. I respectfully passed. That year, terrorists, bent on disrupting the election, wired car bombs that killed and wounded hundreds of people. The Taliban later targeted hotels catering to foreigners. Nine died at the luxurious Kabul Serena resort. Ashraf Ghani won less than 3 percent of the vote in 2009. He did become president in 2014 but had to flee in 2021, when the Taliban regained power.

Hope can sometimes triumph over experience. But if you're weighing whether to take a chance, try imagining the worst-case scenario. If you can handle the risk, roll the dice. Otherwise, move on.

Despite the vagaries of foreign travel, I tried to obey my own rule: **take the meeting**. In late 2014, Bibi Netanyahu invited me to Israel. I was a little surprised by his overture. I'd worked against him in 1996, when I'd advised Shimon Peres. But Peres had lost that race, giving Netanyahu his first term as prime minister. He obviously considered it ancient history. So I flew to Jerusalem. When we sat down, Bibi told me that he'd been keeping an eye on me and was impressed by my instincts. We talked for five hours about Israeli politics, particularly Israel's relations with the United States. He didn't need to tell me he wasn't a fan of our current president. He believed Obama's efforts to negotiate a nuclear deal with Iran endangered Israel. He said he never would have imagined that he'd be closer to the leaders of Egypt and Saudi Arabia than to America's commander-in-chief. He asked me how he thought he should respond. I suggested that he go over Obama's head and directly appeal to Congress and the American people. We talked about specific legislators he might approach. At the end of our long conversation, he seemed pleased. He told me I was hired.

I never heard from him again.

Not long afterward, Netanyahu addressed a rare joint session of Congress. House Speaker John Boehner and Senate Majority Leader Mitch McConnell, both Republicans, invited him without consulting the Obama administration. For forty-five minutes, Netanyahu railed about the "bad deal" Obama was making with Iran. I was flattered, in a way, that Netanyahu had followed my advice. I didn't mind so much that no one on his team had invited me to attend his address. It did bug me that Netanyahu didn't pay my consulting bill or even reimburse my airfare as he'd promised. I'd never been stiffed by a world leader before but, when I mentioned it to other Israelis, they shrugged. "That is Bibi," they explained. "He does that to everyone." Eventually, though, he stepped on too many people. I wasn't surprised when he was indicted for bribery, fraud, and breach of trust.

Don't be shortsighted. Small insults add up. Snubs, slights, and broken promises aren't just rude. They have a way of biting you in the ass.

★ ★ ★

Still, I remained open to far-flung assignments. For some time, a friend had been telling me about a Ukrainian businessman named Victor Pinchuk. Born in Kyiv in 1960, Pinchuk was the son of two engineers who'd been forced to hide their Jewish faith during the Soviet era. A brilliant student, he'd earned a doctorate in industrial engineering. His innovations in the manufacture of seamless piping and railcar wheels became the foundation of his wealth. The collapse of the USSR and the privatization of state enterprises brought him more lucrative opportunities. It also challenged him to pioneer a new frontier—call it the Wild East—that was crawling with ruthless fortune-hunters. I wasn't sure why this master of survival wanted to talk to me. But when he asked if I'd come to Kyiv, I packed my bag.

Getting to that meeting was an ordeal. A missed connection imprisoned me in Paris's Charles de Gaulle Airport for five hours. I arrived in Kyiv almost half a day late. Nevertheless, Pinchuk was gracious when I finally joined his team in a conference room.

"Doug, you must be very tired," he said. "Why don't you first get some rest at the hotel?"

"Victor, I've flown eighteen hours to be here," I said. "Let's get to work."

"I like you already," said Pinchuk.

Pinchuk wanted me to help him forge closer relations between Ukraine and the West, particularly the United States. I was happy to assist. I believed that a democratic Ukraine was an essential bulwark against revived aggression by Russia, whose new president was a former KGB officer named Vladimir Putin. My first surveys sounded out how the West perceived the newly independent Ukraine. Regrettably, even sophisticated European investors were foggy about it. Some thought it was still part of Russia.

While Pinchuk and I pondered ways to raise Ukraine's profile, a more urgent need arose. In 2004, the Ukrainians were voting for their third post-Soviet president. The current president, Leonid Kuchma, who happened to be Pinchuk's father-in-law, had endorsed Prime Minister Viktor Yanukovych, popular among the Russian speakers in the country's east. Viktor Yushchenko, a vocal critic of Kuchma and committed to European Union integration, was the hero of Russo-phobic nationalists in the west. The campaign threatened to split the country in two—especially after someone poisoned Yushchenko with dioxin. In a matter of weeks, the handsome, young politician came to resemble a horribly disfigured old man. Yanukovych's camp denied any involvement. Incredibly, Yushchenko kept campaigning even though he relied on a morphine drip to cope with his pain.

The first round of voting was inconclusive, so a runoff was scheduled for November 21. During the three weeks before the voting, I saw the passions of both sides reach a boil. On election day, an exit poll funded by Western embassies showed Yushchenko ahead by 11 percent. But official results gave Yanukovych a three-point lead. Yushchenko and his supporters claimed fraud and voter intimidation. On the day after the election, an estimated 200,000 demonstrators filled downtown Kyiv. Soldiers and police stood on alert. Unofficially, Yushchenko declared himself the winner.

For weeks, in freezing weather, Yushchenko's supporters camped out in Independence Square in what came to be called the Orange Revolution (after Yushchenko's campaign color). One cold night, an unlikely visitor strolled into this tent city—Victor Pinchuk. During President Kuchma's two terms, his government had sold Pinchuk major factories that produced steel and ferroalloy. There were allegations of favoritism. The protest camp was festooned with unflattering caricatures of Kuchma and Pinchuk. And yet there stood Yanukovych-supporter Pinchuk. He wanted to hear what the demonstrators had to say.

"Something historic was happening," Pinchuk later recalled in *Tablet* magazine. "If you are a patriot of your country, it doesn't matter which candidate you support. [If] you love this country, you want to take part in building it."

I was confident that Pinchuk was committed to doing the right thing. Behind the scenes, he served as a back channel between Yanukovych and the U.S. government. Pinchuk helped defuse an Interior Ministry plan to mobilize troops for a Tiananmen Square–style crackdown on demonstrators. Instead, the government and the opposition reached a peaceful agreement to hold a third round of voting on December 26.

Pinchuk asked me and Republican pollster Frank Luntz to conduct a definitive exit poll for ICTV, the Pinchuk-owned television station. Two weeks before the election, he announced that ICTV would call the election soon after the polls closed. It was a brave stance. Most observers expected Yushchenko to win and saw the Yanukovych camp as complicit in electoral irregularities. Yet, despite his past support for Yanukovych, Pinchuk believed the nation deserved an unflinching assessment of the people's will.

The stakes were high. To guarantee an accurate count, ICTV agreed to conduct an extraordinary number of interviews on Election Day—three separate rounds that would query roughly 50,000 people. The day before the election—Christmas—I flew into Kyiv to oversee the operation. Despite the bone-chilling weather, Yushchenko supporters of all ages continued to occupy the center of the city.

On December 26, everything appeared to be going smoothly. By noon, we had our first numbers. Viktor Yushchenko was making a strong showing. His lead shrank in the afternoon. But by 6:00 p.m., our polls showed him ahead by 10 or 11 points—a decisive margin. When the polls closed, Luntz and I briefed Pinchuk. I wondered how he would react to his candidate's defeat. He showed no disappointment. He never questioned the results. After chatting for a bit, he said, "It's time for you to go to the studio."

At 9:00 p.m., we went live with ICTV's news anchor, Dmitry Kiselyov. He noted that exit polls in America had gotten the 2000 Bush-Gore race wrong. Why should viewers accept these results? I explained that our Ukrainian survey was proportionally much bigger than American exit polls. We could now say with confidence that Yushchenko was ahead by double digits. While Yanukovych refused at first to acknowledge his defeat, the following month Viktor Yushchenko was sworn in as Ukraine's third elected president.

★　★　★

The Orange Revolution proved costly for Pinchuk. Yushchenko's government declared that he'd underpaid for his steel mill, clawed it back, and sold it to a foreign investor at a much higher price. Pinchuk struggled in court to keep a grip on his other assets. But even as his wealth was under siege, he kept investing in Ukraine's future.

I helped his foundation devise initiatives to foster education, culture, health, human rights, and democracy. The Zavtra. UA scholarship program pays for Ukrainian students to study abroad—with the understanding that they'll bring their new skills home. The free Pinchuk Art Center not only features work by contemporary stars like Jeff Koons, Damien Hirst, and Takashi Murakami but gives young artists the chance to learn from them. Pinchuk teamed up with Steven Spielberg to produce *Spell Your Name*, a documentary about the Babi Yar massacre of over 33,000 Jews during the Holocaust.

Victor's wife, Elena, has a foundation dedicated to the prevention and treatment of AIDS. Knowing of Elton John's commitment to the same mission, I called his manager to see if the singer might play a benefit concert. The manager politely told me to get lost. When I shared the discouraging news with Victor, he asked, "Doug, have you tried all the angles? Can you call someone else?" Time and again, he's shown me how to pivot off rejection.

"No" is simply a mispronunciation of the word "yes."

In the case of Elton John, I tried the head of his AIDS foundation, Anne Aslett. The concert idea excited her and, in 2007, Elton performed for the first time in Ukraine. He's since done two more shows. In 2009, he and his husband, David Furnish, tried to adopt an orphaned Ukrainian boy. Authorities did not see the couple as "suitable parents." But they provided for the child anyway and, in the process, raised awareness of LGBT equality.

The year after Elton's first show, we had an idea for another concert, this one aimed at unifying the country's polarized west and east regions. At the time, I tended to take rock 'n' roll for granted. Pinchuk reminded me that music from the West—and the fashion that came with it—had long been forbidden in Ukraine. "To us," he recalled, "blue jeans and rock represented the chance to dream beyond our world." He was ready to dream big. This time, we set our sights on Paul McCartney. I knew John Eastman, the brother of McCartney's late wife, Linda. Again, there was some back and forth. Pinchuk would end up shelling out $5 million to import the former Beatle. But he considered it money well spent. On one extremely rainy June night, McCartney lit up the Kyiv square where Orange demonstrators had camped. Televised across the country, the free show's highlight was "Back in the USSR."

"I've been waiting a long time to say that," McCartney told the soggy throng.

The extravaganza—seen by 350,000 people—was the perfect way to remind Ukrainians they were no longer locked in a Soviet gulag. As with all the Pinchuks' projects, it was about injecting the idea of possibility. It was also part of our plan to put Free Ukraine on the map.

As fun as the concerts were, we also wanted to have serious conversations with Western leaders about how Ukraine's politics and economy could become more democratic and transparent. Toward that end we organized Yalta European Strategy (YES), aimed at looking for ideas to stimulate European, Ukrainian, and global development. Each year, we hold a lunch at the World Economic Forum (WEF) in Davos, Switzerland. We host another lunch at the Munich Security Conference (MSC). The centerpiece of our dialogues became the annual Yalta European Strategy Forum, first held in 2004 in Crimea at the Livadia Palace, where Franklin Roosevelt, Winston Churchill, and Josef Stalin had their Yalta summit in 1945. The YES summit has brought together hundreds of heads of state, diplomats, journalists, and business leaders from more than 50 countries. I spend a good deal of time wrangling speakers. Over the years, we've welcomed UN Secretary-General Kofi Annan, U.S. diplomats Condoleezza Rice, Richard Holbrooke, and Strobe Talbott, Britain's Tony Blair, Germany's Gerhard Schröder, Turkey's Recep Tayyip Erdoğan, Israel's Shimon Peres, Poland's Aleksander Kwaśniewski, generals Wesley Clark and David Petraeus, International Monetary Fund head Dominique Strauss-Kahn, U.S. Treasury secretary Larry Summers, World Bank president James Wolfensohn, business titans Richard Branson and Jimmy Wales, economist Arthur Laffer, and thought leaders Eric Lander, Niall Ferguson, Paul Krugman, and Bernard-Henri Lévy, among others.

Conversations were usually cordial. But we had to be ready for anything. The year of the first conference, I had to strengthen security after an anarchist group called The Brotherhood poured glue on Open Society founder George Soros and hurled eggs at him.

★　★　★

I wasn't just booking rock stars and prime ministers. My work got trickier when, in 2010, Viktor Yanukovych ran again for president and won. He wasted no time in punishing the opposition. This included launching criminal prosecutions against his political opponents. His principal target was former Prime Minister Yulia Tymoshenko. Steely yet angelic looking in her halo of blond braids, Tymoshenko had almost defeated Yanukovych in the 2010 election. Even before her trial on charges of abuse of power and misuse of funds, the government jailed her. Many European and American organizations viewed her detention as politically motivated. Tymoshenko was an oligarch in her own right (known as the "gas princess"). She'd been a business partner of Pinchuk, then a rival. Later, as prime minister, she became the driving force behind the government's clawback of his steel and alloy plants. Nevertheless, Pinchuk believed that her seven-year sentence was unjust. He hoped he might talk sense to Yanukovych. He also asked if I could assist in getting the Obama administration to put pressure on the new president.

Advocating for a foreign entity in the United States is a regulatory bramble. Pinchuk and I agreed that I should register as a lobbyist and follow every rule. Back in 2004, I'd introduced Pinchuk to Bill Clinton and then-senator Hillary Clinton. Now that Hillary was Obama's Secretary of State, it made sense to bring Tymoshenko's incarceration to her attention. The European Court of Human Rights had condemned Yanukovych's treatment of Tymoshenko. The U.S. Senate had passed two resolutions calling for her release. But just as we seemed to be making some progress, we encountered some mysterious headwinds. News reports suggested that Pinchuk's contributions to the Clinton Foundation amounted to layaway payments for access. A *New York Times* story questioned whether his meetings with Hillary had more to do with his steel business.

"Mr. Pinchuk's relationship to the Clintons became the subject of scrutiny last summer when American steel makers filed a case alleging that Ukraine—and by extension Mr. Pinchuk's company, Interpipe Ltd.—and eight other countries had illegally dumped a type of steel tube used in natural gas extraction," the *Times* reported.

The same article stated plainly, "There is no evidence that Mr. Pinchuk or Mr. Schoen discussed anything other than the political crisis in Ukraine with the State Department, or that any United States officials tried to influence the trade case."

When I first brought Pinchuk to meet Bill Clinton at the former president's Harlem office, Pinchuk had assured me, "I will never directly or indirectly try to do business through or with Bill Clinton." I felt confident telling the *Times* reporter that "my lobbying work for Mr. Pinchuk was undertaken and designed solely and specifically to resolve an ongoing crisis in Ukraine that rages to this day."

Even if you never get grilled by a reporter, you may be accused of doing something bad—at work, at home, on the golf course. We live in a contentious world where it's easy to be dragged into court or onto Twitter. My advice: **Defend yourself without becoming defensive. Stay cool. Measure your words. State the facts. Acknowledge undeniable missteps, but also point out what you did right. Keep it brief.**

I didn't know it then, but this baloney about our hidden intent was part of a disinformation campaign. (More on that later.) At the time, Pinchuk and I carried on—still trying to free Tymoshenko, to tilt Ukraine toward Europe, and to keep Vladimir Putin at bay.

Secretary Clinton underscored America's commitment to Ukraine when she attended our 2013 YES conference with husband Bill. Urging Ukraine's citizens to be "agents of change," she noted the country's resources, its educated population, and, especially, its "excellent chocolate." The line got a big laugh because, as part of his effort to derail Ukraine's trade and association agreement with the European Union, Putin had blocked the Russian import of chocolate manufactured by Petro Poroshenko, a Putin critic who would later become Ukraine's president. Poroshenko himself wasn't feeling jocular. He lashed into Putin's chief economic adviser, Sergei Glazyev, for the Kremlin's heavy-handed attempts at intimidation. Glazyev responded by threatening Russian retaliation if Ukraine signed the E.U. agreement. That included assisting pro-Russian separatists.

The same conference saw opposition leader Vitali Klitschko, a world heavyweight boxing champion, look President Yanukovych in the eye and ask what he would do if the E.U. deal fell through because of Yanukovych's record of corruption.

"Will you have the guts to resign?" the towering fighter asked.

Fellow opposition leader Yuriy Lutsenko, who only recently had been pardoned after serving almost two years in prison, implored Yanukovych to free Yulia Tymoshenko. The boldness of Klitschko and Lutsenko stunned many in the audience, including me. That kind of talk could get you locked up. But, with so many Western onlookers, Yanukovych made nice. He claimed he wanted to see Tymoshenko released; he just hadn't found the legal means to do so. Seeming to defy the Kremlin, Yanukovych even declared: "We have to move towards European integration."

That September's conference ended with a gala dinner. After dessert, everyone danced on the beach of the Livadia Palace. It was lovely scene but, within a few weeks, the country plummeted into chaos. That November, Yanukovych sided with Russia and refused to sign the E.U. deal, even though the Ukrainian parliament had overwhelmingly approved it. Protesters set up camp again in Kyiv's Independence Square. Anti-demonstration laws fanned their rage. At first, Pinchuk watched from a distance. But after police violently tried to evict the protesters, he showed up at their camp to cheer them on. Behind the scenes, Pinchuk was strategizing with business and political leaders.

In January and February of 2014, the face-off turned bloody. Demonstrators burned police trucks and barricades. Police torched a government building seized by protestors. When thousands of demonstrators marched toward parliament, snipers fired at will. Pinchuk's team dispatched medical supplies to the wounded. All told, the clashes left 108 protesters and 13 officers dead. Many more were wounded. In response, Yanukovych and opposition leaders reached a deal calling for an interim unity government, constitutional reforms, and early elections. Police withdrew from central Kyiv, ceding control to the demonstrators. Yanukovych fled the city. That day, the parliament voted 380–0 to remove him from office. They also authorized the release of Yulia Tymoshenko. Yanukovych escaped to Russia. The Putin regime called his overthrow an illegal coup fomented by the United States. Former Ukrainian Prime Minister Arseniy Yatsenyuk has alleged that, while Yanukovych was in office, treasury funds of up to $70 billion were transferred to foreign accounts.

During the Revolution of Dignity, as it came to be called, other Ukrainian billionaires fled the country. Pinchuk stayed. I believe his years of quiet diplomacy wound the spring for Yanukovych's ejection. Some in the opposition may have wished Victor had been more vocal. But his television channel and his YES events gave them the microphones and audiences they needed.

During a tempest, the center path will get you to higher and drier ground.

Pinchuk himself has come to see the inequities of the windfall he enjoyed when privatization of state plants made him Ukraine's second-richest man. "A few rich people emerged and a great many poor," he told *Tablet*. "The gap is crazy . . . I, by the way, also think that it's unfair." Having surrendered some of those assets, he has also embraced the Giving Pledge of Bill Gates and

Warren Buffet—committing at least half his money to charity. I'm not saying everything we did was perfect. We were learning the "grayscale" in an evolving democracy. But I fundamentally bought into Victor's vision for Ukraine. I believe he's done as much as anyone to enhance life there. He might disagree. The bravery of the protesters, he once said, "makes you feel small compared to them."

If you trust someone, you can stick with them through the rough patches.

25

DROPPING IN ON THE DONALD

President Yanukovych's ouster ignited violent protests in Russian-speaking regions of Ukraine. Putin quickly seized the opportunity to "restore order" by annexing Crimea to Russia. His "protection" of the peninsula made it impossible for us to hold the 2015 Yalta European Strategy Forum in Yalta. It would have to be in Kyiv. I began to cast about for speakers. A name came to mind: Donald Trump.

I'd met Trump almost three decades earlier through Roger Stone, the dapper and cunning Republican consultant who'd worked for Richard Nixon, Ronald Reagan, and George H. W. Bush. For a couple of years, Stone and I counseled Trump on the political aspects of his real estate and casino businesses. I quickly learned his quirks. I once came to a meeting with him with a presentation deck of fifty or so slides. I got through three or four slides before he grew impatient. He also became distracted if there were more than two people in the room. Particularly if a woman was present, he'd start to dominate the conversation. But I rolled with it.

In 1990, Trump brought us on to help market the Trump Shuttle—the commuter airline he'd bought from Eastern. Roger Stone told the *New York Times* that the airline business was "like a political campaign. Two candidates fighting for at least a 51 share,

using the same tools: TV, radio, print, direct mail, telephones."
Stone and I were miles apart politically, but Trump thought our
differing viewpoints would enhance the campaign. Less excited by
our input was Robert Levenson, vice chairman of Scali, McCabe,
Sloves, the advertising agency Trump had recently hired and
whose first ads he'd publicly mocked. I tried to reassure the ad
guys that we respected their work. "Instead of fixing something
that's broken, we're coming in to add a strategic dimension," I
told the *Times*. I'm not sure any of us could have kept the Trump
Shuttle in the air. Despite Trump's attempt to pamper his passengers with steak, champagne, and golden lavatory fixtures, the
airline defaulted on its debt a few months after he'd hired us. It
went out of business in 1992.

A few years earlier, in 1987, Trump had registered as a
Republican and placed full-page advertisements in three major
newspapers, declaring that "America should stop paying to defend
countries that can afford to defend themselves." The ads also
recommended "reducing the budget deficit, working for peace in
Central America, and speeding up nuclear disarmament negotiations with the Soviet Union." He did some more chest-beating
at a gathering of Republican presidential candidates in New
Hampshire. He demurred that he himself was not a candidate but
confidently told a reporter: "If I did run for President, I'd win."

Privately, he wasn't so sure. If you got him one-on-one, Trump
would listen to you. He asked me to see what his chances were.
Our polling found that his name recognition was low outside of
New York. Those who did know of him didn't necessarily trust
him. He had just 15 to 20 percent favorability.

That probably had to do with his escalating bankruptcies. Yet
even when his casinos were going under, I saw him swagger up to
the gaming tables, where people would swarm around him like
he was a messiah. His painstakingly crafted illusion of unlimited
wealth spoke to their aspirations. Gamblers wanted to shake his

hand, as though it were a lucky rabbit's foot. I could see then that he had something that, someday, might have currency in politics. But, at the time, I was mostly interested in getting paid. He may not have owed me what he owed Citibank, but I wasn't blasé about getting stiffed for $80,000. One cold, rainy afternoon, after having lunch at the Harvard Club, I was walking up Fifth Avenue when I happened upon Trump Tower. Fixing my gaze on the brassy name on the building, I decided I was going to get paid.

I marched into the lobby, got on the elevator, and ascended to the 26th floor headquarters of The Trump Organization. Walking straight past the receptionist, I strode into the office of Donald J. Trump. He was sitting at his desk. Before he could speak, I said, "Donald, I'm here for my money."

Chuckling, he pointed to a pile of bills about a foot high.

"I got all these invoices, and you want me to pay just yours?" he asked.

"Yes," I said. "I only need one check."

He must have been impressed by my brass. "Okay," he said, opening his checkbook. Grabbing one of his beloved Sharpies, he affixed his electrocardiogram-like signature to a check.

I thanked him and went straight to the bank to deposit it. My debt collection left no ill will. We stayed in touch but didn't do much business. He was always perfectly nice to me. But he preferred to take his own counsel, and I wasn't eager to be part of his scene. Life went on.

I didn't think he had a chance of becoming president in 1987 but, twenty-seven years later, the timing was right. Veteran analysts wrote him off. He had no political experience. His policy proposals—building a giant wall at the southern border, banning Muslim immigrants, bringing back American manufacturing jobs—defied conventional wisdom. His rhetoric—branding Mexicans as "criminals, drug dealers, rapists"—defied political correctness. And yet he was clearly connecting with blue-collar whites. It was the rebellion I'd forecasted in my earlier books. Thirty-eight years earlier I'd shown how Britain's Labour party had underestimated the appeal of Enoch Powell's anti-immigrant jeremiad. More recently, I'd explored the rise of the Tea Party and voters' loss of faith in professional politicians. Now, in op-eds and on TV, I predicted Trump would be the GOP nominee.

About ten years earlier, I'd introduced Trump to Victor Pinchuk. I thought that he might fit into our roster of YES speakers for 2015. You could depend on Trump to be provocative, and Trump was always up for burnishing his foreign policy profile. It looked like a win-win.

On the day of the conference, Trump was due to speak to the assembled dignitaries via video link. I was to interview him. Trump started by calling me "a wonderful person" and Pinchuk "a tremendous guy." Unfortunately, there was a delay of several seconds between my questions and his responses. He seemed flummoxed. He also presumed that his remarks were being translated, which led to more awkward pauses. Some guests at the dinner tittered. Others ignored him and talked among themselves. Nevertheless, he pressed on.

"My feeling toward the Ukraine and towards the entire area is very, very strong. I know many people that live in the Ukraine, they're friends of mine, they're fantastic people," said Trump, apparently unaware that patriotic Ukrainians view "the Ukraine" as an offensive Soviet coinage.

The previous month he'd said he "wouldn't care" whether NATO accepted Ukraine as a member. But now he contended, "I don't think that the Ukraine is given the proper respect from other parts in Europe." He added, "Ukraine is an amazing place. These are people who know what's right and they're not being treated right."

I asked him what changes he'd make to the U.S. military.

"Our military would be very, very strong," he said, adding that President Obama "is not strong. So far, we have all lip service. Part of the problem that Ukraine has with the United States is that Putin does not respect our president whatsoever."

We'd spoken for about twenty minutes when Trump's video link was suddenly cut, depriving guests of a chance to question him. Britain's *Guardian* called Trump's appearance "bizarre." Terming it an "unusual foray into foreign affairs," the *New York Times* reported that some attendees felt Trump spoke in "platitudes." Oleksandr Bohutskyy, the president of Pinchuk's ICTV network, remarked, "I am a little bit concerned whether Trump can find Ukraine on the map."

Well, at least the evening got some attention. I'd also managed to elicit Trump's most pro-Ukrainian, anti-Putin speech, before or since.

As I foretold, the GOP went on to nominate Trump as its candidate. The leftward media regarded Trump as a buffoon and remained convinced that the election was Hillary Clinton's to lose. For all my history with the Clintons, I remained troubled by her use of a private email server for State Department communications. Then, eleven days before the election, FBI director James Comey told Congress that the bureau was looking into newly discovered emails. Comey's announcement convinced me that, if Hillary won, we faced the real possibility of a criminal investigation of the president elect.

"We simply cannot face a situation where the president elect may need or want a pardon from the president to govern," I wrote in my column in *The Hill*. "Or worse yet, need to pardon herself after she takes office."

"I still share her worldview and am much closer to her approach to policies than I am to Donald Trump," I went on. "That said, with America facing a potential constitutional crisis after her election, I am not able, under the circumstances we are now facing, to vote for Secretary Clinton."

That November, I abstained from voting for a presidential candidate. Ultimately, the FBI found that Clinton's server did not contain any information marked classified. I do believe Comey's unprecedented announcement cost her the election. But Federal agencies determined that 100 of her emails *should* have been deemed "Secret" or "Top Secret" when they were sent. Moreover, I believe Hillary had prior knowledge of the Steele dossier—the largely unverified opposition research report alleging cooperation between Trump's campaign and the Russian government. The *Wall Street Journal* reported that the Democratic National Committee and the Clinton campaign paid $12.4 million to the Perkins Coie law firm for legal and compliance services. At least $1.02 million of that went to Fusion GPS, the investigative firm that produced the Steele Dossier. Having worked with both Clintons, I don't believe Hillary's campaign would spend that amount of money without the candidate knowing where it was going. With what I know now, I still would not have voted for Hillary.

Sometimes you make the right decision for the wrong reasons.

★   ★   ★

In the final weeks of the race, many polls predicted Hillary as a shoo-in. The Princeton Election Consortium put her chances of victory at 99 percent. I estimated her odds at around 60 percent. Yes, I too got it wrong. Why were we all blindsided? First, it's become more and more difficult to get a representative sample because fewer voters—certainly fewer young voters—will answer their phones. If they do answer, it's hard to get them to say openly what they're going to do. Many conservative Republicans disdain the political establishment and the mainstream media and won't speak to pollsters. Trump compounded the problem. Even moderate Republicans were embarrassed to admit to strangers that they were voting for him. We called these people "shy Trumpers." We've started to get around this shyness by asking indirect questions. Like: "Will any of your family or friends be voting for Trump? Can you understand why they'd vote for Trump?" Nonpolitical preferences, such as churchgoing and favorite magazines, also tell you a lot.

Anyway, two weeks after Trump won the Electoral College (but lost the popular vote) the media stepped up its reporting on laws he may have broken. The *Washington Post*'s David A. Fahrenthold discovered that Trump's charitable foundation had admitted to the IRS that it had violated self-dealing rules by using charitable funds to pay Trump's personal, political, and legal costs. (The candidate famously used $20,000 from the foundation to buy a six-foot-tall portrait of himself.) Among the Trump foundation's contributors was Victor Pinchuk's foundation. It had paid $150,000. I explained to reporters that the payment was an honorarium for Trump's speech at the Yalta European Strategy Forum. That seemed to put an end to it—until April 2018.

By then Special Counsel Robert S. Mueller III was almost a year into his investigation of alleged Russian interference in the 2016 U.S. presidential election. Pinchuk's aspirations for a free Ukraine are obviously at odds with Vladimir Putin's wish to reclaim it. Nevertheless, Mueller's team was reportedly scrutinizing Pinchuk's donation to Trump's foundation. "The timing of the transaction," *Slate* stated, "raises questions about whether the money was, in essence, a thinly veiled alternative campaign donation in an attempt to curry favor." A former IRS official told the *New York Times* that the honorarium "looks like an effort to buy influence." The speculation was absurd. How, in September 2015, when Trump was one of seventeen Republican candidates and Hillary was still the favorite, could Pinchuk and I foresee that the host of *The Apprentice* would one day sit in the Oval Office?

Most likely, Mueller turned his scope on Pinchuk because of Trump's personal lawyer, Michael Cohen. Back in 2015, after I'd invited Trump to the forum, I heard from Cohen. He said his client usually received a speaker's fee—which Cohen said would benefit Trump's foundation. It seemed like a reasonable request at the time. Flash forward to spring 2018. "Trump's fixer" was alleged to have violated campaign finance laws by making "hush money" payments to his client's reputed paramours, including porn star Stormy Daniels. FBI agents had just raided Cohen's office when I got a call from the *New York Times'* Maggie Haberman. I was straight with her: we paid fees to *all* the YES conference speakers. It's standard. Trump's foundation may have been playing games, but that had nothing to do with me or Pinchuk.

Later in 2018 Cohen was sentenced to three years in federal prison after pleading guilty to tax evasion and campaign-finance violations. Mueller's team never contacted me or Pinchuk. The Mueller probe did shed light on one lingering mystery. Remember when Pinchuk was trying to win the release of former Ukrainian prime minister Yulia Tymoshenko? Pinchuk and I came up with the idea of hiring a U.S. law firm to do an independent review of the prosecution's case against her. In February 2012, I brought that idea to one of Washington's most respected attorneys, Gregory B. Craig, former White House counsel to President Obama and adviser to the likes of Kofi Annan and Aleksandr Solzhenitsyn. Craig persuaded his firm, Skadden, Arps, Slate, Meagher & Flom, to take the case.

The firm's client of record was the Ukrainian government. But since he was determined to get Tymoshenko justice, Pinchuk somewhat grudgingly offered to advance legal fees, expecting that the government would reimburse him. Having put the investigation in motion, I handed the case off to another American who'd previously worked with Craig—Paul Manafort. Manafort had been a political adviser to Yanukovych since 2004. At the time, in 2012, I didn't know the extent to which he was still doing Yanukovych's bidding. Six years later, as part of his plea bargain with Mueller, Manafort confessed that he'd been conducting a media campaign to *undermine* the Obama administration's support for the imprisoned Tymoshenko. Working with a senior Israeli official, Manafort conspired to link Tymoshenko to an anti-Semitic party in Ukraine. Manafort promised in one memo that he could "plant some stink" on Tymoshenko and get "[O]bama jews [to] put pressure on the Administration to disavow Tymoshenko and support Yanukovych."

Ultimately, the Skadden report offered the carefully parsed conclusion that Tymoshenko's legal defense was "compromised" but that the evidence presented justified her conviction. Hoping this nuanced analysis might get some attention, Craig gave copies to a few journalists and members of Congress. Meanwhile, some in the Trump administration saw a chance to claim a Democratic scalp, namely Craig's. U.S. Attorney Geoffrey S. Berman contended that Justice Department officials pressured him to indict Craig for failing to register as a foreign agent. Berman's investigation found no violation. Not letting up, federal prosecutors in D.C. indicted Craig on a single count of making false statements. I testified about my early role in generating the Skadden report. It was a ridiculous, politically motivated prosecution. Craig was ultimately acquitted. Manafort didn't fare as well. In 2018, he was sentenced to seven and a half years in prison for his role in a decade-long financial fraud scheme related to Yanukovych, whose party allegedly paid Manafort $12.7 million off-the-books. (His indictment had nothing to do with Craig's report.) Fortunately for Manafort, he had a get-of-jail card: he'd served as Donald Trump's campaign chairman. In gratitude, President Trump pardoned him, though not before Manafort had spent nearly two years behind bars—enough time to imagine how Yulia Tymoshenko must have felt in her cell.

What set all this in motion? You might put it down to Manafort's sloppiness, his failure to fill out some simple paperwork. He'd neglected to do what I had done: register as a foreign lobbyist.

Don't cut corners, or the corners will cut you. It's much easier to be honest—and, in the long run, more lucrative. Maintaining your professionalism is not only a matter of success, but also a matter of survival.

★ ★ ★

The president had been in office for less than six months when Jessica Tarlov and I wrote *America in the Age of Trump: A Bipartisan Guide*. In it, we identified what we saw as the country's most pressing crises—failures in education, economic opportunity, and fiscal solvency; erosions in national security, domestic tranquility, and race relations; and deterioration of public trust, values, and governance. We tried to look deeply at the causes and offer proposals based on research documented in fifty-four pages of footnotes and a thirty-three-page bibliography.

We played no favorites. "The tragedy of Barack Obama's presidency," we wrote, "is that its historic promise was squandered willfully by choices that too often reflected a racial analysis of problems that were not exclusively racial, or not racial at all, but in fact transcended race—the problems of a neighborhood watchman frightened by crime, or the timeless problem of a cop menaced by an out-of-control young man (black or white, it doesn't matter) who simply forced him to defend himself." At the same time, we were appalled that Trump, as a candidate, initially refused to reject the support of longtime Klansman David Duke. Apparently, we wrote, Trump "was not willing to risk losing the support of white voters who think [like Duke]."

246

On the first anniversary of Trump's presidency, I was asked on Fox News what grade I'd give him. I hazarded a "B." Trump was apparently pleased. "Thank you . . . to Doug Schoen for the very good grade," he tweeted. "Working hard!"

But when the paperback edition of our book came out in October 2018, we saw no reason to switch off our alarms. Democrats and Republicans showed little inclination to embrace our centrist solutions. We noted that Trump's economic policies had helped bring Black unemployment down to its lowest level in recorded U.S. history. Yet, because of his reckless rhetoric, we wrote, "Trump will almost surely leave behind a more heated racial climate than the one he inherited." At the start of his presidency, we'd hoped for the recovery of "the common moral and cultural glue that had once held the United States together." Trump professed his belief in the old-time religion of his evangelical supporters. But the number of sexual harassment claims against him, combined with the deceptions of Trump and others in his administration, removed "any hope of a revival of traditional values."

"The irony of President Trump's embrace by the conservative wing of the GOP is that his presidency will likely wind up weakening both parties," we wrote. "As polarizing as Trump is along partisan lines, our guess is that the net effect of his term or terms in office will be to hasten the decline of the two-party system and drive an even deeper hunger for alternatives."

★　★　★

I knew how we'd gotten to this impasse. In the run-up to the 2016 election, I wrote *The Nixon Effect: How Richard Nixon's Presidency Fundamentally Changed American Politics*. In it, I traced the evolution of red and blue America to the ruthless battle plans the thirty-seventh president had hatched during his campaigns.

Nixon's pioneering tactics—his Southern Strategy, his perfection of "triangulation," his culture war attacks on "elites"—had shaped political strategy and party identity ever since. The book was in no way a defense of Nixon's cynical appeals to racist voters, his carpet-bombing of Cambodia, his paranoid plots against his perceived enemies, or his cover-up during the Watergate scandal. And yet, I argued, Nixon was the most influential president since World War II. More than anyone else, it was Nixon who pushed the two parties further out to their ideological poles. But it was also Nixon who devised ingenious ways of navigating between those poles. He campaigned from the right but governed from the center. His civil rights record surpassed JFK's and stands as a worthy successor to LBJ's. He also created the Environmental Protection Agency and signed Title IX legislation against gender discrimination in school sports, among other initiatives. He was, I asserted, the last liberal president of the twentieth century. Nixon's skill at adopting the opposition's ideas—which I first learned at the knee of Professor Daniel Patrick Moynihan—animated our campaign to reelect Bill Clinton. So it made sense that Clinton should invite his exiled predecessor back to the White House. Smarter than his adversaries and supporters, Nixon managed to confound them both. Oh, and he won the biggest landslide in American political history. "If that's what we see as 'division,'" I wrote, "the United States today could use more of it."

I thought it could also use the diplomatic acumen Nixon had shown in achieving a détente with China and a landmark arms treaty with the Soviet Union. I worried that our recent presidents had contributed to our current global discord. In 2019, I once again offered a few suggestions in *Collapse: A World in Crisis and the Urgency of American Leadership*. In it, I argued that George W. Bush had lacked a sense of proportion in using America's power—over-reaching by miring its military in Iraq and Afghanistan. Barack Obama had under-reached; his policy of "strategic patience" had let the Islamic State fester and China and North Korea grow into bigger threats. I believed the U.S. has shirked its responsibility to promote freedom and justice.

Was Donald Trump the man to revive what I called "assertive democratic idealism"? I applauded his tougher approach to ISIS, his clear-eyed view of Beijing's ambitions, and his rejection of Obama's 2015 dangerous nuclear deal with Iran. Trump's calls for our NATO allies to pay their fair share were legitimate. Yet he went about it like a bull shopping for china. In *Collapse*, I allowed that Trump might still rise to the occasion. But I recognized his isolationist National Security Strategy, which "begins with building up our wealth and power at home," promised little attention for human rights abroad. Too often, Trump's words seemed to excuse authoritarian leaders.

"Under Donald Trump, the office of the presidency has lost some of its traditional luster as a defender of democracy," I wrote. "Trump's addiction to personal attacks, his reckless use of Twitter, and his contempt for the free press are distressing signals of authoritarian behavior as well. Trump's constant dramas, with firings and instability in his inner circle, also suggest the dynamics of an authoritarian regime—a particularly chaotic one."

But the worst was yet to come.

26

I LIKE MIKE (AGAIN)

Throughout Trump's presidency, I tried to be even-handed in my syndicated columns. One week, I'd warn that a "Socialist Agenda Will Prove Disastrous for Democrats." Another week, I'd explain why "Senate Republicans Urgently Need to Embrace Criminal Justice Reform." I took both parties to task when their budget obstinacy caused the longest government shutdown in U.S. history. I also asked everyone to quit snarling. "We all need to lower our rhetoric, to come together as a nation, and to just stop the hate, the polarization, the division and the finger-pointing," I pleaded in *The Hill*. "It plays into the hands of our enemies, it makes us weaker, and it puts all of us at risk."

I gave Trump his due when he ordered airstrikes on Syrian strongman Bashar al-Assad's chemical weapons plants, when he signed the First Step Act to reduce prisoner recidivism, and when he helped normalize relations between Israel and six Arab League nations. I criticized his withdrawal from the Paris Climate Accords, his failure to reform affordable care, his deceptive Tax Cuts and Jobs Act, his boondoggle border wall, and his blind devotion to his base, including the Proud Boys and QAnon loons.

I was particularly troubled by the way that Vladimir Putin played Trump like an oversized balalaika.

I'd been watching Putin since he'd pointed tipsy president Boris Yeltsin toward the exit. In 2014, Melik Kaylan and I wrote *The Russia-China Axis: The New Cold War and America's Crisis of Leadership*. In it, we documented how Putin and Chinese president Xi Jinping had put aside their countries' longtime rivalry, finding that they had a lot of common interests. Both autocrats enjoyed silencing critics, terrorizing neighboring nations, supporting rogue regimes, and using hackers to steal military and economic intelligence. We reported that, at a Moscow banquet in 2011, Putin had boasted that Russia could "destroy America in half an hour or less." In 2016, Evan Roth Smith and I dove deeper in *Putin's Master Plan*. Some analysts saw Putin as an impulsive tactician who improvised as events arose. We argued that he was in fact a shrewd geopolitical strategist with a grand scheme—namely, to reclaim former Soviet republics, break up the NATO alliance, make Europe his energy slave, and leave America in the dust. I assembled further intelligence in 2017's *Putin on the March*. I warned that, as docile as Obama was, Trump showed even less resolve to combat Russian encroachment.

I didn't buy most of the Steele Dossier, with its unsubstantiated claims that the Russians had sex-party *kompromat* on Trump. But Putin clearly preferred Trump to Hillary Clinton. And having crossed paths with some of the oily characters in Trump World, I wasn't surprised that the FBI should be probing possible ties between Trump associates and Russian nationals. I believed that special prosecutor Robert Mueller's investigation was the only hope of getting unbiased answers. Of course, Trump couldn't abide any suggestion that Putin had helped him. Mueller's team found that, even before the 2016 election, Paul Manafort had begun to spread a Moscow-developed conspiracy theory that Ukraine, not Russia, had hacked the Democratic National Committee and leaked stolen emails. Trump, his personal attorney

Rudy Giuliani, and others promoted the alternative narrative that the Russian government had been framed by the Ukrainian government, which allegedly collaborated with the Democrats, the FBI, and CrowdStrike, the cybersecurity firm that investigated the hacked DNC servers. Trump and his fellow fantasists contended CrowdStrike had planted evidence on the servers to implicate Russia.

The conspiratorialists thickened the plot by stirring in Victor Pinchuk and me. As part of their hallucination of a "coup attempt" against Trump, they archly noted that CrowdStrike's co-founder, Dmitri Alperovitch, was a senior fellow at the Atlantic Council, a Washington think tank to which Pinchuk had donated. It wasn't long before Trump was insinuating that Pinchuk was the secret owner of CrowdStrike. "I heard it's owned by a very rich Ukrainian," Trump told an AP reporter in April 2017. "That's what I heard." Trump's allies pointed out that I, a Democrat, had introduced Pinchuk to Bill and Hillary Clinton. Never mind that CrowdStrike is a U.S.-based, NASDAQ-traded company, and that Pinchuk's donation to the Atlantic Council was less than 1.6 percent of its funding in 2018, and that Trump himself had once called Pinchuk "a tremendous guy."

In March 2019, the Mueller Report found that the Russians had hacked the servers and interfered to help Trump win the 2016 U.S. election. But the report did not establish that members of the Trump campaign "conspired" or "coordinated" with Russia, nor that the president "committed a crime." It would be another four years before special prosecutor John H. Durham would deliver a 306-page report that exonerated the Trump campaign of collusion with Russia and that accused the FBI of being "overwilling" to pursue a theory pushed by Democrats. Even before Durham released his 2023 report, I argued that House Democrats would hurt their party's 2020 election chances by taking up new investigations against Trump—in the same way Republicans had turned off many voters by vengefully pursuing Bill Clinton after he'd been acquitted of covering up his Monica Lewinsky affair.

But Trump got himself into fresh trouble. In August 2019, an unnamed whistleblower told the Inspector General of the Intelligence Community that, in a phone call the previous month, Trump had asked Ukrainian president Volodymyr Zelensky for "a favor"—a public announcement that Ukraine was investigating CrowdStrike, Democratic presidential candidate Joe Biden, and Biden's son, Hunter. The whistleblower alleged that Trump had linked the fulfillment of this favor to delivery of promised U.S. military aid. Several critics likened Trump's language to a Mafia shakedown.

A president using his office for personal political gain is the epitome of an impeachable offense. Having spent years trying to fortify Ukraine against Russian perdition, I was enraged by Trump's bid to hold hostage congressionally mandated arms that Ukraine desperately needed. And yet, in my columns and media appearances, I cautioned Democrats against seeking Trump's impeachment. I argued that it was doomed to fail in the Republican-controlled Senate. I also believed impeachment hearings would distract from what the Democrats should be running on—constructive policy proposals on the economy, health care, and climate change. The hearings would once again focus national attention solely on Trump.

Nevertheless, that September, the House began a formal impeachment inquiry. Several current and former administration officials testified that Trump's phone conversation with Zelensky was part of a broader scheme to get Ukrainian leadership to help injure Biden politically. They also confirmed that White House lawyers and the Justice Department did their best to conceal the call. On December 18, the House of Representatives voted along party lines to impeach Trump on two articles of impeachment: one for abuse of power and one for obstruction of Congress. As

I expected, the Senate acquitted him of both charges in February 2020.

Trump's survival only fired up his base and emboldened him. Following his defiant State of the Union address, his approval rating hit a record high of 49 percent. He reveled in the chaos of the Democrats' Iowa caucus, where technical issues caused a three-day delay in vote counting. Former Vice President Joe Biden, whom many thought would be his party's frontrunner, finished fourth.

★   ★   ★

But another candidate was giving hope to moderates. Back in 2016, Michael Bloomberg had asked me to gauge his chances of winning the presidency if he were to run as an Independent. My polling found that, in a three-way race between Trump, Hillary Clinton, and Bloomberg, Hillary claimed 175 Electoral College delegates, Trump got 75, and Bloomberg got 75; 213 delegates were undecided. That uncertainty was rife with possibilities. But Bloomberg feared he might split the anti-Trump vote and hand Trump a victory. He chose not to run.

Two months later, I did a poll that put Trump at 34 percent and Hillary at 33 percent. Both candidates were viewed unfavorably by 60 percent of those polled. That same poll showed that an "unidentified Independent"—someone voters knew nothing about—got 21 percent, with 14 percent undecided. The survey told me there was broad support for a credible alternative to the two major candidates. I kept thinking of George Allen Sr., the former coach of the Los Angeles Rams and the Washington Redskins. Allen believed in seizing the moment, doing the best with the team you have, rather than waiting to rebuild next season.

Allen's adage (and mine): **"Win now!"**

Still feeling Bloomberg might have won in 2016, I was delighted when he started testing the 2020 waters as a Democrat. He struck me as uniquely qualified to take down Trump. As the former leader of America's largest city and as a businessman far more successful than Trump, he could go toe-to-toe with the president on the economy. He'd also spent his post-mayoral years combating gun violence and climate change. After seeing the disarray of the 28 Democrats who would be president, he declared his candidacy on November 24, 2019.

I liked being back on his team. Bloomberg's competency lies in the leeway he gives his people. Some managers don't do that. New York Yankees owner George Steinbrenner famously harangued executives he should have left alone. I've known several top aides to former governor Andrew Cuomo. If Cuomo called them, they had to stop what they were doing, even if meant walking away from a lunch meeting three times. Yes, he was the governor. But if a governor keeps micromanaging and second-guessing his staff, they can't function. That may be why Cuomo was short on defenders during his impeachment investigation.

Bloomberg generally hired experienced people, paid them well, and trusted them to make sound decisions. If they didn't, he'd get someone else.

Let people do their jobs and judge them accordingly. If you don't show confidence in your staff, they'll lose confidence in you.

As the "Mike Bloomberg 2020" campaign got up to speed, I had the good fortune to be working with Carly Cooperman, my partner at Schoen Cooperman Research since 2007. Carly had led the polling for Bloomberg's political action committee, Independence USA (IUSA). Twenty-one of the twenty-four candidates backed by IUSA in the 2018 midterms had won, helping the Democrats to win control of the House. (Schoen Cooperman predicted the electoral outcome in target districts with 92 percent accuracy.)

Bloomberg's strategy in 2020 was to let the other candidates slug it out in the four earliest primaries while he campaigned in the 15 states that voted on March 4—Super Tuesday. Our research guided the messaging of Bloomberg's historic $500+ million ad buy, helping to catapult Bloomberg into second place in national polls, just three months after he announced his candidacy. But in the February 19 debate in Nevada, his six opponents ganged up on him. No one punched harder than Sen. Elizabeth Warren, who dwelled on a relatively small number of allegations of sexual harassment and gender discrimination at Bloomberg LP. The spectacle of an otherwise thoughtful senator engaging in character assassination brought home everything that was wrong with today's politics. Bloomberg kept his cool throughout the mugging. But, by then, many Democratic voters had gravitated to one of the candidates who'd been campaigning longer. On Super Tuesday, Bloomberg finished third or fourth in most of the states. Biden took 10 of the 15 contests.

The following day, Bloomberg suspended his campaign. He stayed classy. Endorsing Biden as the candidate best suited to defeat Trump, he put his campaign's infrastructure at Biden's disposal. He transferred $18 million to the Democratic National Committee. His contributions forced Republicans to dig much deeper into their war chest. He shook off the price of running, chalking it up to the cost of restoring sanity to American governance. ("The definition of a good life," he liked to joke, "is bouncing the check to the undertaker.")

To me, Michael Bloomberg is the unsung hero of 2020. He got into the race believing that an effective moderate could bring the country together after four years of Trump. As much as he respected Joe Biden's experience, Bloomberg felt he stood a better chance of succeeding. Given President Biden's subsequent failings domestically and abroad, and the challenges of his age, Bloomberg now seems prescient. In the years since that election, Bloomberg has demonstrated his unwavering commitment to educational innovation, climate correction, gun control, and foreign policy—both in his philanthropy and his support of like-minded candidates. His aspirations for his country remain uneclipsed.

A loss isn't a defeat if you put the greater good ahead of your personal disappointment. Don't give up on the cause that drew you to the contest.

27

INFECTIOUS IDEAS

That March, as Bloomberg dropped out of the race, I started to get a cold. It's happened to me a lot after campaigns. You're exposed to a lot of people, and you run yourself ragged. But this was a bad cold. The same month, news spread of the highly infectious novel coronavirus or COVID-19. Fortunately, I tested negative. But as the infection rate grew, I decided, like many New Yorkers, to get out of town. I figured everything would settle down in a week or so.

I flew to Miami, where I have a condo. I'd bought my place thirteen years earlier, but I hadn't visited in months because of the campaign. The pandemic had already infected people with suspicions about who might be a carrier. When I went for a dip in my building's pool, I sensed my neighbors were staring at me. Soon a towel guy came over to ask for my apartment number. I told him but he was skeptical. Another pool attendant insisted on escorting me to the security office to confirm that I was an owner.

My building's management ended up laying off its staff, including the pool police. I enjoyed a twinge of revenge but, after a while, I missed having staff around. I felt the urge to move on. I figured that there might be fewer restrictions on Florida's west coast, where there are more Republicans. I could find only one hotel that was tentatively accepting reservations—a JW Marriott on Marco Island, near Naples. I'd never been there but, at that point, it had few COVID cases. There was a beachfront room available. I booked it.

I'd been trying to get healthy for years. I figured there was no better time than a pandemic. Twice a day, I walked and swam on the beach. I met a trainer. She started putting me through my paces. Another day, I strolled the sand with former House Speaker John Boehner. I asked him if he missed the excitement and power of presiding over Congress. "Not one bit," he said. On still another day on the beach, I met a personal financial adviser. As we watched the seagulls, he pointed out two positive side effects of the pandemic: low interest rates and a soft real estate market.

"You should buy an apartment here," the adviser said.

I already had two apartments—one, just two hours away in Miami. But after touring a turnkey, ocean-view condo for almost nothing down, I found myself owning a third.

As part of my fitness kick, I started playing tennis at the nearby YMCA. I'd often chat with the courts' superintendent, Lee Ross. Sensing that I was idle, Lee kindly offered me a job as his assistant. He said he could teach me how to roll the clay courts in the morning. The job paid $11.50 an hour and, considering that Lee was in his mid-80s and nearing retirement, I stood a good chance of advancement. Lee wasn't kidding. I was touched by his concern for me. I declined his offer, but Lee and his family have become dear friends.

It wasn't my first left-field job proposal. Once, I was on an MGM Grand flight from L.A. to New York. Sitting in first-class, I overheard a Nigerian prince berating his entourage for not getting him suitable accommodations and restaurant reservations in New York. Just for the hell of it, I picked up a phone and got him everything he wanted. The prince was so impressed that he asked me to become his chief of staff. I explained that I had a job.

He said he'd pay me more than I could possibly make. Again, I declined, telling him it had been a pleasure to help him.

Take satisfaction in whatever work you do.

As maddening as the COVID lockdown was, I took pride in adapting to the new realities. I treasured the people I met on the beach—well, aside from that financial planner, whose stock advice proved costly. I was in better shape than I'd been in years. I dropped so many pounds that when you Googled me, up popped, "Doug Schoen weight loss." I think some TV viewers thought I'd had some work done. I don't mean to be glib. I know that over 6.5 million lives were lost during the pandemic, and I feel for those families. But the plague reminded me that every crisis presents opportunities, including chances for self-improvement and new friendships.

I tried to use the downtime constructively. Hunkering down in my new pad, I tried to sort through theories of how the pandemic started. Initial speculation focused on the wet markets of Wuhan, China. But some scientists wondered if the pathogen had originated in the Wuhan Institute of Virology. Whether the virus was manmade or natural, the reluctance of Chinese officials to allow inspections of the Wuhan lab pointed to a cover-up. In *The End of Democracy? Russia and China on the Rise, America in Retreat*, I showed how, from the start, Beijing misled the world about the virus's existence, its prevalence, its transmissibility, about everything. Worse still, China's government orchestrated a campaign to confuse and divide public opinion in the West. The most egregious propaganda claimed the U.S. military had brought the virus to China. Fake social media accounts mined the catastrophe to spread fear and dissension in America. It was a chilling reminder of how, even when Moscow and Beijing aren't working directly together, they are running operations from the same playbook. Six years earlier I'd warned about the bromance between Xi and Putin. By now, the two had met more than two dozen times. They had each other's backs when China menaced Taiwan and Hong Kong and Russia inserted itself into Ukraine, Syria, Venezuela, and Libya. Though they'd flirted with despots in Tehran and Pyongyang, Xi called Putin "my best, most intimate friend."

The pandemic gave both autocrats a new opportunity to destabilize the U.S.—all the better because of the 2020 presidential election. It wasn't too hard for Chinese and Russian trolls to make lies go viral when far-right Americans devoured rumors that COVID vaccines were part of a "plandemic" for medical martial law. Progressives, meanwhile, saw everything Trump did as either too authoritarian or not authoritarian enough.

Despite developing a serious case of COVID himself, Trump was remarkably inept at helping his nation get well. He ignored the advice of his own health experts, abandoned coronavirus task force briefings, held unsafe campaign rallies, and peddled falsehoods about the virus. He didn't even want to be seen wearing a mask. At their national convention in August (held virtually), the Democrats wisely hammered Trump for his mishandling of the pandemic. Putting aside their differences, they nominated Joe Biden, marketing him as a candidate with the competence and empathy that Trump lacked. As I watched Biden accept the nomination, I was pleased to see the seventy-seven-year-old, gaffe-prone warhorse deliver his remarks with energy and precision. Like a maître d' explaining the evening's specials, he recited a menu of policies that catered to the assorted tastes of the party. I personally didn't find this fusion cuisine digestible and doubted that it would entice a potential customer peering through the window of Chez Biden. But I hoped for the best.

In the weeks leading up to the election, Biden held a seven- to ten-point lead over Trump. I still worried that Biden's campaign wasn't doing enough to reach Hispanic, rural, and blue-collar voters in swing states. November 3 was one of the tensest election days I've experienced. Over the next four days, it seemed as though the whole nation was on edge as Americans waited for a victor to be declared. Finally, on November 7, most of the major media forecast that Biden had won Pennsylvania, giving him more than the 270 electoral college votes he needed to win. A final count showed Biden holding 51.3 percent of the popular vote to Trump's 46.8 percent. Biden won 306 electoral college votes to Trump's 232—exactly the margin Trump had declared as a "landslide victory" in 2016.

I don't need to chew over the well-masticated events between the November election and Biden's inauguration. Suffice it to say that, though several Trump aides would later testify that the president knew he'd lost, he publicly claimed there'd been massive voting fraud. His call to supporters to come to Washington to "stop the steal" culminated in the violent demonstrations on January 6. Watching the coverage that day, I could barely believe my eyes as rioters beat and pepper-sprayed police officers. The following day, I wrote on FoxNews.com that "we can rightfully blame President Trump for inciting his followers to storm the Capitol with the intent of jeopardizing the democratic process of certifying President-elect Joe Biden's legitimate election victory." Others on Fox contended that the melee was no worse than the violence of the previous summer's racial justice protests. "I do not see equivalence here," I argued. "The right is not wrong to say that the left has acted in anti-systemic ways in the past. But the attack on the Capitol—the first since British troops attacked during the War of 1812—was certainly more serious because it was armed insurrection. This was an attempted coup to keep Trump in power."

I believed Trump deserved to be held accountable for his actions and I supported his second impeachment. But after the Senate vote fell short of the supermajority needed to convict him, I feared that pursuing the case in the House could hurt the

Democrats politically in 2022. I also believed they could better use their time and their slim majorities in both chambers to advance Biden's agenda. Shortly after the election, Carly Cooperman and I conducted a survey of 1,000 respondents whose party identification was evenly split. Over 60 percent took Biden's victory as a mandate for centrism. Less than 30 percent took it as a mandate to pursue a progressive agenda. Biden's moderate cred was what had lured swing voters away from Trump. During his time in the Senate, Biden had shown his willingness to reach across the aisle. In my columns, I urged him and the rest of my party to do it again. Donald Trump had left the Republican Party in the throes of an identity crisis. Now was the time for the Democrats to consolidate power by enlisting moderate Republicans in legislative compromises.

Instead, during his first weeks in office, Biden issued dozens of unilateral executive orders to fast-track his economic stimulus plan. More and more, it appeared that far-left Dems were wielding outsized influence over in the party. Sen. Bernie Sanders, Rep. Alexandria Ocasio-Cortez, and other progressives pushed for open borders, slavery reparations, student loan forgiveness, unrealistic climate goals, and other initiatives that were destined for defeat. I implored Senate Democrats not to eliminate the filibuster, which I consider an essential tool for bipartisan resolution, especially in today's partisan climate.

My faith in consensus was bolstered in August 2021 when, after months of debate, a bipartisan Senate coalition passed a $1 trillion Infrastructure Investment and Jobs Act. It was a sign that Congress might still end what Biden had called an "uncivil war." But as we approached the first anniversary of the January 6 insurrection, Carly Cooperman and I conducted a survey of likely 2022 midterm election voters. Its findings were disturbing. It showed that distrust and pessimism about American democracy had become pervasive—no longer confined to the fringes of the two political parties. More than half (51 percent) of voters polled said U.S. democracy was at risk of extinction—including 49 percent of Democrats and Republicans, as well as 54 percent of Independents. Young Americans—the future leaders of the country—were even more cynical. Just one in five voters ages 18 to 29 (21 percent) believed U.S. democracy was secure for future generations. Since January 6, Republicans had tried to rewrite history by downplaying the Capitol riot and embracing Trump's "Big Lie" that he'd won the 2020 election. Our poll suggested that they'd succeeded in getting the electorate to swallow these falsehoods. Just 54 percent of Americans believed Biden had legitimately won—10 percent less than when we asked this same question in April 2021.

Contrary to popular belief, it wasn't only the far right that distrusted 2020 election results: just 56 percent of Independent voters believed Joe Biden legitimately won. Three in ten Americans were not confident that votes in the 2022 midterm elections would be counted accurately. Fringe thinking seemed to be infecting the mainstream. And yet an overwhelming majority of those polled (85 percent) were concerned about political extremism, including 53 percent who said they were "very concerned." Two-thirds of voters believed the country had become more divided over the last year (67 percent), while just 18 percent said we'd become less divided.

Carly and I synthesized our takeaways in our book, *America: Unite or Die—How to Save Our Democracy*. Our research showed that eight out of ten Americans wanted their elected officials to work together to *solve problems,* rather than remaining true to their ideological beliefs. That included strong majorities of those polled—Democrats (80 percent), Independents (86 percent), and Republicans (75 percent). And yet, we noted, both Democratic and Republican leaders had let zealots hijack their parties. Republicans had normalized nonsense about the Deep State and voter fraud. Democrats had succumbed to pressure from leftists bent on class warfare and defunding the police. Self-absorbed news networks had fostered alternate realities—so much so that their viewers could no longer distinguish fact from fiction. We'd come to live in two Americas—demonizing those who disagreed with us, resigned to a government paralyzed by partisan gridlock.

Though *Unite or Die* had portended the January 6 riot, we believed a course-correction was still possible. We didn't have to follow the uncompromising dogmatists driving us over a cliff. 2022 brought some signs that someone might be listening. I cautioned Democrats against using a party-line budget reconciliation vote to ram through their Build Back Better social safety net bill—sticker price: $3.5 trillion. I recalled the grim year of 1994, when I'd joined Bill Clinton's campaign. The president's party had lost the House largely because Democrats had passed the then-largest tax increase without any Republican support. Even with the benefit of reconciliation, it took months for Senate Majority Leader Chuck Schumer to convince West Virginia senator Joe Manchin to sign off on a $1 trillion package reworked into the Inflation Reduction Act of 2022. Chuck can be a hothead—witness his "banishment" of me from the Democratic Party—but I give him props for getting Manchin to the altar.

Bipartisanship brought forth another miraculous piece of legislation in June 2022. For nearly three decades, Republicans in Congress had blocked stricter gun control laws, despite polls that consistently showed Americans supported them. Tragically, it wasn't until an eighteen-year-old used a legally purchased AR-15 style rifle to slaughter nineteen children and two teachers in Uvalde, Texas, that common sense prevailed. Senators John Cornyn (R) and Chris Murphy (D) gathered colleagues from both parties to produce a bill that would require background checks for prospective gun buyers ages eighteen to twenty-one, provide incentives for states to pass "red flag" laws, and tighten a federal ban on domestic abusers buying firearms. The bill didn't go as far as a House-passed measure. But I called on Democrats to get real—to dial down their invective and lose their "all or nothing" mentality. Both sides made concessions. In the end, fifteen Republicans, including Minority Leader Mitch McConnell, broke ranks to join Democrats in supporting the bill, which quickly passed in the House. A paralyzed legislature had willed itself to walk.

Shaming and blaming your opponents might impress your allies. But it doesn't accomplish much—aside from chasing people away from the bargaining table. Getting half is better than getting nothing. You can come back later for the rest.

28

AT THE BARRICADES

The same year also brought catastrophic news from Ukraine. For nearly two decades, I'd been warning people about the long-term ambitions of Vladimir Putin. On February 20, 2022, he began massing troops on the Ukrainian border. A few weeks earlier, at the Munich Security Conference, the Atlantic Council presented a Schoen Cooperman poll showing broad support for an independent Ukraine among Ukrainians, Europeans, and Americans. Our report found that Ukrainians were prepared to fight fiercely for their freedom. Putin apparently hadn't seen our research, or didn't believe it, because he continued to test NATO's resolve. In a column, I called on President Biden to assume "a more decisive and forceful posture in defending Ukraine." By pledging only to deploy troops to surrounding NATO-member states, I warned, "Biden is giving Putin the reassurance he needs to invade Ukraine."

Four days after that column, Russia invaded. I was in Miami, watching in horror as tanks rolled into towns I knew well. Missiles struck cities where I had friends. I got in touch with Victor Pinchuk to make sure he and his family were alright. Over the next few weeks, he and I tapped into the network we'd built over twenty years—reaching out to business and government leaders abroad for financial and political aid.

Before the invasion, Victor and President Volodymyr Zelensky had agreed on some issues and disagreed on others. But now that their country was in jeopardy, Victor pledged his allegiance to its leader. Even Victor's past critics came to salute his commitment to saving the democracy he'd helped nurture. He and Elena sold a major Jeff Koons's sculpture for over $12 million, donating the proceeds to help injured soldiers and civilians recover. Victor did his best to keep Ukraine in people's minds—introducing Zelensky (via video) at the Venice Biennale and at the World Economic Forum in Davos, where the Pinchuk Foundation exhibited evidence of Russian war crimes.

Despite the ongoing war, which devastated his enterprises, Victor pressed ahead with the 17th Yalta European Strategy Forum in embattled Kyiv. Moderated by CNN anchor Fareed Zakaria, the conference featured giant banners with Zelensky's reported response to an American offer to evacuate him: "I need ammunition, not a ride." Zelensky promised forum attendees that a free Ukraine would survive. "We must not be broken, disjointed, disconnected," said the president, sporting his trademark army-drab T-shirt. "We must hold our line."

In my columns, I warned that the war in Ukraine was likely to be a long slog. President Biden had showed commendable leadership by rallying the West around Ukraine's defense and contributing billions of dollars in humanitarian and military aid. Still, I pointed out that a few on the far-right and the far-left had formed an odd alliance in opposing American involvement. I noted a recent opinion piece by Jordan Bruneau entitled, "Vote for Peace, Not Perpetual War on Election Day." That piece said the West should press Ukrainian leadership to compromise and hailed J. D. Vance, the Trump-backed Republican later elected as Ohio's Senator, who'd said, "I don't really care what happens in Ukraine, one way or another." Most Americans appeared to disagree. Seventy percent had said in a recent poll that "the United

States must support democratic countries when they are attacked by non-democratic countries." I wasn't saying the United States should act recklessly. But we couldn't cower either. Having spoken to friends and colleagues in Lithuania, Latvia, and Estonia, I could see the Ukrainian war had heightened their own dread of a Russian invasion. Any appeasement, even after almost a year of fighting, I wrote, "would legitimize everything Putin has done up until this point."

★　★　★

Meanwhile, Schoen Cooperman continued to advance democratic causes and political reform. As pollsters for Michael Bloomberg's Everytown for Gun Safety, we developed messaging strategies on reducing gun violence—helping to pass initiatives to expand background checks on gun sales in Nevada and implement universal background checks in Washington state. Our research and ad testing helped elect hundreds of local, statewide, and national officials who support addressing climate change. Working with the Campaign for Tobacco-Free Kids, we sought to educate people about the e-cigarette epidemic among youth. We also helped pass nonpartisan, citizen-based redistricting reform initiatives in Colorado, Michigan, Missouri, and Utah. These measures ensured that districts are not drawn capriciously by the party in charge.

Our research has helped spearhead the passage in Maine, Nevada, and Alaska of ranked choice voting (RCV)—in which voters prioritize their preferred candidates. American politics has grown so divisive partly because of the evolution of the primary system. Each party's candidates are no longer chosen by mainstream-minded party bosses but, rather, by the marshalled voting of a party's most strident activists, whose views are often out of line with rank-and-file Republicans or Democrats. There are different types of ranked choice voting. But in Nevada and

Alaska, for instance, the new RCV system replaced party primaries with a single nonpartisan blanket primary. The top four or five candidates advance to a general election. It's not surprising, then, that a hard-right political blog, Must Read Alaska, should denounce 2022 candidate Bill Walker—a former Republican governor running for his old job as a pro-choice Independent—for hiring me as an adviser. Among my sins, according to the blog: I'd helped to enact ranked choice voting and was "dedicated to increasing bipartisanship." Well, we wouldn't want that.

The blog also blamed me for helping to elect New York City Mayor Eric Adams. I didn't have a big part in that race but I'm proud to say Schoen Cooperman played a role in developing a message strategy for a uniquely qualified candidate. A ghetto-born former gang member once beaten by cops, Adams became a cop and helped reform the NYPD from within. As Brooklyn Borough president, he continued to seek a balance between racial justice and public safety. We helped position him as a corrective to the misguided anti-business and anti-police policies of outgoing Mayor Bill de Blasio. The rest of the country often looks to New York City as a bellwether of progress. To the degree that Adams succeeds, he can demonstrate how moderate Democrats can govern if given a chance.

In many ways, Adams reminds me of the kind of street-smart centrist candidates I worked for at the beginning of my career. If you live long enough, even the tatty strategies of a vintage pollster can come back into fashion. After Bill Clinton left office, young lefties viewed me as evil incarnate. In 2007, then-blogger Ezra Klein called one of my op-eds "almost a parody of the pernicious Democratic consultant." He said I had "a fetish for bipartisanship." To repurpose Mark Twain's adage about his dim-seeming father, it's remarkable how smart I grew fourteen years later when Klein, now a *New York Times* columnist, interviewed David Shor, the *wunderkind* analyst whose forecasts shaped Barack Obama's reelection plan.

"When I first started working on the Obama campaign in 2012, I hated all the last remnants of the Clinton era," Shor told Klein. "When I go back now and think about the fights between the analytics team and the consultants, about 80 percent of the time, they were right. There was an old conventional wisdom to politics in the '90s and 2000s that we all forget. We collectively unlearned those lessons over the past twelve years. We've told ourselves very ideologically convenient stories about how those lessons weren't relevant—that tax phobia isn't real or we didn't need to worry about what conservative white people thought. And it turned out that wasn't true. I see what I'm doing as rediscovering the ancient political wisdom of the past."

Klein didn't agree with all of Shor's premises, but he concurred that "Democrats are often trapped in an echo chamber of their own making . . . and they are too quick to dismiss evidence that their ideas and messages are alienating voters." He added, "They need to campaign with the constant recognition that the pivotal voter is well to their right and skeptical of everything they say. On all of that, Shor is offering a warning Democrats should heed."

If you wait a while, your harshest critics may become your staunchest allies.

Other longtime liberals came around to my way of thinking as the 2022 midterm elections approached. Ruy Teixeira, a political scientist who once worked for Penn & Schoen, had co-authored the 2002 bestseller, *The Emerging Democratic Majority*, in which he predicted that the demographic growth of voters of color would lead the Democratic party to command American politics for the foreseeable future. Barack Obama seemed to fulfill the prophecy but then came Donald Trump. Two years into

Joe Biden's presidency, his poll numbers were dismal. Texeira now shared my view that the Democratic party had become too "woke" for its own good—plagued, he said, by "race essentialist" dogma and the "fallacy" that anything uttered on Fox News must be wrong. In my columns, I beseeched Democratic candidates to stay focused on quality-of-life issues such as the cost of living and surging crime. The Democrats' poll numbers improved after Trump-stacked Supreme Court justices overtured Roe v. Wade—angering roughly two-thirds of voters. But raging inflation threatened to fulfill Trump's dream of "a beautiful red wave" crashing down on Dems snoozing on their battleground beach towels.

Historically, the midterms see a sitting president's party lose a substantial number of Congressional seats. In these midterms, I was bracing for the worst. But the Democrats surprised me—and many others—by yielding only a slight majority to Republicans in the House and hanging on to control of the Senate. Democrats had a net gain of two in gubernatorial elections. Voters largely rejected Trump-backed candidates who denied his 2020 loss. My predictions were a bit off.

Don't take too long to admit you're wrong.

In this case, I was happy to do so. The midterms suggested that moderation wasn't extinct. Voters preferred competent pragmatists—legislators who got things done. Wisconsin Gov. Tony Evers's election takeaway: "boring wins." The backlash against Trump and the loss of a woman's right to choose had helped Democrats survive the midterms. I warned that the better-than-expected outcome was not because of their policies but despite them.

29

APPRECIATING
THE MIDDLEMAN

On October 7, 2023, I was horrified when the Palestinian terror group Hamas attacked southern Israel with a barrage of over 5,000 rockets. Some 3,000 Palestinian militants ambushed Israel Defense Forces, slaughtered civilians, and took more than 240 hostages. By the end of one day, they'd killed roughly 1,400 Israelis. It was the largest single-day massacre of Jews since the Holocaust. The Israeli-Palestinian conflict has long been a polarizing issue in American politics. But polling by Schoen Cooperman Research shortly after the attack revealed that Americans strongly supported Israel's right to defend itself. Furthermore, respondents believed it was in America's interest to protect Israel. We also found that 68 percent of Americans—including 70 percent of Republicans and 69 percent of Democrats—supported U.S. aid to both Israel and Ukraine.

In all my years of surveying American opinion on the Mideast, I'd never seen such numbers. But it didn't take long for America's leaders to become divided. President Biden pledged unwavering allegiance to Israel, and an overwhelming majority of Congressional Democrats agreed with him. But progressive representatives to his left, who'd previously denounced Israel as an "apartheid state," called on the U.S. to cut funding to the country. Typically, Donald Trump amplified the discord. Once,

Trump had been a friend of Prime Minister Benjamin Netanyahu, but their recent beef made Trump brand Bibi a "jerk." While he was at it, Trump hailed Hezbollah, Hamas's ally in Lebanon, as "very smart."

The unfolding war in Gaza gave Congress's bit players new roles for their fringe theater. The Democratic performance artists in the progressive "squad" called for a cease-fire almost before Israel had fired a shot. When Israel did start retaliatory bombing, they bemoaned the truly tragic civilian casualties but paid little mind to the fact that Hamas had prevented civilians from leaving Gaza City, preferring to use them as human shields. Meanwhile, Republican infighting had left Congress without a Speaker of the House, halting all legislation, including aid to Israel.

★　★　★

Back in 1996, in Israel, I met with Shimon Peres, who was then serving as prime minister and defense minister. Peres knew his time in office was coming to an end, thanks to the resurgent Bibi Netanyahu. Reflecting on the security of Israel and of America, Peres told me, "Make no mistake. The problem here is Iran; it isn't going away. It will be a problem for your government long after I've passed from the scene." At the time, I didn't know why Peres was telling me this. I assumed he wanted me to deliver a message to President Clinton. But I see now how prophetic he was. The *Wall Street Journal* learned that, just weeks before the October 7 attack, roughly 500 terrorists from Hamas and Palestinian Islamic Jihad had been training in Iran. Soon after the attack, Tehran's proxy armies twisted their knives. Hezbollah fired rockets into Israel. Houthi rebels fired missiles from Yemen. Iranian-backed militias waged nineteen attacks against American forces in Iraq and Syria.

I applauded President Biden for ordering air strikes on bases used by those militias, as well as for visiting Tel Aviv to pledge America's unwavering support for Israel. But two weeks after his trip, Biden succumbed to pressure from his party's left wing when he called for a humanitarian "pause" to the war—so Palestinian civilians could receive aid and foreign nationals could leave Gaza. Meanwhile, in the House, the GOP's "America First" wing moved to decouple aid to Israel from aid to Ukraine. In a column, I reminded Democrats and Republicans that these wars had linkages. Iranian planes had begun landing at Russia's Khmeimim Air Base in Syria, secure in the knowledge that the Kremlin would turn a blind eye to the planes' weapons cargo. Our adversaries have one thing in common: their contempt for us. We can't afford not to arm our allies. They're fighting our battle. Yes, war is costly, but it would be even costlier to let our enemies exploit our political dysfunction during the defining struggle of our times.

For years, I've offered insights gleaned from polling data that doesn't always jibe with some Democrats' expectations. Those Dems have branded me as a self-aggrandizing crank, a Donnie Downer, a traitor. They see my tough love as betrayal. Listen, it's not that I don't share many progressive aspirations—for social justice, economic empowerment, gun safety, environmental protection. I just want to find ways to achieve them. That usually means prioritizing what policies we can sell right now. Does a reform belong on our wish list or on our must-do list? Passage of a bipartisan federal marriage equality act would have been a fantasy even five years ago. Now it's a reality. Transgender Americans deserve the same protections as the rest of us. But giving gender reassignment for minors the same emphasis on a platform as affordable housing may cost Democrats the swing voters they need. Identity politics is saturated with self-absorption. Some people in the Democratic coalition are so devoted to their group's agenda that they miss the bigger picture. It's easy to scream into the wind from your island. It's harder to paddle over to the mainland and haggle with your competitors. By the way, I also tell Republicans to get real—that they need to stop relitigating past grievances and moderate their positions on abortion and guns.

You must figure out a way to negotiate with people you see as the enemy. You'll never convince some people to think completely as you do. They were born into a different tribe. They hunted with their grandfather. Or they grew up on a commune. Some outliers do rebel against their family's beliefs. Some switch parties. Some move from left to right (Ronald Reagan, Trent Lott, Condoleezza Rice, Mike Pence). Some move right to left (Jay Rockefeller, James Webb, Elizabeth Warren, Hillary Clinton). Occasionally, you have an Arlen Specter, who moved left-right-left. For whatever reason, I've stayed close to the center. It might have to do with my family's mixture of liberalism and conservatism. We were, to borrow my old friend E. J. Dionne's phrase, "tolerant traditionalists." It might have to do with my personality. I was the guy who went to the Harvard antiwar protest but stayed seated while others hurled projectiles at the "warmonger" speakers. I'm inclined to let other people speak. Journalist Joe Klein once said that, while some of his best friends are political consultants, "they have drained a good deal of the life from our democracy. They have become specialists in caution, literal reactionaries—they react to the results of their polling and focus groups; they fear anything they haven't tested."

There's some truth to that. I tread judiciously. I like to stock up on information before I light out into the unknown. You won't find many pollsters lost in the wilderness. You may not find many pollsters, period, given that fewer people are willing to answer their phones. That's troubling, since we need independent data to protect democracy, particularly if sore losers continue to deny they lost elections.

So, yes, I'm cautious. I prefer incremental change. I see progress as being a bit like free climbing. Sure, you can make a death-defying leap across a crevasse—hoping that someone will leave lilies where you land. Or you can pick calculated holds on the rockface, chalking your sweaty palms as you go. It's a slower ascent, but you stand a better chance of getting there and belaying others upward.

A centrist uses shared values to benefit the greatest number of people. Inevitably, someone will charge that centrists have no core values—that they're cynical operators who like making more principled people beg for their approval. First, let me say that there's a difference between a centrist and a moderate, though the two often overlap. The moderate straddles different ideologies. She may be a social liberal and a fiscal conservative. The centrist is someone who tries to reconcile moderates, liberals, and conservatives. I've stood left and right of center on separate issues. True-blue believers on the left see me as a turncoat. Blazing red conservatives find me less objectionable than other Democrats but regret that I still haven't seen the light. What I have seen is that you need to use the whole political palette to paint a legislative masterpiece. You can't get anything done unless you get elected. That isn't to say I would do anything to get my candidate elected. I'm committed to staying within the bounds of decency. And I still believe in backing longshots who probably won't win. Some races need to be run for the principle. That's why I went to Mississippi and Serbia and Mexico and Venezuela.

If you look at my many campaigns and my twenty-three (and counting) books, you'll see I do have convictions and a coherent worldview. I divined Putin's designs long before they became apparent. I believe in democracy and free markets because I've been to countries where people wish they had them. I'm proud to have helped Milan Panić democratically oust Slobodan Milošević, to have helped Menachem Begin stay in office long enough to win a Nobel Peace Prize, to have helped a beleaguered Bill Clinton secure a second term that saw the longest period of peacetime economic expansion in American history, and to have helped give Michael Bloomberg the time he needed to guide New York City to a recovery after 9/11. These and other clients succeeded by seeking consensus—sometimes with the very people who'd vowed to destroy them. Begin's Arab peace partner, Anwar Sadat, once saw him as a terrorist. My clients often have led complicated lives. Pharmaceutical chief turned prime minister Panić was building a Balkans peace summit with Bill Clinton even as Clinton's Security and Exchange Commission was investigating Panić for a stock sale—an investigation ultimately dropped without charges being filed. And you know about Clinton's personal travails. My client Victor Pinchuk has paid for young Ukrainians to study abroad only to have them come home, secure important government positions, and then criticize him. It makes him smile.

I'm not looking to pardon any of these men, all of whom expected controversy the moment they stepped into public life. I'm certainly not an impartial observer. I will say that we in the West often see a black-and-white movie filled with good guys and bad guys rather than characters whose moral integrity is evolving. I believe that we can help it evolve and that, if enough of our interests align, we should engage with those characters.

When I encourage you to "make the deal," I recognize that there's such a thing as a bad deal. **Sometimes, you need to take a step back, or to the side, to move forward.** Sometimes, you can't get to "yes." Sometimes, you need to take a stand. I still wish the United States had stepped in sooner to take down Milošević; if we had, more than 8,000 Bosniak Muslims might have been spared in Srebrenica. I'm still troubled that Presidents Obama and Biden have eschewed grassroots movements in Iran for the sake of a spurious nuclear arms deal. That said, I believe you must always try, earnestly, to bargain.

In America today, we face intense polarization that only seems to be hardening. The left warns us about the growth of fascism and authoritarianism. The right talks about the spread of radical socialism. Both sides make daily vows to destroy each other. I sometimes wonder if we're turning into Italy, which since World War II has had sixty-nine governments (at last count). Sometimes it seems that reason might prevail. Ultraconservative members of Congress' Freedom Caucus call their mainstream Republican colleagues "squishes" because these lawmakers are willing to talk with Democrats and make deals necessary to keep a government running. But after the Freedom Caucus ousted GOP House Speaker Kevin McCarthy, twenty of the "squishes" banded together to keep Trump-enabler Jim Jordan from replacing McCarthy. Death threats from Jordan's far-right base only stiffened their resolve. Alas, after three weeks of infighting, some of the mainstreamers succumbed to fatigue and confirmed Mike Johnson, a Louisiana representative possibly more extreme than Jordan.

I must be doing something right because I manage to irk people on both sides. In June 2023, Donald Trump lumped me among the "failed pundits and losers" who didn't think he could regain the Oval Office or deserved to. "They said I couldn't beat Hillary," he posted on Truth Social. "How did that work out??? Doug Schoen . . . should get a new playbook!" At the same time, some progressives still consider me a deserter. Believe it or not, I admire Bernie Sanders and Alexandria Ocasio-Cortez for broaching daring ideas. But they overreach. Defunding the police would most hurt people of color. It's important to acknowledge the country's ugly past and to continue to fight against racism and sexism. But speaking as someone who campaigned in the Deep South and East Harlem, I've found that if you frame every conversation in terms of race, you start to shut down conversations. **If people can't talk freely, they can't cooperate.** I believe in conciliation, not cancellation. Redemption rather than redaction. We spend our time swearing at each other as Russia, China, Iran, and

North Korea collaborate on our downfall and nervous, smaller countries watch and wait to see who'll win. As we head into the 2024 election, I hope a candidate emerges who can form a coalition. I don't think we can give up on that prospect. Perhaps artificial intelligence will harvest the best of our shared beliefs and guide us toward it.

I don't pretend to have all the answers. It's important for people to dream of a better life, to reach beyond their grasp. But to get there, to make cracks in the status quo, **you need to form alliances.** It's popular in business to talk about "eliminating the middleman." But in politics, you need the middleman. And the middle-woman. You need the go-between, the tiebreaker, the conciliator.

I truly believe that most conflicts can be resolved when opposing parties listen respectfully to each other, treat each other fairly, and creatively explore ways to accomplish what benefits them both. I still think one person can make a difference.

Flipping through my back pages, I have new appreciation for my mentors—my parents, teachers like Martin Kilson, Bill Schneider, and Pat Moynihan, as well as Arthur Deutsch, Ted Kheel, David Garth, Bob Squier, and many others who gave me a leg up. I often learned the most from people I was getting paid to advise. Maybe that's the definition of the perfect job.

I hope that a few of my Schoenisms prove useful—that I've given you a better sense of how to leave your comfort zone, pick your battles, learn the grayscale, deflate your ego, and make the deal. Permit me one more: **Don't give other people advice unless you're willing to take some.**

I intend to keep peddling my two cents to anyone who'll listen. And if I run out of takers, it's nice to know my Florida friend, Lee, might still have a job for me at the YMCA tennis courts.

SCHOENISMS
FOR EVERY OCCASION

Leave your comfort zone.

Work all the time. It will serve you well.

Don't assume everyone is like you.
If something seems creepy, it probably is.

It's good to be clever, but clever only gets you so far.

Self-sacrifice is great—unless it renders you useless.

Whenever you hire people,
understand their needs as well as your own.

Where possible, make that deal.

Sleeping alone has its advantages.

Be wary of people whose vision of a better world
doesn't include reforming themselves.

SCHOENISMS FOR EVERY OCCASION

Pick your battles.

Anger can be a superpower
if you use it constructively and rationally.

Wherever you go, look for a mentor.

Don't guess! Do your fieldwork!
Ask questions until you get answers.

Winning isn't always the point.
A defeat can get you closer to victory.
Lose the battle but win the war.
Know your goal.

Brains and money only get you so far.
You need to connect with people.
Know your whereabouts and assess situations accurately.

Never grant interviews to anyone
whose agenda you don't know.

Never be afraid to borrow—and improve upon—your
opponent's good idea. And be prepared to acknowledge
where the idea came from.

If you're offered a way into a powerful institution,
take it, you dummy!

Most people are self-contradictions—
mixtures of light and darkness. Life is about learning
the moral gradients—the grayscale—and deciding
how much shadow you can live with.

Not sure what to do after college? Try more college!
Especially if it enhances your life skills. There's no such
thing as being overeducated. You often won't know why
a class is useful till after it's helped make you a success.

Find a partner who can do what you can't.

Don't drink on the job.
Your work will survive longer and so will you.

Never assume an opponent's beaten till he's truly beaten.
Always be ready to step up your game.

Before you take a bow, make sure the rest of the cast is
onstage—and that they think you deserve applause.

Problems are opportunities.
Make it your business to take work other people don't want—
and take it seriously, whatever it pays.

Make the trip. Take the meeting.

Underdogs can become top dogs. Be prepared
to compromise for the sake of a longer relationship.
Taking less now can mean making more later.

Invest in a good shredder.

You can be critical without being vicious. You can win without
defiling your opponent's dignity. Even if you're trying to
stay positive, you need to differentiate yourself from the
competition. Whether it's politics, business, or romance, you
need to explain why you're best qualified for the job.

285

If you can't get a dream out of your head,
get it out of your system. Give it a shot. You may succeed.
You may not. At least you tried.

Even if you are the smartest guy in the room,
don't act like it. Don't talk down to people.
You can be smart without being a smartass.

Feed your family first! Don't sell others till you've sold yourself.

Go general!

Wisdom can come from people you don't immediately
recognize as wise.

Whenever you land in a new terrain, find a fixer—someone
who can get you out of trouble or, better yet, keep you from
getting into it.

Martyrdom is overrated. Don't fall on any swords
unless there's an ambulance on the way.

When you have something sold, shut up and leave!

Authenticity works—
even if it takes a little work to become authentic.

Take the offensive and play to win.

Start yesterday: front-runners tend to be winners.

Define the issues before others define them for you.

Keep your finger on the pulse and be ready to respond.

Let no attack go unanswered.

When somebody important wants to see you,
make yourself available, regardless of your schedule.

When someone you want to work with asks you if you can
solve a problem, the answer is always Yes.

When you can't do it yourself, call in reinforcements.

Nothing impresses like discretion.

Smart, small plays gain more yardage than Hail Mary passes.
One silver bullet may kill a werewolf but, if you want to build a
house, you'll need 10,000 nails.

Doing a job well may be its own reward but someone else's
gratitude gives you the strength to start the next job.

Foresight isn't flawless. The best binoculars
won't stop you from running into a wall.

If you're the boss, act like the boss.

Even if you're angry, remain professional.
No temper tantrums. Just do your job.
Do what your client has asked to the best of your ability.

There is no such thing as perfect information.
Get the best evidence you can find, then act on it decisively.

Influence depends on access. If you don't have
as much juice as you want, get close to someone who does.

Know your adversary and act on his fears.

An analyst must sometimes become an advocate.
When all else fails, stop observing and do something!

Data can give courage to your convictions.
Persuasive research is a call to arms.

Support democracy! It's cheaper than its alternatives
and it lasts longer.

Take on a despot when he first threatens you.
Bullies only get bigger.

Clients want a firm recommendation. They don't want you to
give them a bunch of pros and cons and let them decide. They
pay for an informed opinion. It helps if the opinion is correct.
But first, it should sound convincing.

Don't talk about your innovation until you know it works.

If you do what you think is right,
things will resolve themselves to your benefit
and the greater good.

If you're going to a knife fight, bring an AK-47.

Data can tell you what people are thinking
and how to change their thinking.

Don't dicker with people who have more to gain than you do.
Stay attuned to your own needs.
Deal only with those who can help you.

Expect to be blamed, even when your predictions come true.

Don't mistake confidence for stubbornness.
Don't refuse help when you need it.

Every loss is a lesson.

Doing business with mysterious strangers can be profitable.
But, before you get into bed with them, check the sheets
for scorpions. And be ready to get out of bed quickly.

Never accept conventional wisdom.

Don't try to persuade someone who can't be persuaded.

The meeting starts when the boss shows up.

The only thing you have is your integrity. It's more important
than any client, even a head of state.

Don't let your personal dignity overpower your professional
responsibility. Nothing heals an ego like getting the job done.

Therapy can work—if you make sure it's solving your
problems, not creating new ones.

You may need to make mid-course corrections.
When you must reposition, it helps to sit down with trusted
friends, your team of advisers.

Don't waste time on feuds. Grudges sap your strength
and hurt you almost as much as the person you're fighting.

If you truly believe you're right,
take criticism as a compliment.

Don't be afraid to modify your position.
It's not a crime to change your mind.

Hope can sometimes triumph over experience.
But if you're weighing whether to take a chance,
try imagining the worst-case scenario. If you can handle
the risk, roll the dice. Otherwise, move on.

Don't be short-sighted. Small insults add up.
Snubs, slights, and broken promises aren't just rude.
They have a way of biting you in the ass.

"No" is simply a mispronunciation of the word "yes."

Defend yourself without becoming defensive. Stay cool.
Measure your words. State the facts. Acknowledge undeniable
missteps, but also point out what you did right. Keep it brief.

During a tempest, the center path
will get you to higher and drier ground.

If you trust someone, you can stick with them
through the rough patches.

Sometimes you make the right decision
for the wrong reasons.

Don't cut corners, or the corners will cut you. It's much
easier to be honest—and, in the long run, more lucrative.
Maintaining your professionalism is not only a matter of
success, but also a matter of survival.

Let people do their jobs and judge them accordingly.
If you don't show confidence in your staff,
they'll lose confidence in you.

Win now!

A loss isn't a defeat if you put the greater good ahead of your
personal disappointment. Don't give up on the cause
that drew you to the contest.

Take satisfaction in whatever work you do.

Shaming and blaming your opponents might impress your
allies. But it doesn't accomplish much—aside from chasing
people away from the bargaining table. Getting half is better
than getting nothing. You can come back later for the rest.

If you wait a while, your harshest critics
may become your staunchest allies.

SCHOENISMS FOR EVERY OCCASION

Don't take too long to admit you're wrong.

Sometimes, you need to take a step back,
or to the side, to move forward.

If people can't talk freely, they can't cooperate.

You need to form alliances.

Don't give other people advice
unless you're willing to take some.

ABOUT THE AUTHORS

DOUGLAS E. SCHOEN, author of *Power: The 50 Truths*; *Four Presidents: Kennedy, Nixon, Biden, Trump*; *Putin's Master Plan*; *Putin on the March*; *The End of Democracy*; and *America: Unite or Die*, has been one of the most influential Democratic campaign consultants for more than forty years. He is the founder of Schoen Cooperman Research, a premier strategic research consulting firm, and he is widely recognized as one of the co-inventors of overnight polling. His political clients include former New York City mayor Michael Bloomberg and President Bill Clinton, and internationally, he has worked for the heads of state of more than fifteen countries. He is a graduate of Harvard College and Harvard Law School, and has a doctorate of philosophy in politics from the University of Oxford.

GEORGE RUSH has contributed to *Vanity Fair, Esquire, Rolling Stone*, the *New York Times*, and the *Wall Street Journal.* His books include *Scandal: A Manual* and *Confessions of an Ex-Secret Service Agent.*